INTERNATIONAL CONFLICT
RESOLUTION

International Relations for the Twenty-first Century

Series Editors: R. J. Barry Jones, *University of Reading*, Charles Hauss, *George Mason University*, Mary Durfee, *Michigan Technical University*

Ranging from international political economy to security, migration, human rights and the environment, this series is designed to explore the issues that make International Relations such an exciting, controversial and, at times, confusing field in a world undergoing unprecedented change.

The books are designed as core texts for advanced undergraduate and specialized graduate courses, and each volume follows a standard format. The first section is devoted to general theories and concepts. The second includes carefully selected case studies which students can use to deepen their understanding of the theoretical issues. The books include, as an integral part of the text, addresses of particularly helpful websites, and the series also has its own website with links to internet-based resources in International Relations: <http://www.continuumbooks.com/irseries.htm>.

Published titles in the series
International Law and International Relations by Craig Barker

Forthcoming titles in the series

The EU Enters the Twenty-first Century by Michael Huelshoff
The Global Environment by Elizabeth De Sombre
Global Migration by Joanne Van Selm

INTERNATIONAL CONFLICT RESOLUTION

CHARLES HAUSS

CONTINUUM
London and New York

Continuum

The Tower Building, 11 York Road, London SE1 7NX

370 Lexington Avenue, New York, NY 10017–6503

First published 2001

British Library Cataloguing-in-Publication Data

A catalogue record for this book is available from the British Library.

ISBN 0–8264–4775–9 (hardback)
    0–8264–4776–7 (paperback)

Library of Congress Cataloging-in-Publication Data

Hauss, Charles.

    International conflict resolution / Charles Hauss.

      p. cm.— (International relations for the 21st century)

    Includes bibliographical references and index.

    ISBN 0-8264-4775-9 (hardback) — ISBN 0-8264-4776-7 (pbk.)

    1. Pacific settlement of international disputes. 2. International relations. 3. Conflict management. I. Title. II. Series.

JZ6010. H38 2001

327.1′7—dc21   00-065696

Typeset by YHT Ltd, London

Printed and bound in Great Britain by Biddles Ltd, Guildford and King's Lynn

CONTENTS

PREFACE AND ACKNOWLEDGMENTS

When I started writing this book, I thought it would be an easy one to finish. After all, I had been involved in the peace movement since my high school days in the 1960s. I also have been teaching and writing about comparative politics and international relations since the mid-1970s. Since the mid-1980s, my political and professional vocations have come together in a number of efforts to build support for win-win conflict resolution.

However, this book proved anything but easy to write. In large part, that reflects the fact that it was my first work on international conflict resolution that could not be written from a partisan perspective. The premise underlying this series is that students learn the most about general concepts and specific examples in international relations by considering a wide variety of theoretical perspectives, not just those a particular author finds most appealing.

Furthermore, I have long been convinced that what are commonly portrayed theoretical 'debates' miss the central role theories could and should play in political science. In other words, I have rarely found that one theory 'works' across the board. Rather, all the major theories I have worked with – including those I don't particularly like – help me understand and teach about political life. In short, theories tend to complement more than they contradict each other – at least at the current level of theoretical development (or lack thereof) in the social sciences.

Yet, I discovered that actually blending the key theoretical concepts in the discipline proved to be easier said than done. To some degree, that is the case because the various theorists I drew on had not covered the same material in some cases or extended their general ideas about international relations to conflict resolution in others. But even more important, it was simply difficult intellectually to do two of the things I discuss in chapter 1.

First, international conflict resolution is a topic that evokes passionate and even polemical responses from the people who work on it. While I have not tried to minimize the emotional side of the issues we will be considering below, I struggled to find ways of emphasizing the analytical rather than the normative aspects of the ways we handle international disputes.

Second, moving between theory and case studies just was not as easy to do as I had anticipated. In particular, by considering the traditional or mainstream theories those of us who work on international conflict resolution typically give short shrift to, I found myself doing two unexpected things – questioning many of the ideas from the newer theories I had all but taken for granted and finding major ways in which the traditional theories helped me understand the conflicts I was writing about.

In the end, this was a difficult but immensely rewarding book to write. As I point out in the first and final chapters, writing it demonstrated once again the power of an approach that asks instructors and authors as well as students to constantly shuttle back and forth between the abstract concepts of theory and the concrete examples of case studies. I hope you find it as rewarding to read a book written that way.

* * *

Writing is a solitary act. Like most authors, I write in the privacy of my study. I work best when there are no interruptions. My wife is at work. The dog doesn't want to go for a walk. The phone doesn't ring. FedEx doesn't deliver any packages.

The solitary nature of writing often leads readers to think we actually do it on our own. Nothing could be further from the truth. Most authors accumulate massive personal and intellectual debts, and that certainly has been the case here.

I owe the most to my wife, Gretchen Sandles. As a veteran foreign policy analyst for the U.S. government, the practical demands of the policymakers she writes for has made her a good foil for the idealistic traps I often fall into. She was particularly helpful in this project. It was her posting to the U.S. Embassy in London that got me to the United Kingdom, sparked my interest in Northern Ireland, and enabled this entire series to get off the ground. In the other good move she made for my career, she took a new position as a Balkans analyst just as I began writing this book.

The editorial team for this series has also been a tremendous help. In their very different ways, my coeditors, Barry Jones and Mary Durfee, have forced me to be more disciplined in my approach to theory. The two acquisitions editors we have worked with at Continuum, Petra Rechter and Caroline Wintersgill, have provided great advice and much-needed encouragement when my energies flagged. For a second time, Gary Kessler has mucked his way through my gnarled prose and made it far more consistent and readable.

I have benefited from working with people in the conflict resolution field, primarily people outside of academe. As I noted earlier, I have a long career as an activist and have actually worked as such on each of the cases covered in this book. I am especially indebted to my friends in the Beyond War Movement (now the Foundation for Global Community) for getting me into the field professionally in the first place and Rush Kidder of the Institute for Global Ethics for broadening my horizons beyond conflict resolution.

Academically, I have learned the most from Joel Peters. Now of Ben Gurion University of the Negev, Joel taught a graduate course with me on international conflict resolution at the University of Reading when we were both teaching there. We have worked together ever since on a number of political and academic projects. And I will be eternally grateful to Joel for organizing a cricket match as my going away party when my wife and I moved back to the States. For those who care (or understand), I got a duck but took three wickets in two overs.

A number of other colleagues have also helped me see the big picture. David Last of the Royal Military College in Canada appeared in my life as this book and his book on peacekeeping were falling into place. It was amazing to see how a career pacifist and a career artillery officer had reached virtually identical conclusions. Fran Harbour, Jim Barry, and Kevin Avruch at George Mason University have been soul mates on at least some of the issues I cover here. Guilain Denoeux of Colby College and Roger Bowen, president of SUNY New Paltz, team taught with me early on in my obsession with conflict resolution and also have done a lot to temper my often blind, early enthusiasm.

Others helped on the case studies. Theuns Eloff, founder of the National Business Initiative, convinced me that I could and should write on South Africa. T. R. Reid of the *Washington Post* urged me to keep Northern Ireland in the book when I was considering dropping it for space reasons. Dr. Mahdi Abdul Hadi and the students at PASSIA (Palestinian Academic Society for the Study of International Affairs) showed me that as a Jew, I had to be involved in what 'my people' were doing. Cheshmak Farhoumand directed me to the growing literature on reconciliation that took on a much more important role in this book than I had originally expected.

The book is dedicated to two people whose work entered my life too late to have much of an impact on this book but who have had a tremendous impact on my life in conflict resolution since I finished writing. Bernie Mayer is a partner at CDR in Boulder, Colorado. We have known each other since we were undergraduates protesting the Vietnam War and have frequently exchanged ideas on conflict resolution over the years. His new book, *Dynamics of Conflict Resolution*, is simply the best overall treatment of the field, covering everything from interpersonal to international disputes. Shortly after Bernie's book came out, I joined the staff of Search for Common Ground, where I am part of a team working to transform the way we deal with conflict here in the United States. On my second day at the office, my boss took me to meet the executive vice-president, Susan Collin Marks, who gave me her just-published book on South Africa. *Watching the Wind* documents the transition from apartheid to majority rule in Susan's native West Cape. It is a stunning book that reflects the commitment and passion Susan brings to this work. This is a commitment and passion I now get to experience first hand every week.

Last but by no means least, I have to thank Jessie, the mostly border collie who joined our family after I had drafted the first three chapters. I quickly discovered that if I took her for walks whenever I hit a writer's block, she would be a good sounding board for my ideas; at least she never objected to any of them.

To Bernie Mayer and Susan Collin Marks

Part 1

THEORY

PASSION, ARGUMENT, EVIDENCE, INSIGHT

Decimation means the killing of every tenth person in a population and in the spring and early summer of 1994 a program of massacres decimated the Republic of Rwanda. Although the killing was low-tech – performed largely by machete – it was carried out at dazzling speed; of an original population of about seven and a half million, at least eight hundred thousand were killed in just a hundred days. Rwandans often speak of a million deaths, and they may be right. The dead of Rwanda accumulated at nearly three times the rate of Jewish dead during the Holocaust. It was the most efficient mass killing since the atomic bombings of Hiroshima and Nagasaki.

– Philip Gourevitch

In April 1994 two momentous events occurred. On 6 April an airplane carrying the presidents of Rwanda and Burundi was shot down, killing all aboard. The crash was the catalyst for the genocide in Rwanda described in the passage by Philip Gourevitch (1998) that begins this book. Three weeks after the crash, South Africa held its first democratic election, which swept Nelson Mandela into power and marked the formal end of apartheid.

Those two events symbolize what this book is about.

The killings in Rwanda and Burundi are but the tip of a much larger iceberg of war and violence in the post-Cold War world. Many academics look longingly back to the Cold War when geopolitical pressures at least seemed to impose some limits on human cruelty. Others go further, like the journalist Robert Kaplan (1994, 1996), who warns of a 'coming anarchy' in which the combination of crime, poverty, environmental decay, and war will make our world a far more volatile and violent place.

The experience of South Africa, conversely, suggests that political life does not have to remain that violent. Those of us involved in the 1980s campaign to force American universities and pension funds to divest their holdings in companies that cooperated with the South African government frankly worried that we might never see the end of an apartheid regime that still seemed so very strong. Yet, just as the 1990s dawned, the South African government released Mandela after twenty-seven years in prison. He and his former jailers then led negotiations that produced the transition to majority rule. The former inmate became one of the world's most respected and adored political leaders. South Africa remains very troubled, with more than its share of political violence and one of the highest murder rates in the world. Nonetheless, an important corner toward peace and reconciliation has been turned, one that many of us are convinced can be adapted and used elsewhere to gradually redirect the world away from the coming anarchy.

PASSION

Most academic books are dispassionate. Their authors weigh evidence and arguments in a reasoned way, downplay their own values, and reach what they believe to be rational conclusions given what is known at the time.

We cannot, however, ignore either our values or our emotions in trying to come to grips with international conflict and its resolution. As Gourevitch implies in the epigrah to this chapter, it is usually something like revulsion against the killings in Rwanda or hopes for the tentative and fragile agreements reached in South Africa that draw most of us to the subject in the first place.

What's more, the stakes of international conflict are high indeed. The twentieth century was the most violent on record. The Carnegie Commission on Preventing Deadly Conflict's final report (1997) shows that more than 100 million people died in wars during the twentieth century.

Over the last twenty years, somewhere between twenty and thirty-five wars were being fought during an average year (see tables 1.1 and 1.2). In the 1990s alone, forty million people fled their countries as refugees. Ethnic cleansing brought genocide back onto the political agenda. The first war crimes tribunals since the end of World War II were created, and we will soon see the establishment of a permanent international criminal court to deal with crimes against humanity. As a report prepared for the International Committee of the Red Cross put it,

> The [most] fundamental shift in the character of war is illustrated by a stark statistic: in World War I, nine soldiers were killed for every civilian life lost. In today's wars, it is estimated that 10 civilians die for every soldier or fighter killed in battle. (International Committee of the Red Cross, 1990a:v)

Table 1.1 The number of wars in progress each year since 1950

Year	Number of wars
1950	11
1955	10
1960	12
1965	15
1970	17
1975	20
1980	24
1985	33
1990	33
1995	34

Source: International Global Futures Review, 15 February 1998. Distributed from <igfr@peg.apc.org>. Based on Worldwatch Institute data.

Table 1.2 Wars in progress each year between 1990 and 1998, by region

Region	Number of wars
The Americas	5
Africa	16
Central and eastern Europe	2
Former Soviet Union	4
Middle East	5
South and Southeast Asia	6

Source: Adapted from Carnegie Commission, *Preventing Deadly Violence*. New York: Carnegie Commission on Preventing Deadly Violence, 1997: 12.

Today's violent conflicts also take a terrible toll on the survivors, because they undermine the economies and environments of the countries in which they are fought. For example, the estimates for rebuilding Kuwait and Bosnia after their wars started at $50 billion each, which is more than all the money the industrialized countries spend on foreign aid each year.

They also are different from those of even a generation ago, Most at least started as domestic rather than international wars though many have spilled across national boundaries (Wallensteen and Sollenberg, 1995). Most revolve around emotionally charged religious, ethnic, linguistic, and racial disputes, which are much harder to resolve than the geopolitical issues that have sparked most previous wars.

Although the media tend to focus on the violence, there are thousands of people who have dedicated their intellectual and political lives to finding a better way of settling international disputes. Especially since the end of the Cold War, there has been an upsurge of interest in positive-sum or win-win conflict resolution that leaves all parties satisfied and open to cooperative problem-solving in general. In time, that kind of dispute resolution can lead to what Kenneth Boulding (1979, 1988) called stable peace in which war is all but impossible because the parties to past violence have learned to settle their differences without considering the use of force.

Such prominent politicians as former U.S. president Jimmy Carter and senator George Mitchell have built new careers as mediators in international disputes. Similarly, Bernard Kouchner moved on from his post as head of *Médecins sans frontières* to become, first, a cabinet minister in France, and then head of the UN's reconstruction efforts in Kosovo. Georgia's president (and former Soviet foreign minister) Eduard Shevardnadze is among a growing number of national leaders who have set up government-sponsored centers to promote conflict resolution.

Attempts to resolve conflict nonviolently often come from previously unexpected sources. Peacekeeping and peacebuilding are now part of the training of all senior officers in the U.S., Canadian, and Scandinavian armies. One European think tank has identified more than 500 NGOs (nongovernmental organizations) that devote all or part of their efforts to international conflict resolution (Miall, Ramsbotham, and Woodhouse, 1999:37). Perhaps most impressive of all, there are now tens of thousands of people who have full-time careers in governments, NGOs, and consulting firms specializing in conflict resolution.

ARGUMENT

But, this *is* an academic book and thus cannot rest on passion alone. Like all the books in this series, it is based on the premise that students (and other readers interested in international relations) can make the most sense of international conflict resolution by using theoretical arguments to sift through the evidence and reach deeper and more insightful conclusions.

There is no shortage of general analyses that can help people come to grips with international conflict and its resolution. However, those theoretical works have only been put to limited use because their authors have typically focused all but exclusively on the optimistic or the pessimistic sides of the field. Some see international conflict and violence as an inescapable part of the human condition. Others (including me in my own previous work on the subject) conclude that there are better ways of settling our disputes that puts them to rest once and for all.

In the pages that follow, I will make the case for at least giving new approaches to conflict resolution that stress win-win outcomes, reconciliation, and stable peace serious consideration. Those ideas are not new. There was a similar burst of optimism at the end of the nineteenth and beginning of the twentieth centuries just as there is now shortly after the dawn of a new century and millennium. Moreover, the theories to be discussed in chapters 3 and 4 have roots in the world's major spiritual traditions, which means they can be traced back for thousands of years. If I am right, however, the changed nature of conflict today and our growing, though still limited, experience with these strategies and techniques suggest that it would be foolhardy not to take them seriously.

That is only partially the case because of evolution in international politics. Win-win problem-solving and alternative dispute resolution have a long and rich intellectual pedigree in other disciplines, most notably business management and interpersonal dynamics (see, for instance, the summary in Abu-Nimer, 1999:1–28). To cite but the most obvious example, the most influential book in the field, Roger Fisher and William Ury's *Getting to Yes* (1981) has sold well over a million copies and is used by most corporate human resources departments.

That does not mean that the realists and others who argue for the continued use of more traditional analytical models and foreign policies are wrong. While today's conflicts are qualitatively different from those that traditional international relations theory is based on, it could well be that the next period in international relations could be one in which states, geopolitics, and wars fought by conventional arms are again the norm. More important, win-win conflict resolution is still very much the exception to the rule. To understand why that is the case, we have to turn to the more traditional theories and the less optimistic conclusions they typically lead to.

In other words, I do not want to seem too optimistic. As Pat Caplan (1995) among others has shown, conflict is an inescapable part of our lives at everything from the interpersonal to the international level. And, if the first signs about globalization are true, there could well be more conflict, not less, in the years to come.

Nonetheless, I will be insisting that there is what I have elsewhere called a 'rational basis for hope' for the medium to long term (Hauss, 1989). As we gain more experience using the new approaches to conflict resolution to be described in later chapters, we should be able to learn to use them more effectively and to build more support for them in the process.

It is important to underscore the importance of taking each school of thought seriously from a slightly different viewpoint before moving on, because it will make this book different from most on conflict resolution or, for that matter, international relations in general.

In academic life, there is a tendency to pit theories against each other in a 'debate' over which of them is correct. I will not be doing that in the pages that follow. I do have a strong personal preference. I very much want to live in a world in which win-win conflict resolution becomes the norm because individuals, organizations, and states learn to settle their disputes 'better.' However, my task here is to help the reader understand the way conflict is addressed today. That is a very different matter. Writing this book convinced me more than ever that we need both the new and the traditional theories in trying to explain conflict and its resolution, because they *complement* more than they contradict each other.

EVIDENCE AND INSIGHT

Theory is important, but it is not enough. Our goal may be to reach general and even abstract conclusions that shape both our analyses and our actions. However, research by scholars who study how people learn suggests that few of us can assess theory by working solely at an abstract level.

Therefore, like the other volumes in this series, this book uses carefully selected case studies to allow readers to test the theories and reach their own conclusion. Part 2 develops five examples that illustrate the variety of conflicts that exist as the twenty-first century dawns, from those in which major strides toward resolution have occurred to others in which the dispute festers and ongoing violence is the norm. Together, they allow us to get a first glimpse at the conditions under which win-win conflict resolution and stable peace are most – and least – likely to occur and, as a result, where traditional and new approaches to international relations are most effective. They are:

- the transition to democratic rule in South Africa
- efforts to end the 'Troubles' in Northern Ireland
- the peace process between Israelis and Palestinians
- the breakup of Yugoslavia and the war in Bosnia
- the Gulf war and its aftermath

The rest of this book will demonstrate that combining theory and case studies leads to new insights into international conflict resolution and the state of international relations in general. Outlining them here, however, would be premature. The conclusions we can reach do depend on the joint consideration of theories and cases, and it only makes sense to defer discussing specific insights. Each case study chapter will start with theoretical questions and end with the broader implications about conflict resolution in general that can be derived from that example.

TWO PRACTICAL MATTERS

Each chapter will have a box with useful web sites for the material covered in it. Furthermore, the series as a whole has a web site: <http://www.continuumbooks.com/irseries.htm>. This allows you to go beyond what is in the books. Among other things, you can:

- investigate the link between theory and cases as you read, using the more flexible approach to contrasting the two offered by hypertext-based software;
- seek links to other sources of information on the concepts and cases covered in this book;
- explore overlapping themes between this and other books in the series;
- participate in a forum with other students, instructors, and nonacademics who are using these books;
- ask questions of and make suggestions to the series editors and most of the authors of individual books.

Each chapter also has a select bibliography that includes everything cited in it. The bibliographies are not meant to be exhaustive lists of books and articles on the cutting edge of scholarship. Rather, they direct you primarily to works that are particularly useful to people who are not specialists in either international relations theory or the conflicts covered in part 2.

Useful Web Sites

The best place to begin is with the web site which was created for this book and which includes all the sites mentioned here and others that have appeared since this book went to press.
`<http://classweb.gmu.edu/classweb/chauss/irseries/index.htm>`

As is almost always the case in academic life, the Virtual Library has an outstanding and well-documented collection of sites, which can be reached at either the main site `<http://www.vlib.org>` or the specific conflict resolution one,
`<http://www.pitt.edu/~ian/resource/conflict.htm>`.

Also helpful are the Centre for Security Studies and Conflict Research in Switzerland `<http://www.fsk.ethz.ch>`, INCORE on ethnic conflict based in Northern Ireland
`<http://www.incore.ulst.ac.uk>`, and the Colorado Conflict Resolution Consortium
`<http://www.colorado.edu/conflict/index.html>`.

SELECT BIBLIOGRAPHY

Abu-Nimer, Mohammed. *Dialogue, Conflict Resolution, and Change: Arab-Jewish Encounters in Israel.* Albany, N.Y.: SUNY Press, 1978.

Boulding, Kenneth. *Stable Peace.* Austin: University of Texas Press, 1978.

————. 'Moving from Unstable to Stable Peace.' In *Breakthrough: Emerging New Thinking: Soviet and American Scholars Issue a Challenge to Build a World Beyond War,* edited by Martin Hellman and Anatoly Gromyko, 157–67. New York: Walker, 1988.

Carnegie Commission for the Prevention of Deadly Conflict. *Preventing Deadly Conflict.* New York: Carnegie Commission, 1997. Also available at <http:www.ccpdc.org>.

Fisher, Roger, and William Ury. *Getting to Yes.* New York: Penguin, 1981.

Gourevitch, Philip. *We Wish to Inform You That Tomorrow We Will Be Killed with Our Families.* New York: Farrar-Strauss-Giroux, 1998.

Hauss, Charles. 'A Rational Basis for Hope.' In *Peace: Meanings, Politics, Strategies,* edited by Linda Rennie Forcey, 203–18. Westport, CT: Praeger, 1989.

International Committee of the Red Cross. *People on War: General Report,* 1999a. <http://www.onwar.org>. Accessed 20 December 1999.

Kaplan, Robert D. 'The Coming Anarchy.' *Atlantic* (February, 1994).
————. *The Ends of the Earth: A Journey at the Dawn of the 21st Century*. New York: Random House, 1996.
Wallensteen, Peter, and Margareta Sollenberg. 'After the Cold War: Emerging Patterns of Armed Conflict.' *Journal of Peace Research*. 23 (1995): 345-60.

2

THE ROLE OF THEORY

> I pass with relief from the tossing sea of Cause and Theory to the firm ground of Result and Fact.
>
> – Winston Churchill

People who actually try to solve international disputes rarely think about the role theory plays in their work. Many go so far as to reject the premise of this series – that theory is vital to their work. Winston Churchill certainly did that in the statement that begins this chapter. More recently, the same sentiment found its way into the second paragraph of Richard Holbrooke's memoir about the diplomatic initiatives that led to the Dayton Agreement that ended the war in Bosnia, '[t]his was not a theoretical game between nation states, but a dangerous and unpredictable process' (1998:xv).

The likes of Churchill or Holbrooke can, of course, be excused for not worrying about theory at the most charged moments of their political lives, when the pressure of events simply did not leave them with the time to do so. That is not true for us academics, however. In the kind of teaching and research most of us do, we cannot make much progress without theory.

In fact, everyone uses theories all the time, even in the midst of an international crisis. While we may not be aware of how they shape our thoughts or even that we are using them, theories serve as the mental lenses through which we view and interpret the world. As such, they determine how we make the judgments that govern how we act – average citizens and policymakers alike. Churchill's implicit theory revolved around the need for democracies to remain resolute in the face of totalitarian regimes such as the one in Nazi Germany. Holbrooke's expectations were different, reflecting the more optimistic times of the first years after the end of the Cold War.

WHAT IS THEORY?

As with everything else in academic life, there is no simple or universally accepted definition of theory. As it will be used here and in the other volumes in this series, a theory is an attempt to reach general conclusions about a broad body of material.

There are two main types of theories. (For overviews of theory in international relations, see Viotti and Kauppi, 1999; Dougherty and Pfaltzgraff, 1996; Booth and Smith, 1995.) Empirical theories seek to explain why certain phenomena occur and, therefore, focus on cause and effect relationships. Normative theories are designed to prescribe what we should do in dealing with those phenomena. Thus, empirical theories of conflict resolution analyze why, at some times, we can settle our disputes peacefully, while, at others, we turn to violence and war. A normative theory would lay out options we should use in trying to reach a certain goal, such as a nonviolent outcome that satisfies all parties to the conflict.

The two types of theories will be treated separately here. However, keep in mind that no theory is entirely empirical or normative. Theories that purport to be empirical invariably reflect the ideological and other biases of their creators. Similarly, the best normative theories are based on solid analyses of 'what is' as well as of 'what ought to be.'

We should not expect any theory to satisfy everyone. To begin with, there are gaping holes in what we know about international relations, especially about what motivates leaders to act as they do. Those uncertainties are especially important during times like ours, when things are changing so fast that some pundits claim that change is the only constant in our lives. Furthermore, we disagree too much, especially about normative goals and how to reach them. And those disagreements get in the way of reaching agreement on empirical issues as well, something we will see time and time again in the case studies in part 2.

USING THEORY

Still, we should never underestimate the importance of theory, because it is by contrasting different theories that we make the most progress in understanding a contentious field like international relations. That is the case because of four ways we can use theory in empirical analysis.

First of all, we need theory to help us organize our studies or research. The *New York Times* masthead proclaims that it includes 'all the news that's fit to print.' In fact, that isn't true. The *Washington Post*, for instance, gives American national politics far more attention. All the British dailies cover politics there more thoroughly than the *New York Times* covers American politics.

The *Times* includes all the news that its editors think is worthy to print and that fits in the number of pages they have available for the paper that day. They make their decisions using some simple rules about what they think is important and what will sell newspapers, which form a rudimentary theory of what it takes to run a successful 'quality' daily.

At the very least, then, theories help us organize our work. They point us toward some information or issues and away from others. They give us intellectual cubbyholes (for example, the domestic news, foreign news, sports, business, and other sections of a newspaper) into which to put the information we gather and an order in which to analyze it.

Different theories do that in different ways. Realists have us focus on the international system, the balance of power, geopolitical issues, and the (hoped for) rational actions of leaders. Their mainstream critics, usually dubbed pluralists, liberals, or idealists, draw our attention to the often-complicated and anything-but-rational nature of domestic politics. Globalization theorists broaden our horizons even further by including international organizations, multinational corporations, and nongovernmental organizations.

Second, theory allows us to think at a more general and abstract level (Nicolson, 1996). Educational theorists argue that one of the toughest challenges students have to face is learning to take a concept encountered in one context and apply it in another. What does learning about the Holocaust teach me about genocide in general? Can I use the insights gleaned from the horrid history of the Third Reich and its 'final solution' to help me understand ethnic cleansing in Bosnia or Kosovo?

To do that, Rosenau and Durfee tell us we have to move up the 'ladder of abstraction.' In this case, we do that by asking a syntactically awkward question. 'Of what is this an instance?' (2000:3). The Holocaust was an instance of European fascism. Even more generally, it was an example of genocide, the most horrific kind of human rights violation.

Put in slightly different terms, a theory helps us understand common patterns or similarities and differences we find in a large number of related phenomena. Why is it that the most authoritarian regimes engage in such massive abuses of human rights? By contrast, why is it that democracies rarely – if ever – do so?

We can then use those conclusions in other cases that might not have even occurred when the theory was initially developed. In this example, we could explore if and how the authoritarian nature of Slobodan Milosevic's regime in Serbia contributed to the horrors that have gripped the Balkans since 1991 and if the more democratic nature of the Czechoslovakian government made it easier for that country to split in two peacefully.

Third, empirical theory can be a powerful tool for reaching abstract conclusions in what may strike you as an odd way at first glance. No theory can ever be proven true.

Useful Web Sites

After years of looking, I still have not found any outstanding web sites dedicated to international theory.

That does not mean that the Internet is of no use to people studying international theory. If you go, for instance, to the Virtual Library's site on international relations, you will find that almost all of the entries will provide some links to theoretically rich sites <http://www.vlib.org>.

Realistically, however, you are most likely to find useful material from sites such as CIAO (Columbia International Affairs Online), Infotrac, ProQuest, Project Muse, Jstor, and similar reference sources that include full texts of journal articles. I have not provided the URLs for these sites here, since they are typically services that can only be reached through a library or research institute that has paid the relevant subscription fees.

Researchers can gather all the available evidence. However, it is always possible that they missed a case in which they would have found that the theory's predictions and explanations were inaccurate. Similarly, researchers can never be certain that there will not be some future event that undermines the theory.

Instead, the critical characteristic of a theory is that we can falsify it or show that its predictions or explanations are wrong. Once we have done that, we can go on to another, even more vital, step and ask ourselves why the theory failed in the cases under consideration. In so doing, we can improve the theory and, with it, our overall understanding of the subject under consideration.

To see what it means to falsify, start with Thomas Friedman's variation of the controversial theory that democracies do not go to war with other democracies because of the values, cultures, and other phenomena they share. In early 1999 he argued that 'no two countries that both had McDonald's had fought a war against each other since each got its McDonald's' (1999:195). He claimed that what he called the 'golden arches theory of conflict prevention' existed because of the economic, cultural, and other 'globalizing' links that drew such societies together and raises the cost of their going to war with each other.

Friedman actually understood that his theory had its limitations, because he went on to point out that someday there would be a war between countries with McDonald's. In fact, it happened in the first weeks after his book was published. The heavily McDonaldized NATO powers went to war with Yugoslavia, whose seven McDonald's were shut when the war broke out but were back in business within a few days.

To see where falsification can take us, consider a more intellectually contentious example – the contemporary critiques of realism. Traditional realists claim that wars arise when states cannot otherwise adjust to changes in the balance of power among the leading states. Thus, they focused on such trends as the shifting European balance of power after the Napoleonic wars and the events leading up to the two world wars. Similarly, they were able to account for superpower involvement in many of the regional conflicts between 1945 and 1990 as being proxy struggles between the superpowers.

Realists, however, have had a much harder time so categorizing the wars of the 1990s. I am not saying that they have failed completely. We can develop realist analyses of the two major conflicts of the decade – the Gulf war and the on-again, off-again fighting in the former Yugoslavia. However, it is far more difficult to use realism to come to grips with the genocide in Bosnia, which began as an almost purely domestic dispute. As a result, some international relations analysts have decided that realism has been falsified.

The next step is not in itself empirical, since we cannot determine what is wrong with a theory simply by looking at the facts. Instead, the theorist has to take a step back from the data and use his or her intuition and creativity to amend the old theory or develop a new one altogether. In this case, because the state is no longer the one and only unit of importance in international political life, we have to concentrate on domestic politics, ethnicity, and other factors in explaining what gave rise to most of today's most vexing conflicts.

A fourth reason theory is useful is that normative theory is also a powerful and inescapable part of international relations. This can be illustrated using examples from the academic literature. However, it is easier to do so with personal examples, because normative concerns frequently lead people to become interested in international relations in the first place and shape the way they view the world as students, scholars, or average citizens alike.

My father, who was born in 1920, was drawn to political life because of the economic difficulties he experienced during the depression and then as a Jew and member of the U.S. military at the height of the Holocaust. I became a political scientist rather than a physicist during my under-graduate years in the late 1960s out of a desire to end the war in Vietnam. During the 1980s, many of my students became Soviet studies majors because of their interest in the heightened tensions of the first half of the decade and the remarkable events that led to the end of the Cold War under Mikhail Gorbachev. Today, students are more likely to be fascinated by the economic, environmental, and political aspects of globalization.

Normative differences also frequently lead people from different theoretical schools of thought to talk past each other because their values lead them to answer the 'of-what-is-this-an-instance' question differ-ently.

I started writing this book just as the war over the treatment of ethnic Albanians in Kosovo began, and it was thus constantly on my mind as I put the first pieces of this manuscript together. Like many 1960s pacifists, I found myself in the unusual position of supporting a war for the first time in my life. I was convinced that this case was different from all the others from Vietnam to the Gulf war because the level of human rights abuses being committed by the Milosevic regime outweighed my commitment to peace. A good friend who teaches high school and is a practicing Quaker opposed the war because her beliefs put the prohibition against killing above all other values and goals. A conservative Republican friend who is a retired Defense Department employee and a realist opposed the war because he saw it as a regional conflict that did not in any way directly imperil vital American interests.

THEORY AND CASES

This book is also written on the assumption that most people deal with those four aspects of theory by moving up Durfee and Rosenau's ladder of abstraction from specific examples to general conclusions. That approach, however, flies in the face of scientific orthodoxy, which is deductive. Most experts are convinced that, because we need theory as an intellectual road map and as a tool for falsification, we need to start with it and then assess it in the light of the data we uncover.

Unfortunately, most teachers find that students have a hard time getting beyond the theory if we focus on issues of an abstract nature from the beginning. To get around this problem in my classes, I rely heavily on the case study method, which is widely used in business and other professional schools. In it, I guide the class through a discussion of the critical issues in the case so that that I can move the class up that ladder and get them to see the general arguments that flow from it. Unfortunately, a book is more linear than a classroom discussion. It has to go from page 1 to page 2, chapter 1 to chapter 2, part 1 to part 2 and simply cannot be as flexible as a teacher in a classroom. Therefore, this book is structured more along the theory to cases to revised theory lines of conventional scientific work than are my classes.

However, there are three things you can do to give reading this book more of the flavor and power of the traditional case study method. First, after reading chapters 2 through 5, go back and review chapter 1, because it gives you a substantive agenda with which to make some first assessments of the theories and, even more important, to begin bringing it down to earth. Second, use the guidelines in the first box in chapter 6 in assessing the individual cases in part 2 and others you may work on. Finally, take advantage of the online study guide for this and the other books in this series at our web site. It uses the nonlinear nature of hypertext programming to allow you to move back and forth between theory and cases at your own pace and using your own learning style.

SELECT BIBLIOGRAPHY

Booth, Ken, and Steve Smith. *International Relations Theory Today*. Cambridge: Polity Press, 1995.

Dougherty, James, and Robert Pfaltzgraff. *Contending Theories of International Relations*. Boston: Addison-Wesley, 1996.

Durfee, Mary, and James Rosenau. *Thinking Theory Thoroughly: Coherent Approaches in an Incoherent World*, 2d ed. Boulder, CO: Westview, 2000.

Friedman, Thomas L. *The Lexus and the Olive Tree: Understanding Globalization*. New York: Farrar-Strauss-Giroux, 1999.

Holbrooke, Richard. *To End a War*. New York: Random House, 1998.

Nicholson, Michael. *Causes and Consequences in International Relations: A Conceptual Study*. London: Pinter, 1996.

Viotti, Paul, and Mark Kauppi. *International Relations Theory*. Boston: Allyn and Bacon, 1999.

3

UNDERSTANDING CONFLICT

In the years ahead crises and threats will grow more numerous, not less, and will pose significant threats to international peace and security and to the interests of many nations.

– Michael Lund

It is tempting to leap right into the theories we will use to explain international conflict and its resolution. Doing so, however, would be premature. Instead, we have to start with a more basic theoretical question. What is international conflict like? How observers answer that question is actually an important first step in seeing why they reach different theoretical conclusions about the field.

THE NATURE OF CONFLICT

Protracted Violence

Until recently, scholarship on international conflict focused on wars fought between countries. Indeed, the definitions of war used most frequently a generation ago were based on battle deaths in fighting between the armies of internationally recognized states.

To be sure, there have always been civil wars in which two or more internal groups vie for power in a single country. Similarly, the last two centuries have seen a large number of revolutionary wars of national liberation in which a colonized people fought for their freedom. Still, given the destruction of international wars over the last several centuries, it is hardly surprising that they remained the focus of theoretical and empirical research in international relations through the Cold War years.

In the last generation or so, however, intrastate conflicts have become the rule, not the exception. One typical study found that only twenty-eight of the eighty wars fought between 1945 and 1995 pitted two or more states and their armies against each other (Kaplan, 1996:8). In the conflicts of the 1990s, only the Gulf war was primarily international in origin.

About two-thirds of these wars have taken place in the world's poorest countries, Many of those failed states have lost all or most of their ability to maintain order let alone forge policies to help their societies and economies develop. In short, wars not only kill soldiers and civilians but they also make life even harder for the millions of people who struggled to survive even before the fighting began.

Furthermore, many of these wars have turned into what Robert Kaplan calls 'mini-holocausts.' For instance, 10 percent of the Rwandan population was killed in six weeks. Well over half the ethnic Albanians living in Kosovo were forced to flee their homes in a briefer period. The fighting in Rwanda and the former Yugoslavia was so horrid that the United Nations established a war crimes tribunal that had been put in political mothballs once the trials at the end of World War II were completed. Now a treaty has been signed that could eventually lead to the creation of a permanent international court, though it is by no means clear yet whether the United States and other key countries will participate.

Research in fifteen of the most deeply affected countries that was conducted for the International Committee of the Red Cross (1999a:vii–xi) is especially telling in this regard. Just about one-quarter of the combatants have been either killed or injured. One in six were imprisoned. Of them, about 20 percent claim to have been tortured. In the civilian populations that were surveyed for the study, the two most commonly used adjectives to describe the fighting were 'horrible' and 'hateful.' That is hardly surprising. The majority of the casualties have been civilians. Almost a third of the respondents reported having had at least one close relative die. In addition, 40 percent cited having permanently lost touch with at least one family member, many of whom, of course, are dead but not accounted for. A third had their homes destroyed, while another quarter had their property looted. In perhaps the most tragic example of all, hundreds of thousands of children as young as ten years old are fighting on the world's battlefields today.

These are not easy conflicts to resolve because they have nonpolitical aspects that make negotiations more difficult than in most 'traditional' wars. In the twentieth century as a whole, about half the interstate wars ended as a result of a mediated settlement; for civil wars, the figure was only 15 percent (Stedman, 1999:16). In many of them, ill-disciplined groups of guerrillas do much of the fighting, much of which seems like

---

Useful Web Sites

The Carnegie Commission for the Prevention of Deadly Conflict issued a mammoth report on international conflict in late 1997. The commission has since gone out of business but its main report and other publications remain available on line.
<http://www.ccpdc.org>.

The Center for Security Studies and Conflict Research in Switzerland maintains an exhaustive set of links to other sources of material on international conflict. <http://www.fsk.ethz.ch/>.

INCORE, located at the University of Ulster in Northern Ireland, does the same for ethnically based conflicts.
<http://www.incore.ulst.ac.uk/>.

The Institute for War and Peace Reporting has outstanding material, especially on conflict in what used to be the communist world. <http://www.iwpr.net/>. So, too, does a project headed by Roy Gutman of *Newsday*. <http://www.crimesofwar.org>.

The International Committee of the Red Cross has commissioned surveys of public reactions to war in fifteen of the countries that have been hardest hit since the late 1980s. The results and analyses of those surveys can be found at <http://www.onwar.org>.

The Conflict Resolution Consortium at the University of Colorado also has a wide range of links to both data sources on conflict itself and tools for those working on its resolution.
<http://www.colorado.edu/conflict>.

---

little more than random acts of violence against citizens who are members of the groups they oppose. That makes it hard to differentiate purposive political violence from organized crime, especially in cases like the combined war being fought by revolutionaries and drug lords against the government of Colombia. Many of them are also asymmetric disputes in which one side is far more powerful than the other, and the imbalance of their strengths also makes resolution difficult because the weaker side typically feels deeply aggrieved and is reluctant to cooperate with its more powerful adversary. Thus, as we will see in chapter 7, until recently there were almost twice as many Protestants as Catholics in Northern Ireland. Protestants controlled an even larger share of the province's economy and enjoyed far closer links to the British government.

Donald Snow, who has long studied the role of the military in politics, puts it this way:

There is no common center of gravity to which combatants appeal; in many cases it is not clear that the 'insurgents' have any interest in or intent on gaining political power or responsibility; and there is little sense of boundaries on the extent of violence both sides would commit. These conflicts seem, indeed, to be a new kind of war. (Snow, 1996:ix)

The travel and political journalist, Robert Kaplan, goes even further:

It was in Sierra Leone that I first considered the possibility that just as states and their governments were meaning less and less, the distinctions between states and armies, armies and civilians, and armies and criminal gangs were also weakening. (1996:45)

The International Dimension

We should not, however, conclude that these are *purely* domestic conflicts. International factors are almost always among their causes and consequences. And, perhaps most important of all for our purposes, the international community is increasingly involved in attempts to resolve them.

On a few occasions, the actions of other states are consciously intended to provoke or sustain conflict as was the case with Soviet aid to the Palestine Liberation Organization and African National Congress for much of the Cold War and American support to Iraq during its war with Iran. More frequently, the impact is indirect and unintentional. Thus, Stephen Stedman (1999) has argued that the economic dislocations caused by the international financial institutions' demands for structural adjustment have exacerbated tensions in much of the third world and contributed to the escalation of many of the conflicts in sub-Saharan Africa. Similarly, the European Union's failure to strictly adhere to its own rules for extending diplomatic recognition to new states sped up Croatia's declaration of independence and the beginning of the fighting that would embroil the former Yugoslavia for the bulk of the 1990s. Stedman goes on to suggest that even the provision of humanitarian aid can make things worse. In such places as Bosnia and Rwanda, the food, clothing, and medicine the international community sent in served to strengthen the resolve of one side to the conflict and thus helped prolong the fighting. (Also see the discussion of hurting stalemates later in this chapter and in chapter 5.)

Some of the wars did spill across national borders. Most produced waves of refugees, which were estimated to top seven million in Africa alone in mid-1999. In some cases, the fighting itself spread to neighboring countries or drew other regional powers into the struggle, as we will see most clearly in the discussion of the former Yugoslavia in chapter 9.

The international community has played an increasingly active role in trying to resolve these disputes. While the United Nations has gotten the most attention – and criticism – for its involvement, it is often not a major factor, since it lacks either the legal right or the economic and human resources to intervene. Rather, as we will see in part 2, most of these efforts are spearheaded by private citizens, nongovernmental organizations (NGOs), individual states, or regional alliances.

THE LIFE CYCLE OF INTERNATIONAL CONFLICT

Other recent research (see, especially, Stedman, 1999; Lund, 1996:38; and Miall, Ramsbotham, and Woodhouse, 1999:ch. 3–7) has documented a common life cycle spanning four stages that most international conflicts have in common. Not all conflicts pass through each one of them. Nonetheless, the onset of each phase does make the next one more likely. More important for our purposes, the stages offer us a useful way for making sense of the evolution of any dispute and, as we will see in the next two chapters, why all conflict resolution techniques work better in some situations than others.

Crisis Creation

In the first stage of a conflict, tensions deepen to the point that violence becomes possible. In considering conflict resolution at this stage, political scientists have begun regularly using a term we borrowed from the physicians. Almost all doctors now practice preventive medicine, trying to convince their patients that they should lose weight or change their diets to reduce their risks of heart attack, stroke, and other debilitating conditions. Thus, we now speak of preventive diplomacy in which states, NGOs, or international bodies try to literally prevent a conflict from turning violent.

They frequently point to the UN mission sent to Macedonia in the early days of the fighting as Yugoslavia fell apart. It has largely succeeded (so far at least) in its 'trip-wire' mission to detect and react to signs that the fighting might spread into Macedonia. Such operations are seen as an opportunity to avoid the outbreak of fighting and move directly into a situation in which it is possible to reduce tensions in the short term and, over time, to (re)build stable peace.

For reasons that will become clear in the next two chapters, politicians rarely are able to summon the political will to do that. Instead, they more often make weak or belated efforts at preventive diplomacy. Thus, the Serbs had been eroding the rights of Kosovars and laying the groundwork for rebellion for almost a decade before the international community made a serious attempt to find a negotiated settlement.

There is no better or more tragic testimony to the awareness that we should intervene as early as possible but also to the practical difficulties in doing so than two recent reports prepared for the Carnegie Commission on the Prevention of Deadly Violence. John Stremlau and Francisco R. Sagasti (1998) entitled their report *Preventing Deadly Conflict: Does the World Bank Play a Role?* In fact, they focus on what the Bank could and should do once the fighting has ended. While a laudable goal (see the end of this section), the Bank's efforts are aimed at preventing the next war, not the one looming immediately on the horizon. Similarly, the BBC's Nik Gowing (1997, also see Strobel, 1997) paints an ambiguous picture of the impact of the media. To be sure, CNN's Christiane Amanpour, *Newsday's* Roy Gutman, and former BBC correspondent (and now Member of Parliament) Martin Bell head a list of journalists whose work has helped propel human tragedies around the world onto the global political agenda, giving rise to what is often called the CNN effect. However, just as frequently the pressure of deadlines, the lack of correspondents in places like East Timor, the need to keep ratings up, and the limits imposed by a half-hour or hour-long program mean that the media simply do not cover many of the world's hot spots.

Turning to War

As with preventive diplomacy, there is reason to believe that timely intervention when the fighting begins can lead to a quick cessation of hostilities. However, the parties to the conflict and the international community rarely commit themselves to any sort of conflict resolution until the fighting has become intense.

Indeed, the failure to do so has been one of the most consistent criticisms of the leaders of the world's major powers during the 1990s. In perhaps the most tragic example, Romeo Dallaire, the Canadian head of the UN peacekeeping mission in Rwanda, was convinced that he could have stopped the genocide as it began if he had been given a few thousand more soldiers. The Security Council refused (Feil, 1998). Criticism also comes from some who have long been involved in the peace movement or the academic field of peace studies. Jane M. O. Sharp

(1998), for instance roundly criticizes the United States and the major European powers for their reluctance to get involved and their continuing indecision, which, she feels, made the death and destruction in Croatia and Bosnia much worse than it had to have been.

Instead, at that stage, the international community tends to concentrate on helping people who are caught up in the fighting. In recent years, the United Nations and other international organizations, NGOs, and national governments (including their militaries) have stepped up their humanitarian intervention (Weiss, 1999; Weiss and Collins, 1996). Perhaps because development agencies and dozens of NGOs are already working 'on the ground' when the fighting starts, they have become the vehicle through which food, medical supplies, and other aid is channeled in attempts to ease the damage of what are euphemistically known as 'complex emergencies.' One sign of how such efforts have grown is the fact that Bernard Kouchner, one of the founders of *Médecins sans frontières*, became a cabinet minister in the French government until he was named head of the UN-led civilian reconstruction effort in Kosovo. The scholarly community, however, has not come close to reaching an agreement about how such intervention affects the outcome of a conflict; some observers even argue that sending of food, medicine, and other aid can, in some circumstances, actually prolong the war.

A New Taxonomy

In 1992 then United Nations secretary-general Boutros Boutros-Ghali issued his report, *An Agenda for Peace*. In it, he pointed out that in the early 1990s, the UN (and by implication, other international organizations) had gone beyond the peacekeeping role that it had used most frequently during the Cold War years. Since then, other writers have suggested changing some of his terms or adding some new ones. For our purposes, his list will do and included:

- peacemaking – the attempt to bring fighting to an end using peaceful means
- peace enforcement – the armed effort to stop the fighting
- peacekeeping – monitoring and reinforcing a cease-fire that is already in place before the UN or other forces come in
- peacebuilding – steps taken to settle the disagreements that led to the fighting in the first place, which, in other words, entails building stable peace.

Stopping the Fighting

Until recently, political scientists have been convinced that it is all but impossible to stop the fighting until the parties reach what I. William Zartman (1989) and Richard Haass (1990) call a 'mutually hurting stalemate.' At that point, serious negotiations can begin, often mediated by a neutral third party drawn from the international organizations or the growing group of former politicians who have taken on international conflict resolution as a retirement job.

Historically, too, the most attention has been focused on peacekeeping by the United Nations and other, regional international organizations. The UN's lightly armed blue berets were only introduced once a cease-fire agreement was reached, and they have normally played a limited role – preventing the resumption of the fighting (United Nations, 1996). As with UNFICYP, which has been in Cyprus since the mid-1960s, these troops are only sent in after the fighting stops and their primary goal is to see that it does not break out again, usually by keeping the former antagonists apart.

But in the last decade, the scope of the international community's efforts have expanded – and become far riskier. There is a greater willingness to intervene early in the fighting to produce what has come to be called peacemaking or peace imposition (Snow, 1996:133). On some occasions, the international community is willing to send in troops even while there was still fighting going on, as was the case in Somalia, Sierra Leone, and Haiti. They are not the lightly armed or unarmed blue helmets. Rather, in this kind of intervention forces expect to have to do some fighting and take some casualties. The international community often is not neutral but weighs in against a government whose human rights violations sparked the mission in the first place. And, in the most unsettling example of all, the U.S.-led NATO force actually went to war against Yugoslavia in 1999 as part of its attempt to end the ethnic cleansing and resolve the conflict in Kosovo.

As the still-raging debates regarding the Kosovo mission, in particular, make clear, we have not had enough time to determine how successful these more ambitious actions can be.

Building Stable Peace

In the writing on international conflict before the end of the Cold War, most observers stopped their analyses with peacekeeping and its less-than-stellar track record. That made sense, since the UN and other bodies did not and could not go any further than that.

The events of the late 1980s, however, led some observers to give new attention to the areas of the world in which stable peace is the norm. Though rare in the third world, there is little doubt that stable peace is the rule rather than the exception among the industrialized democracies. Although they use the term zone of peace instead, the conservative analysts Max Singer and Aaron Wildavsky (1996) make a convincing case that war between the major western European, East Asian, Antipodean, and North American states is all but impossible.

Other observers looked at domestic and international efforts to 'build bridges' between former combatants and create what comparative politics specialists call civil society and the other preconditions of a system in which people use nonviolent means to settle their disputes. The most widely cited such example is the remarkable ongoing transition in South Africa. When the 1990s began, it still had a repressive, Whites-only regime. When the decade ended, it had just held its second all-race election following six years of reasonably successful democracy and majority (that is, African) rule. One of the highlights of those years has been the efforts by leaders – Black and White alike – to overcome the horrors of the past and build true reconciliation between their communities.

In that sense, stable peace is the only true form of conflict resolution. Literally speaking, resolution is the harmonious solution to a problem, as when a 'resolved' chord ends a piece of music. To achieve stable peace, states and other actors must find ways to solve the problems that gave rise to the violence to the degree that people no longer consider it an option, because it is no longer 'needed' in working out their differences.

Stable peace does not mean that conflict disappears or that citizens of the societies involved like each other. Thus, when I lived in France and then in Great Britain, it was rare to find French people of my generation (born shortly after World War II) who had nice things to say about the Germans. Nonetheless, relations between them are now good enough that there no longer is any real chance that they would turn to violence to solve the conflicts over trade, foreign policy, or immigration that are still a common feature of their joint political lives.

Stable peace is rare. It takes the kind of time and patience that is uncommon in political life. Still, there are signs that the international community is taking the idea more seriously than ever before and is experimenting with new strategies to take societies closer to it.

As Minow (1998) has shown, South Africa is but the most prominent example of a country whose leadership has tried to ferret out the truth about the political crimes of the past as a first step toward building reconciliation between former adversaries. The Dayton Agreement that ended the war in Bosnia had provisions for civilian-military cooperation to (re)create the civilian institutions needed to bolster a legitimate and effective state (Joulwan and Shoemaker, 1998). The U.S.-led NATO coalition went even further after Yugoslavia capitulated in the summer of 1999 by calling for the systematic rebuilding of Kosovo's economy and civil society as well as its political institutions. Thus, more and more observers acknowledge that stable peace and the prevention of violent conflict requires a concerted effort aimed not just at the specific issues that led to fighting but at all the social, economic, environmental, and cultural issues that underlie the dispute as a whole (Cortright, 1997).

Stable peace, in short, requires a very different attitude on the part of those involved from what one normally finds in international political life. In the words of the seventeenth-century philosopher, Baruch Spinoza:

> Peace is not an absence of war; it is a virtue, a state of mind, a disposition for benevolence, confidence, justice.

TOWARD STABLE PEACE?

This discussion of the way disputes play themselves out itself opens the door to the two schools of thought that dominate the study of international conflict resolution today.

Traditionally, international relations experts have focused on the causes and nature of war. Realists, in particular, have assumed that international conflict and war are common and inescapable aspects of political life. From their perspective, the statement by Flavius Vegetius Renatus, 'If you want peace, prepare for war' is as valid today as it was when it first made nearly 2,000 years ago.

A Fifth Stage?

While acknowledging the possibilities of stable peace, we should also briefly consider a fifth stage. As is often the case, if the parties fail to build stable peace, it is only a matter of time until we 'loop' back and a new issue creates a crisis and the possibility for more violence. And, as we will see in the former Yugoslavia, all too frequently the next outbreak of violence is far deadlier than the previous one, and the prospects for stable peace grow even dimmer.

All too often, however, deterrence and the other strategies realists believe *can* keep the peace fail to do so and states and their citizens are plunged into war. Once that happens, realists are convinced that wars end with either a win-lose or lose-lose outcome followed by a negative peace in which the tensions that gave rise to the dispute persist.

People who work on the new forms of conflict resolution, however, are convinced that we can do better than the alternation between armed defense and war around which traditional international relations revolve. Their approach is based on two related assumptions. First, it is best to deal with a crisis using preventive diplomacy before it turns violent. Second, win-win conflict resolution can be part of a broader process of reconciliation in which the tensions between the parties are reduced because the root causes that originally gave rise to the conflict are addressed in ways that eliminate the divisions that gave rise to the dispute in the first place.

A GLASS PARTLY EMPTY OR PARTLY FULL?

The preceding section also allow us to get a first glimpse at one of the central conclusions – and ambiguities – of this book and of the study of international conflict resolution in general. Depending on your perspective, the 'glass' of international can seem both partly empty and partly full.

From a purely statistical point of view, it is mostly empty. We have had precious little success preventing conflict from turning violent, ending it once it has done so, or building stable peace once the fighting has come to a halt.

If we focus primarily on the last ten to twenty years, however, we can see what is at least the potential for 'filling' the glass. Events in Europe, Central and South America, Africa, and Asia suggest that we can realistically hope to do a 'better' job with all the stages of conflict discussed above.

The next two chapters conclude part 1 by suggesting some reasons to be both pessimistic and optimistic about the future of international conflict resolution.

SELECT BIBLIOGRAPHY

Boulding, Kenneth. *Stable Peace*. Austin: University of Texas Press, 1978.
————. 'Moving from Unstable to Stable Peace.' In *Breakthrough:*

Emerging New Thinking: Soviet and American Scholars Issue a Challenge to Build a World beyond War, edited by Martin Hellman and Anatoly Gromyko, 157–67. New York: Walker, 1988.

Boutros-Ghali, Boutros. *An Agenda for Peace*. New York: United Nations, 1992.

Burton, John, ed. *Conflict: Human Needs Theory*. London: Macmillan, 1990.

Carnegie Commission for the Prevention of Deadly Conflict. *Preventing Deadly Conflict*. New York: Carnegie Commission, 1997. Also available at <http:www.ccpdc.org>.

Cortright, David, ed. *The Price of Peace: Incentives and International Conflict Prevention*. Lanham, MD: Rowman and Littlefield, 1997.

Crocker, Chester, Fen Osler Hampson, and Pamela Aall. *Managing Global Chaos: Sources of and Responses to International Conflict*. Washington, D.C.: United States Institute for Peace, 1996.

Feil, Scott R. *Preventing Genocide: How the Early Use of Force Might Have Succeeded in Rwanda*. New York: Carnegie Council for the Prevention of Deadly Conflict, 1998.

Gowing, Nik. *Media Coverage: Help or Hindrance in Conflict Prevention*. New York: Carnegie Commission on Preventing Deadly Violence, 1997.

Haass, Richard. *Conflict Unending*. New Haven: Yale University Press, 1990.

International Committee of the Red Cross. *People on War. General Report*, 1999a. <http://www.onwar.org>. Accessed 20 December 1999.

Joulwan, George A., and Christopher C. Shoemaker. *Civilian-Military Cooperation in the Prevention of Deadly Conflict: Implementing Agreements in Bosnia and Beyond*. New York: Carnegie Commission on the Prevention of Deadly Conflict, 1998.

Kaplan, Robert D. *The Ends of the Earth: A Journey at the Dawn of the 21st Century*. New York: Random House, 1996.

Kelman, Herbert C. 'The Interactive Problem-Solving Approach.' In *Managing Global Chaos: Sources of and Responses to International Conflict*, edited by Chester Crocker, et al., 501–19. Washington, D.C.: United States Institute for Peace, 1996.

Lund, Michael S. *Preventing Violent Conflict: A Strategy for Preventive Diplomacy*. Washington, D.C.: United States Institute for Peace, 1996.

Miall, Hugh, Oliver Ramsbotham, and Tom Woodhouse. *Contemporary Conflict Resolution*. Oxford: Polity, 1999.

Minow, Martha. *Between Vengeance and Forgiveness: Facing History after Genocide and Mass Violence*. Boston: Beacon Press, 1998.

Sharp, Jane M. O. 'Dayton Report Card.' *International Security* 22 (Winter 1997): 101–38.

Singer, Max, and Aaron Wildavsky. *The Real World Order*. 2d ed. Chatham, N.J.: Chatham House, 1996.

Snow, Donald M. *Uncivil Wars: International Security and the New Internal Conflicts*. Boulder, CO: Lynne Reinner, 1996.

Stedman, Stephen. *International Actors and International Conflicts*. Rockefeller Brothers Fund, Project on World Security, 1999. <- Accessed 18 December 1999.

Stremlau, John, and Francisco R. Sagasti. *Preventing Deadly Conflict: Does the World Bank Have a Role?* New York: Carnegie Commission on Preventing Deadly Conflict, 1998.

Strobel, Warren P. *Late-Breaking Foreign Policy: The News Media's Influence on Peace Operations*. Washington, D.C.: United States Institute for Peace, 1997.

United Nations. *The Blue Helmets: A Review of United Nations Peace-Keeping*. 3d ed. New York: United Nations, 1996.

Weiss, Thomas. *Military-Civilian Interactions: Intervening in Humanitarian Crises*. Lanham, MD: Rowman and Littlefield, 1999.

Weiss, Thomas, and Cindy Collins. *Humanitarian Challenges and Intervention: World Politics and the Dilemmas of Help*. Boulder, CO: Westview, 1996.

Zartman, I. William. *Ripe for Resolution*. 2d ed. New York: Oxford University Press, 1989.

TOWARD STABLE PEACE

> Stable peace can almost be measured by the amount of dust on the plans
> for the invasion in the various war offices.
>
> – Kenneth Boulding

The final chapters of part 1 outline the two main theoretical approaches
to the study of international conflict resolution. Here, we will concentrate
on the new theories that show us why win-win conflict resolution and
stable peace are at least possible. In chapter 5, we will continue with
more traditional theories that lend themselves to less optimistic
conclusions. As noted in chapter 1, the two schools of thought will not
be treated as opposites. Instead, we will use the case studies in part 2 to
show that they both help us understand both the nature of international
conflict and how we end it.

UNDERPINNINGS

We do not have sophisticated theories that explain why win-win conflict
resolution occurs. That should not be surprising, since it has only been in
the last generation that scholars have begun examining international
conflict beyond the 'mere' ending of the fighting. (See Fisher, 1969,
however.)

That does not mean that there are no useful analytical perspectives for
us to use. In fact, there are two broad schools of thought we can draw on.
However, as is often the case in a new field of inquiry, their intellectual
roots lie in other fields, not international relations.

Systems Theory

The first is based in systems theory and its spinoffs in chaos and complexity studies (for nonscientific audiences, the best introductions are to be found in Capra, 1982; Senge, 1990, 1999; Gleick, 1987; Waldrop, 1992) and among journalists studying globalization (Horsman and Marshall, 1995; Friedman, 1999). They have begun to get an airing among international relations specialists (Jervis, 1997; Rosenau, 1990), but they are still far from reaching the academic mainstream.

Systems theory uses interdependence as an intellectual starting point and leads us to win-win conflict resolution and stable peace as possible empirical as well as normative outcomes. As such it offers a new paradigm not just of conflict resolution but of international relations as a whole, a point we will return to in chapter 11.

Because a system is completely interdependent, the analyst has to explore how the behavior of each actor affects every other actor. (See box.) This has vital implications for such basic concepts in international relations as the national interest. Thus, if a state tries to get what it wants but provokes a powerful response from its adversaries, its apparent pursuit of its self-interest can turn out to be highly counterproductive, as we will see in the case of Iraq's invasion of Kuwait in chapter 10.

Systems and the Systemic Level of Analysis

There is a potential point of terminological confusion here. Many realists and other traditional international relations theorists often work at what they call the systemic level of analysis. In so doing, they focus on the interaction of states with each other.

Systems theory goes much farther in three respects. First, it leads us to consider all actors, not just states. Second, it forces us to focus on all international political issues and not just geopolitical ones. Finally, because it brings feedback into the intellectual picture, it forces us to use a much longer-term perspective in which the rationality of traditional theories in general and of zero-sum decision making in particular lose a lot of their luster.

Systems theory also leads us to take the medium- and long-term effects of our actions on the entire system into account. Thus, we cannot understand today's events without exploring their historical roots, often stretching back for many generations. Traditional international relations theories are mostly based on short-term analyses that are more or less like intellectual snapshots. Systems theory provides the intellectual equivalent of a videotape, and an extended play one at that.

This does not mean that systems theorists always anticipate positive outcomes. In fact, many proponents of it use the two Chinese characters for the English term 'crisis' in discussing how a system works. The first character represents 'danger' and the meaning most Westerners have in mind when they think about a crisis. The second is 'opportunity.' To use a different metaphor drawn from complexity studies, a system can behave like a vicious circle and deteriorate. By contrast, it can behave like a virtuous one and improve its performance over time.

The potential for decay can be seen most easily in environmental studies. As most ecologists see it, the earth is a single life support system. If it is disrupted in one place, unpredictable and often undesirable consequences can occur everywhere, something we see most clearly in the threats posed to the global and regional ecosystems by the accumulation of greenhouse gases producing 'global warming' or the destruction of the ozone layer.

By contrast, management theorists have pointed out, systems can also improve over time through what they call social learning. The executives and line workers of successful companies take the feedback or information about past acts and develop new strategies to build on prior successes and overcome earlier failures. (The most sophisticated theoretical version is provided in Senge, 1990 and 1999.)

The capacity for growth and decay plus the need to consider the long term have profound implications for international relations and conflict resolution. Put simply, anything other than a win-win outcome tends to produce systems that decay at least over the medium to long term.

The traditional theories we will discuss in the next chapter assume that conflict will end either with a winner and loser or, in the most tragic case, nothing but losers. Systems theorists have shown that such outcomes normally lead to deterioration over time. Thus, the United States and its allies won a decisive victory over Iraq during the Gulf war of 1991. However, the nature of Iraq's defeat only served to deepen its leaders' hatred of the West and stiffen its resolve to resist the UN sanctions that have remained in place ever since.

In sum, win-lose or lose-lose conflict resolutions tend at best to produce temporary victors, while the vanquished lick their wounds and sew the seeds of more – and often more intense – conflict at some later point. There are times when win-lose outcomes are so definitive that the relationship starts again from scratch afterward, as was the case between the Allies and Germany and Japan after 1945. However, such cases are few and far between in international relations today.

From a systems perspective, win-win outcomes *can* set the participants off in a very different and more constructive direction by providing feedback. Thus, if my actions harm you today, you are likely to come back and try to respond in kind in the not-so-distant future. Conversely, if I try to do something that helps reach an agreement that we can both benefit from, we lay the groundwork for more sweeping cooperation down the line. Thus, in this sense, power is something we exert together for the good of the whole – and of ourselves at least, again, in the medium to long term.

The word 'can' was emphasized in the preceding paragraph because even the most optimistic advocates of systems theory acknowledges that interdependence and win-win outcomes do not always produce a more harmonious relationship. Complexity and chaos theorists, in particular, note that the behavior of even simple systems cannot be predicted all that accurately and that actions today may have profound, unpredictable, and destructive effects tomorrow.

Conflict Resolution Theory

There is an even more extensive literature on conflict resolution outside of international relations that offers other useful theoretical insights (Yankelovich, 1999; Pruitt and Carnevale, 1993; Fisher and Ury, 1991; Mitchell and Banks, 1996; Susskind and McKearnan, 1995; D. Johnson, et al., 1995). Win-win conflict resolution is now the 'dominant paradigm' in interpersonal and corporate relations. That does not mean that theorists working in the field think it is the norm. Instead, most acknowledge the difficulties in reaching win-win outcomes that grow out of cultural differences, time pressures, dysfunctional relationships among those involved, and other issues that make cooperation difficult.

Scholars working in those other fields argue that it is almost always possible to envision a win-win outcome that would satisfy all parties to a conflict. Making it happen is far more difficult but is most likely to occur when all or most of the parties:

- Understand that in most cases, it is in everyone's interest to reach a mutually satisfying agreement. (See box on interests.)
- Look for new and creative solutions to their problems. This is especially important for the more powerful party in an asymmetric relationship that typically has the most room for maneuver and resources to offer.
- Focus on their general goals, not their specific demands.
- Treat each other with dignity and respect.

- Use trained, neutral mediators or other 'third parties' to help antagonists see new options and reach an agreement.
- See the conflict as part of a larger relationship that can improve or deteriorate over time, depending on the choices they make.

Interests

Conflict resolution theorists focus on interests just as much as the traditional scholars do. However, they view self-interest and national interests differently. As we will see in more detail in the next chapter, scholars have typically assumed that people and the institutions they form try to maximize their wealth, power, territory, and whatever other resources they value. And, because those resources are normally in short supply, those actors rather selfishly compete for those they want the most. That competition quickly leads to conflict that frequently ends with only one side getting what it wants.

The theorists considered here focus on shared or common interests as well because of their interest in the medium to long term. From that perspective, pursuing one's interests as tradition- ally defined and winning today may be counterproductive if doing so leaves the other side angrier and more frustrated. Similarly, it is only finding common ground that leads to a solution that satisfies everyone's needs and can help ease the tensions that gave rise to the dispute in the first place.

Two Motivations

Although they do not explicitly draw on systems theory, Hugh Miall, Oliver Ramsbotham, and Tom Woodhouse (1999:5–9) have developed a simple chart (reconfigured here as table 4.1) that highlights much of what we know about how win-win conflict resolution can occur, but also why it happens so rarely.

Participants in conflict can be influenced by two main sets of motivations. The first is one's own perceived self-interest. The other is concern for the impact of what happens on the other side. As noted earlier, traditional international relations theory focuses all but exclu- sively on the former, while systems analysis compels us to consider the latter as well.

Combining the two produces four main kinds of outcomes:

Table 4.1 Approaches to conflict

Concern for self	Concern for others	
	Low	**High**
High	Aggression	Cooperation
Low	Withdrawal	Capitulation

Source: Adapted from Miall, Ramsbotham, and Woodhouse (1999:6).

- Withdrawal from the conflict is most likely to occur in conflicts that do not matter all that much to the parties involved in it.
- Capitulation more often occurs when the issue does not matter much to one party and that person or group has a deep concern about what happens to the other side.
- Aggression is a common outcome when a party feels its own interests are at stake and has little concern for what happens to the other side.
- Cooperation is most likely when both sides have a strong self-interest and a strong concern for the people each side is in conflict with.

The table reinforces a central conclusion in the literature on interpersonal conflict resolution that often gets short shrift from critics. Effective conflict resolution, reconciliation, and the creation of stable peace do not simply involve being nice. People cannot ignore their own self-interest, however one chooses to define the term. Giving in to the other side tends to leave the actor who did so feeling as dissatisfied as someone who actually lost and can thus also lay the foundation for future conflict. As noted earlier, successful conflict resolution, then, requires meeting everyone's needs at least in the medium to long term.

It also reinforces the importance of thinking about how one's actions affect everyone else in the system, including one's opponent. This may be a relatively new idea in international relations. It is not, however, unprecedented in other parts of political science. While traditional international relations theory focuses all but exclusively on national self-interest, other analytic schools (for example, on the link between political culture and democracy) emphasize less selfish actions in which such incentives as the good of the community as a whole come into play.

Effective win-win conflict resolution occurs when the parties to a dispute reach an agreement that satisfies them all. Win-win or positive-sum outcomes are more creative in that they recast the terms of the debate in a way that gives all participants something they value. In the best of circumstances, they are able to resolve the conflict once and for all by eliminating the issue(s) that gave rise to it in the first place. More often, all a single win-win outcome does is provide some of what both sides seek, thereby reducing tensions between them. If done 'right,' win-win decisions can also build trust between the parties and, thus, make it possible for the parties to go further and faster toward ending their dispute once and for all later on.

Many political scientists (especially pluralists in the United States) focus on compromise. Win-win conflict resolution is more than that. In a compromise, the various sides grudgingly give up some or all of what they seek in an agreement that hurts them all the least. In win-win conflict resolution, all parties are happy with the outcome because, at least over time, they all will benefit from it.

Herbert Kelman, who has been a pioneer in bringing Israelis and Palestinians together, put it this way:

> [T]he satisfaction of the needs of both parties is the ultimate criterion for a mutually satisfactory resolution of the conflict. Efforts should ideally be directed not merely toward settling the conflict in the forms of a brokered political agreement, but toward ... arrangements and accommodations that ... address the basic needs of both parties, and to which the parties are committed. Only this kind of solution is capable of transforming the relationship between societies locked into a protracted conflict ... There is no presumption, of course, that conflicts can ever be totally or permanently resolved; conflict resolution is a gradual process conducive to structural and attitude change, to reconciliation, to the development of a new relationship mindful of the interdependence of the two societies and open to cooperative functional arrangements between them. The real test of conflict resolution in deep-rooted conflicts is how much the process by which agreements are constructed and the nature of the resultant agreements contribute to transforming the relationship between the parties. (Kelman, 1996:503–04; also see Burton 1990)

Win-win conflict resolution does not appear magically out of thin air. It requires hard work, creativity, and flexibility on the part of everyone involved. The solution itself typically involves stepping back from the specific demands each side has to broader concerns they both share. It also requires at least one of the parties taking the initiative to seek an outcome that works better for them all. The party that takes the initiative typically is the one with the most power in the relationship. Finally, all parties need to understand that no one agreement will solve the problem overnight.

As a political scientist who works in Washington, D.C., I know that concern for others is in short supply, especially in intense conflicts. Similarly, many politicians who worry about their standing in the polls and how they will do in the next election find it hard to take the long-term consequences of their actions into account when making foreign policy.

However, there is no denying the importance of Miall, Ramsbotham, and Woodhouse's second dimension as we will see most clearly in the chapter on South Africa. And, as the work on reconciliation by academics and practitioners alike have shown, people can learn to factor that concern for others into their decision making, whether in a nuclear family or the family of states. In short, the most powerful normative conclusion that emerges from the work on conflict resolution is the 'need' to change our political practices so that we do pay more attention to the concerns of those we disagree with and take the long-term into account.

Useful Web Sites

For this chapter, the best web sites come from nongovernmental organizations (NGOs) and international organizations that are actively involved in conflict resolution.

Search for Common Ground is the largest organization in the world working on international conflict resolution. <http://www.sfcg.org>.

The Carter Center emphasizes the work done by former president Carter and his colleagues. <http://www.cartercenter.org>.

CRS is one of the leading consulting firms with a large international as well as nonpolitical practice. <http://www.mediate.org>.

The Conflict Management Group was founded by Roger Fisher and has a large international practice. <http://www.cmgroup.org>.

George Mason University's Institute for Conflict Analysis and Resolution (ICAR) is one of the world's leading academic departments specializing in conflict resolution. <http://www.gmu.edu/departments/icar/>.

The OSCE (Organization for Security and Cooperation in Europe) has done more innovative work than any of the other international organizations, especially in the former Yugoslavia. <http://www.osce.org>.

TEN FACTORS THAT CAN LEAD TO AND/OR OBSTRUCT WIN-WIN OUTCOMES

The principles of systems theory and insights drawn from the conflict resolution literature can be distilled into the following ten factors that will be at the heart of the case studies and conclusion that follow. Because the authors whose work underlies these ideas believe strongly in win-win conflict resolution and reconciliation, their emphasis is on factors that contribute to cooperative problem-solving. However, given the 'danger' as well as the 'opportunity' side of systems theory, the factors are presented here to suggest that they can hinder as well as bolster win-win conflict resolution.

1. The most momentous changes in the international system over the last generation have put conflict resolution more squarely on the world's political agenda. The end of the Cold War has done away with the old bipolar distribution of power that made intervention by the international community into domestic political life and disputes extremely difficult for almost half a century. Meanwhile, globalization in all its guises has both shown people the horrible consequences of war even in such faraway places as Somalia or East Timor and convinced many of us that we can and should be involved in trying to improve such dire situations.

That is easiest to see in the changed role of the United Nations, especially in the first half of the 1990s. The threat of a veto made it very difficult to deploy peacekeeping forces in countries that one or another of the permanent members of the Security Council felt it had vital interests in, which covered most of the world. In the late 1980s and early 1990s, there was a tremendous expansion in the UN's role. It deployed more peacekeepers during those years than it had throughout the Cold War. Perhaps more important, it took on new kinds of peace enforcement, building, and making activities, which ranged from supervising elections to authorizing the use of force.

As noted in chapter 3, the ethnic, linguistic, or religious nature of many of today's conflicts make them hard to settle peacefully. The international community's inability to solve many of the most visible conflicts of the 1990s has cost the UN and other international bodies much of the support they gained in the first half of the decade. The United Nations, furthermore, does not have the money or the troops to intervene quickly and effectively in all of the world's hot spots and has actually had to cede control of many operations to NATO and other regional bodies. What's more, the international community still finds it impossible to act when a crisis occurs that directly involves a major power (Northern Ireland,

Chechnya) or breaks out in a region that none of them care strongly about (Rwanda, Burundi).

In sum, the world's new geopolitical arrangements have provided the UN and other regional organizations unprecedented opportunities to intervene and try to solve conflicts. In contrast, the sheer number and the severity of those conflicts have also made it abundantly clear that the international community lacks the experience, expertise, or resources to intervene effectively on a consistent basis.

2. It is not difficult to find an intellectually plausible win-win solution for just about every international conflict on the world's political agenda today. For instance, the status of Jerusalem has long been a major stumbling block in the Arab-Israeli peace process. There are, however, dozens of proposals on the table to turn Jerusalem into an international city or for the Israelis and Palestinians to share it in some way as a joint capital of what would be two states.

The hard part lies in finding the political will to put these proposals into practice. Indeed, there are some issues that are so divisive that such win-win outcomes are not given serious consideration. In this case, each side has made a nonnegotiable demand that the city must be the capital of its state.

3. Many academics stress the importance of preventive diplomacy, which works best before a conflict turns violent or otherwise gets out of hand. As we also saw earlier, the international community in any of its guises rarely is able to address a conflict before the fighting starts. Nonetheless, the success of the Organization for Security and Coopera-tion in Europe's 'trip-wire' mission in Macedonia or the U.S. intervention in Haiti in 1994 do provide us with evidence that preventive diplomacy can be effective, just like the preventive medicine for which it was named (Evans, 1998; Kittani, 1998).

Few observers doubt the value of preventive diplomacy. However, it is simply not something that politicians rely on very often or very effectively for two main reasons. First, a simmering crisis is not likely to reach their busy agendas, which are filled with what seem like much more pressing issues both at home and abroad. Second, even if diplomats or politicians see the need for early action, it is not easy (at least in democratic states) to raise the money or get the popular support to put its soldiers 'in harm's way.' Third, there are at least some scholars who are not convinced that preventive diplomacy is all that effective or at least will remain so until serious assessment of its effects is carried out.

4. Win-win outcomes only occur if the parties involved can break down the image of the enemy, hatred, and other psychological factors that lead them to demonize each other. Psychologists such as Herbert

Kelman (1996) and Ralph White (1984) have demonstrated that attitudes that put the blame for our problems on 'the other guy' and that portray ourselves as wholly virtuous are a major reason why so many conflicts escalate into violence. From this perspective, conflict resolution advocates have to replace those attitudes with others that reflect the concern for others discussed above, reassure worried adversaries, build on positive incentives, create trust, and transform the relationship into one in which cooperation and win-win outcomes are at least possible.

Three of the case studies will include information about reasonably successful track-two diplomacy by academics and other private citizens that built initial bridges between communities in conflict. This is not work that is easily done by professional diplomats who are hemmed in by official protocol, the often antagonistic formal positions taken by their governments, and more. Rather, the barriers tend to be broken down through the kinds of professional exchanges, student trips, and twin-cities projects during the 1980s that went a long way toward showing people on both sides of the iron curtain that, as the singer Sting put it, 'the Russians love their children, too.' The new mood in public and elite attitudes can, in turn, lead to effective formal diplomacy and policy changes. Thus, shifts in public opinion made it easier for Presidents Ronald Reagan and Mikhail Gorbachev to point their two countries away from confrontation during the second half of the 1980s.

But these successful examples also illustrate one of the major problems associated with such attempts at conflict resolution. It usually takes a long time to change people's attitudes and values, because the most effective work is done on a person-by-person basis. For instance, I spent most of the 1980s as an active volunteer in the Beyond War movement, which tried to convince people to change their 'modes of thinking' about conflict resolution in their personal as well as their political lives. Though we were well funded, only about five hundred thousand people (mostly Americans) participated in the three-evening seminars that were at the heart of our work. And, even among them, the new values did not translate into practical political changes that had an impact on U.S. foreign policy.

5. The fourth factor points to the fifth. Leadership is critical. In the last few years, we have seen an unusual number of political leaders who took risks to increase the chances for peaceful conflict resolution – Mikhail Gorbachev and others who brought East and West closer together, Nelson Mandela and F. W. de Klerk who ended apartheid, or the British and Irish politicians who made the 1998 Good Friday Agreement possible.

Moreover, some negotiation theorists now argue that the diplomatic challenge requires more of our leaders than was the case before the end of the Cold War, because building stable peace requires much more than 'simply' stopping the fighting. Rather, as Cecilia Albin (1995) suggests, we need a new type of diplomacy and leadership that addresses the fundamental injustices and inequalities that gave rise to the conflict in the first place. This is never easy. It is especially difficult today when states have different priorities and resources, which means that they often end up talking past each other. What's more, today's negotiations are much more complicated even than those of the Cold War years when two states and their national security interests dominated so much of international life. Now we have to deal with literally dozens of issues, nearly 200 states, and countless other actors.

Conversely, history provides us with even more examples of intransigent leaders such as Saddam Hussein or Slobodan Milosevic who make reaching agreements exceptionally difficult. Even politicians like U.S. president William Clinton who talk about building bridges also engage in the rhetoric that drives wedges between states.

6. There is even more compelling evidence that the parties to intense conflict rarely settle their disputes on their own. There are examples like South Africa in the early 1990s. Mandela, de Klerk, and their supporters were able to reach their landmark agreement without significant outside support. More often, however, the services of a neutral third party are critical, especially in the prenegotiation stage during which it is difficult to get the antagonists to the table.

Third parties are most effective if they have no vested interest in the outcome of the conflict. With time, they can use their impartiality and negotiating skills to ease the tensions that typically accompany this kind of bargaining by, among other things, instilling trust.

The 1990s have seen a dramatic expansion in the number and types of third parties. Some of the work has been carried out by the UN and other regional organizations as in the work Secretary-General Kofi Annan did in preventing the bombing of Iraq in 1998. Sometimes it is done by individuals appointed by national governments as in the mediation by Richard Holbrooke and Dennis Ross in Bosnia and the Middle East respectively. Sometimes it is a private individual or consulting firm as we will see in the universally applauded role former U.S. senator George Mitchell played in Northern Ireland.

Similarly, little-known average citizens working through NGOs now play an important role in helping solve conflicts on a local or regional basis (Mathews, 1997). Traditionally, NGOs were not involved in politics and 'simply' provided relief, development aid, and other support to societies in conflict and crisis. In recent years, however, NGOs have found themselves involved in conflict management if not resolution, and a growing number of them are now explicitly dedicating various aspects of conflict resolution as in workshops held to bring Palestinians and Israelis or Turkish and Greek Cypriots together for 'problem-solving' sessions. Such groups can play a particularly important role in getting the rivals to the negotiating table, because they often have more credibility with the parties to the conflict than states and formal international organizations do.

But, third parties are not a panacea. To begin with, despite the recent rapid growth of university and nonacademic training programs, there are not enough mediators. Furthermore, it is often difficult to find a third party that is both influential and impartial enough. That is particularly true when the United States is involved. It often has to play a role given its strengths and interests, as is the case in the Middle East. However, it is often too identified with one side of the dispute, and its representatives have a hard time establishing a trusting relationship with the other party.

There are even times when third parties can make mistakes that make a bad situation worse. As we will see in chapter 9, there are critics who are convinced that Lord Carrington's lack of involvement and Lord Owen's agreement to 'cantonment' that would effectively divide Bosnia into a number of ethnically determined ministates unnecessarily prolonged the fighting there.

7. The mass media – especially television – can also facilitate conflict resolution. At a time when CNN and the other global news services have reporters working almost everywhere, it has become much easier to follow global events. While it is hard to pin down with any accuracy, it seems certain that televised reports of the horrors in Bosnia and, then, Kosovo strengthened support for intervention in the former Yugoslavia in 1995 and 1998.

The CNN effect, however, can not be taken for granted. There are quiet crises in places like Sierra Leone or Eritrea that rarely make it into the *New York Times* let alone the nightly news. Moreover, while the CNN effect may have shrunk the world so that we can get more information, it has also shrunk most of our time horizons. As the news becomes available to us instantaneously, there is a parallel expectation that problems can be solved almost as quickly. To cite but the most recent and most absurd example, at the very moment that Kosovo International Security Force troops were being deployed in Kosovo, journalists had already started asking NATO officials when they expected the peace-keepers to complete their mission.

Furthermore, the media can be a part of the problem as well as the solution. Coverage of setbacks in Somalia, for example prompted the international community to withdraw rather than to intervene more forcefully.

The media are never unbiased either in what is covered or in how the stories are presented. Thus, Tim Pat Coogan only half jokingly refers to the British and Irish press having looked at each other across the Irish Sea during the Troubles using 'telescopes with the cap on' (1996:296). The English government frequently put pressure on the press not to carry favorable coverage about the nationalist cause, let alone the Irish Republican Army. The Irish press just as frequently chose to carry only stories that stressed the extremism of the Protestants in Ulster or the intransigence of the authorities in London.

Finally, in the most extensive book on the subject, Walter Strobel (1997) argues that the media tend to follow rather than shape public opinion and therefore have at most a limited impact on decision makers at the elite level.

8. Stable peace cannot be built as the result of a single win-win decision. Instead, it entails a much longer and more difficult period of what former UN secretary-general Boutros Boutros-Ghali called peace building (1992). In Fen Osler Hampson's words, peace has to be 'nurtured' (1996). As the South African leadership has understood as well as anyone, a permanent end to a conflict requires transforming the relationship between the antagonists into one of cooperation through reconciliation. In the most comprehensive book on reconciliation, John Paul Lederach (1997:29) argues that reconciliation includes the following steps that, in time, can alleviate the root cause(s) of the conflict:

- **Truth** – acknowledging the wrongs that had been committed
- **Mercy** – forgiveness of those wrongs and a new beginning to the relationship
- **Justice** – the establishment of new rights and programs for the oppressed
- **Peace** – the security of all and the harmony and respect that come with it

States and international organizations have played a role in this regard (Last, 1999). However, NGOs have generally been more effective than states, because they have been 'on the ground' longer, have better local contacts, and are therefore better able to work with the parties to a conflict (Anderson and Woodrow, 1989; Anderson, 1996; Natsios, 1997). There is considerable disagreement about the form reconciliation takes other than the fact that it will vary considerably from case to case and that it will take time. Some observers stress democratization, others social and economic equality. Some praise efforts like South Africa's

Truth and Reconciliation Commission, others find them too forgiving of an old, repressive regime.

Unfortunately, the pressures of practical politics often make it hard to keep the political momentum needed to move a peace process forward. Understandably, there is a collective sigh of relief when the violence stops. However, ending the combat almost always leaves the two sides far from a lasting agreement, because the issues that gave rise to the conflict in the first place have not been settled (Lipschutz and Jonas, 1998). In democratic countries, politicians also rarely have the luxury of making plans for the long periods needed to build a stable peace. Prudent politicians cannot realistically pursue policies that are going to harm their chances at the polls in at most a few years' time. Moreover, in these days of the spin doctor and focus group, politicians are always paying attention to their poll numbers as well as (and perhaps more than) the demands of a conflict occurring thousands of miles away.

This is not only true of mainstream politicians. Thus, the American peace movement peaked during the Vietnam War and, again, during the renewed Cold War tensions and arms buildup of the early 1980s. As soon as those immediate crises eased, the movement all but disappeared. Even hard-core activists are reluctant to take on tasks that may take a generation or more. Along these lines, John Paul Lederach is by no means alone when he notes that he was nearly thrown out of a conference on reconciliation in Northern Ireland in the early 1990s when he remarked that it might take as long to end that conflict as it did to create it in the first place.

9. The first students of conflict resolution were properly criticized for not devoting enough attention to the social, economic, and environmental issues that give rise to conflict in the first place (Miall, Ramsbotham, and Woodhouse, 1999:48-64). In the simplest terms, if the international community and/or the parties to the dispute do not address the root causes of the conflict, it is likely to reappear (Edwards, 1999).

While most students of conflict resolution now have broadened their agendas to include these other types of social change, doing so makes us all the more aware of how difficult it is to achieve stable peace. Even though South Africa will be treated as the most successful case in part 2, there is reason to believe that the transition to a stable multiracial democracy is far from assured. Supporters and critics of the new regime alike worry about the social and economic dilemma it faces in having to balance the interests of both Whites and Blacks. Most Blacks expect to see noticeable improvements in their living conditions in the next few years, which has prompted the government to set ambitious social and economic goals. They will be hard to meet unless it can redistribute income and wealth from Whites to Blacks. So far, it has been unwilling to do so given the implicit agreement in the negotiations following Mandela's release that the White standard of living would not be eroded. Meanwhile, several hundred thousand jobs have been lost, and the unemployment rate among Blacks tops 40 percent.

Similarly, the various agreements reached between Israel and the Palestinians have called for substantial economic development and other aid to the Palestinian authority. The World Bank and the other international economic agencies have funneled grants and loans to Gaza and the West Bank and helped organize a series of forums designed to lure private sector investment. Similarly, the United States has used such different agencies as USAID and the CIA to help build a civil society and democratic political infrastructure. It is, however, too early to tell how much of a difference such steps can make, especially when the political fault lines are as old and as deep as they are in the Middle East.

Ironically, the best example we can point to is one that has developed largely without conscious planning by political leaders. In the thirty years since the Troubles began in Northern Ireland, the social status and economic conditions of the Catholic minority in Northern Ireland has improved dramatically. While the causal connections in such developments are always hard to determine, polling data suggests that those improvements helped convince many Catholics that they could adopt 'inside the system' tactics rather than revolutionary strategies for achieving their long-term goals.

10. There is no single approach to international conflict resolution that 'works,' however you define that term. That will be clearest in chapters 7 and 8 in which we will see two very different kinds of third-party mediation efforts. There is little doubt that George Mitchell's low-key, bridge-building work as chair of the negotiations was needed to help reach the Good Friday Agreement in 1998. So, too, was the more forceful (and some would say bullying) efforts of Richard Holbrooke in forging the Dayton Agreement that ended the war in Bosnia in 1995. Mitchell would not have been as effective in Bosnia, nor would Holbrooke have been in Northern Ireland.

REPLACING DANGER WITH OPPORTUNITY?

International conflict resolution is a new field. It is also a daunting one.

Most of this chapter has discussed theories about how win-win conflict resolution, reconciliation, and stable peace can be reached. On balance, however, the track record of international conflict resolution is not all that impressive. Academic theorists and practitioners in the field have learned a lot about how to settle disputes in recent years, but they have also learned that we have a long way to go before we are as effective at building peace as we are at preventing war.

In short, that makes the following comment on the 'Troubles' in Northern Ireland by Tim Pat Coogan an appropriate way to end this chapter and set the stage for the far more pessimistic theoretical arguments to follow.

> Just as a blade of grass can deflect a speeding bullet, so can a fragile peace process be deflected. To succeed, the process needs two things, momentum and reconciliation. ... A window of opportunity, unequalled in the history of the Anglo-Irish relationship, is not being opened with anything like the flair, imagination and generosity that is called for. It is my hope that this book will do something to jolt both consciences – and momentum. (1996:xv)

SELECT BIBLIOGRAPHY

Albin, Cecilia. 'The Global Security Challenge to Negotiation: Toward a New Agenda.' *American Behavioral Scientist* 38 (1995): 921-49.

Anderson, Mary B. 'Humanitarian NGOs in Conflict Intervention.' In *Managing Global Chaos: Sources of and Responses to International Conflict,* edited by Chester Crocker, et al., 343–54. Washington, D.C: United States Institute for Peace, 1996.

Anderson, Mary B., and Peter J. Woodrow. *Rising from the Ashes: Developmental Strategies at Times of Disaster.* Boulder, CO: Westview, 1989.

Boulding, Kenneth. *Stable Peace.* Austin: University of Texas Press, 1978.

————. 'Moving from Unstable to Stable Peace.' In *Breakthrough: Emerging New Thinking: Soviet and American Scholars Issue a Challenge to Build a World beyond War,* edited by Martin Hellman and Anatoly Gromyko, 157–67. New York: Walker, 1988.

Boutros-Ghali, Boutros. *An Agenda for Peace.* New York: United Nations, 1992.

Capra, Frijtof. *The Turning Point: Science, Society, and the Rising Culture.* New York: Simon and Schuster, 1982.

Cohen, Raymond. *Negotiating across Cultures: International Communication in an Interdependent World*. Rev. ed. Washington, D.C.: United States Institute for Peace, 1997.

Coles, Robert. *The Call of Service: A Witness to Idealism*. Boston: Houghton-Mifflin, 1993.

Coogan, Tim Pat. *The Troubles: Ireland's Ordeal 1966–1996 and the Search for Peace*. Boulder, CO: Roberts Rinehart, 1996.

Edwards, Michael. *Future Positive: International Co-operation in the 21st Century*. London: Earthscan, 1998.

Evans, Gareth. 'Preventive Diplomacy and Conflict Resolution.' In *Peacemaking and Peacekeeping for the New Century*, edited by Olara A. Otunnu and Michael W. Doyle, 61–88. Lanham, MD: Rowman and Littlefield, 1998.

Fisher, Roger. *International Conflict for Beginners*. New York: Harper Colophon, 1969.

Fisher, Roger, and William Ury. *Getting to Yes*. New York: Penguin, 1981.

Friedman, Thomas L. *The Lexus and the Olive Tree: Understanding Globalization*. New York: Farrar-Strauss-Giroux, 1999.

Gleick, James. *Chaos: Making a New Science*. New York: Viking, 1987.

Hampson, Fen Osler. *Nurturing Peace: Why Peace Settlements Succeed or Fail*. Washington, D.C.: United States Institute for Peace, 1996.

Horsman, Matthew, and Andrew Marshall. *Beyond the Nation State*. London: HarperCollins, 1995.

Jervis, Robert. *System Effects: Complexity in Social and Political Life*. Princeton, NJ: Princeton University Press, 1997.

Johnson, David W., Roger T. Johnson, Bruce Dudley, and Douglas Magnuson. 'Training Elementary School Students to Manage Conflict.' *The Journal of Social Psychology* 135 (1995): 673–86.

Kaplan, Robert D. *The Ends of the Earth: A Journey at the Dawn of the 21st Century*. New York: Random House, 1996.

Kelman, Herbert C. 'The Interactive Problem-Solving Approach.' In *Managing Global Chaos: Sources of and Responses to International Conflict*, edited by Chester Crocker, et al., 501–19. Washington, D.C.: United States Institute for Peace, 1996.

Kittani, Ismat. 'Preventive Dipolmacy and Peacemaking: The UN Experience.' In *Peacemaking and Peacekeeping for the New Century*, edited by Olara A. Otunnu and Michael W. Doyle, 89–110. Lanham, MD: Rowman and Littlefield, 1998.

Last, David. 'Soldiers and Civilians in Peacebuilding: Reliable Partners?' Paper prepared for the 1999 meetings of the International Studies Association, Washington, D.C.

Lederach, John Paul. *Building Peace: Sustainable Reconciliation in Divided*

Societies. Washington, D.C.: United States Institute for Peace, 1997.

Lipschutz, Ronnie D., and Susanne Jonas, eds. 'Beyond the Neoliberal Peace: From Conflict Resolution to Social Reconciliation.' *Social Justice*, special issue. 25 (1998): no. 4.

Mathews, Jessica Tuchman. 'Power Shift.' *Foreign Affairs* 76 (January/February): 50–67.

Mearsheimer, John. 'Back to the Future: Instability in Europe after the Cold War.' *International Security* 15 (1990a): 5–56.

————. 'Why We Will Soon Miss the Cold War.' *Atlantic Monthly* 266 (1990b): 35–50.

Miall, Hugh, Oliver Ramsbotham, and Tom Woodhouse. *Contemporary Conflict Resolution*. Oxford: Polity, 1999.

Mitchell, Christopher, and Michael Banks. *Handbook of Conflict Resolution: The Analytical Problem-Solving Approach*. London: Pinter, 1996.

Natsios, Andrew S. 'An NGO Perspective.' In *Peacemaking in International Conflict: Methods and Techniques*, edited by I. William Zartman and J. Lewis Rasmussen, 337–64. Washington, D.C.: United States Institute for Peace, 1997.

Rosenau, James. *Turbulence in World Politics: A Theory of Change and Continuity*. Princeton, NJ: Princeton University Press, 1990.

Senge, Peter. *The Fifth Discipline: The Art and Practice of the Learning Organization*. New York: Doubleday Currency, 1990.

————. *The Dance of Change: The Challenges to Sustaining Momentum in Learning Organizations*. New York: Doubleday Currency, 1999.

Strobel, Warren P. *Late-Breaking Foreign Policy: The News Media's Influence on Peace Operations*. Washington, D.C.: United States Institute for Peace, 1997.

Susskind, Lawrence, and Sarah McKearnan. 'Enlightened Conflict Resolution.' *Technology Review* 98 (1995): 70–4.

Waldrop, M. Mithchell. *Complexity: The Emerging Science at the Edge of Order and Chaos*. New York: Simon and Schuster, 1992.

White, Ralph. *Fearful Warrior: A Psychological Profile of U.S.-Soviet Relations*. New York: Free Press, 1984.

Wilson, James Q. *The Moral Sense*. New York: Free Press, 1993.

Yankelovich, Daniel. *The Magic of Dialogue: Transforming Conflict into Cooperation*. New York: Simon and Schuster, 1999.

5

TRADITIONAL PERSPECTIVES

> Our opinion of the gods and our knowledge of men lead us to conclude
> that it is a general and necessary law of nature to rule whatever one can.
> The strong do what they have the power to do and the weak accept what
> they have to accept.
>
> – Thucydides

We do not have to start with theoretical works in other disciplines to see
how more traditional international relations experts have analyzed
international conflict. Indeed, international relations is one of the
theoretically richest parts of political science, and the study of conflict
has been at the heart of the field for well over two thousand years.

That does not mean, however, that there is a large and sophisticated
'mainstream' literature on international conflict resolution, because such
scholars have typically focused more on the conflict than on its
resolution. (See box on frames of reference). Indeed, the best brief book
on the subject (Nye, 2000) focuses on the causes of major international
disputes and does not even have an entry in its index for 'resolution.'
Therefore, here, too, we will have to extrapolate from a series of
underlying theoretical principles to specific factors that affect the way
international disputes are settled.

Different Frames of Reference

There are many reasons why the theorists covered in chapters 4
and 5 reach such different conclusions but also why their ideas
complement more than they contradict each other. None is more
important than the issues or 'dependent variables' they focus on.

As we saw in chapter 4, analysts exploring the new approaches to
conflict resolution concentrate on strategies for ending disputes
before they reach the crisis point and on building stable peace once
a conflict has run its course.

By contrast, the theorists we will consider here focus on why
some crises turn to war and how the fighting is (finally) stopped.

UNDERPINNINGS

Given the long-standing interest of international relations experts in war and conflict, no author can hope to do justice to the diversity of their analytical approaches to justice in a single chapter. Therefore, I have chosen to concentrate only on the central aspects of the two most widely used theories – realism and pluralism (also referred to as idealism and liberalism) – that are of the most use in understanding the way disputes are settled.

Realism

Realism is by far the oldest and most widely used theory in international relations. Indeed, its lineage can be traced back to Thucydides' *Melian Dialog*, an extract from which begins this chapter.

Realists reach more pessimistic conclusions about the possibilities for win-win conflict resolution, reconciliation, and stable peace than the theorists considered in chapter 4 because, like Thucydides, they are convinced international relations is power politics.

As Hans Morgenthau, the founder of modern realism put it:

> All history shows that nations active in international politics are continuously preparing for, actively involved in, or recovering from organized violence in the form of war. (Kegley and Raymond, 1999:3)

As recently as the Gulf war in 1991 and the bombing of Kosovo in 1999, the United States and its allies demonstrated to Iraq and Yugoslavia that Thucydides' simple statement still carries plenty of weight in explaining the outcome of conflict.

This state of affairs is no accident. Originally, realists and similar theorists saw it as a reflection of our human nature. Today's 'neorealists,' however, emphasize how the nature of the international system makes conflict, violence, and war so common in political life. (Among others, see Waltz, 1959; Buzan, 1991.)

States do many things. To realists, however, protecting national security, which they define in terms of key geopolitical and other vital resources, is by far the most important challenge any state faces. If political leaders fail to do so, they put their people and the very existence of the state at risk. Because such resources as wealth, population, and territory are in short supply, states invariably compete with each other for them.

That competition is different from other arenas of conflict, because the system is anarchic. Realists do not use the term to suggest that states are at each other's throats all the time. Rather, they mean that there is no international state, no equivalent of the government in Washington or Warsaw that can maintain order and enforce the law or regulate the interstate competition. Realists often call this a 'self-help system' in which states have to look out for their own interests or work with allies in a hostile environment.

The Gulf crisis, again, is instructive. There was no international state the Kuwaiti authorities could turn to in order to stop Iraq from invading. Similarly, while far too weak to stop Baghdad on its own, Kuwait did have allies who could build a force that eventually forced Iraq to withdraw.

The stakes of a conflict can be magnified by security dilemmas in which the actions of one state to protect its own security actually serve to weaken that of its opponents. Thus, as Yugoslavia was falling apart, Croats tried to protect their compatriots living outside the republic, which threatened the Serbs and thus helped fan the flames of their already substantial nationalism (Rose, 2000).

The State as Level of Analysis

Four of the case studies in part 2 are not primarily interstate in nature. It could also be argued that some of them do not involve the vital interests of the world's leading powers.

Therefore, the purest of realists might not include them in a list of conflicts they would focus on. However, given the changes and uncertainties of the last few years and the disruptive potential that each of them has, there are very few realists who have not expanded their frame of reference to include conflicts such as these.

In sum, conflict is an inescapable feature of international political life. And, because the international system is anarchic, there is no equivalent of a national state that can effectively and routinely adjudicate disputes. Furthermore, because neither state is likely to give in willingly to its rival(s), that competition can become extremely tense. States have to look out for their own interests in what realists call a 'self-help' system.

As a result, they also have to resort to the use of power, which political scientists typically define as one side's ability to get its opponent to do *what it otherwise would not do*. Those last five italicized words in the definition of power are all-important here. The exercise of power is an attempt to get another state to act contrary to its own wishes and interests. Not surprisingly, it requires the state trying to exert its power to at least threaten the use of force. That does not necessarily mean violence and war. Deterrence, alliances, and other strategies that the realists stress can keep the fighting from starting. In fact, as the quantitative studies of warfare have shown, well under a quarter of the world's intense conflicts in which one side or the other threatens to use force actually leads to a full-scale war.

That is the case because realists expect states to behave rationally by calculating the likely costs and benefits of the various courses of action open to them and acting accordingly. They should, thus, only use force when the likely gains in terms of vital national interests outweigh the losses they can realistically expect to incur.

These last few paragraphs suggest why cooperative problem-solving is so difficult to achieve in international relations. Once in a conflict, realists do not expect states to seek any sort of resolution as long as one of them is convinced it can win or at least avoid losing. Win-win outcomes are possible only when both sides have reached the mutually hurting stalemate mentioned in chapter 3 (Zartman, 1985). More often, they keep the conflict going until one side wins and the other loses in the so-called win-lose or zero-sum outcome.

To see that from a different angle, consider a recent typology of five types of security arrangements listed in table 5.1 (Kolodziej, 1998:17–19). Each type depicts a way states and their allies go about trying to ensure their security. On one end of the spectrum is the creation of a security community, Kolodziej's equivalent of stable peace. On the other are situations in which force is 'needed' because the parties cannot readily reach agreements because of their own insecurity, ongoing tensions, and imbalances in the distribution of power.

The security arrangements at the top of the table do not lend themselves to win-win outcomes because of the particularly tense and unequal relations among the states involved in them. The closer you get to those in the bottom rows, the easier it is for states to cooperate and resolve whatever conflicts arise without coming close to the use of force. But, as the realist would be quick – and correct – to point out, the 'need' for win-win conflict resolution is greatest in cases that fall near the top of the table, where it is least likely.

The focus on vital national interests also leads many realists to be skeptical about the kind of military involvement the United States and many other major powers have engaged in since the end of the Cold War. From their point of view, prudent leaders are concerned only about their direct, national interests. The business of international relations is dangerous and risky, and states should focus only on their most vital interests in protecting their territory, population, and other critical

Table 5.1 Security arrangements

Type of security arrangement	Characteristics	Examples
Insecurity	Open hostilities or close to it	The former Yugoslavia after 1991
Balance of power	Security through deterrence, arms	India and Pakistan most of the time since 1947
Spheres of influence	Coercive leadership by a strong power	Russia with Belorus today
Concert of states	Loose cooperation among somewhat differing regimes	NATO and the Partnership for Peace
Hegemonic security community	One state dominates a cooperative alliance	NATO
Security community	Voluntary alliance, stable peace, cooperation	European Union

Source: Adapted from Kolodziej (1998:18).

resources. And, while it is tempting for a state like the United States to want to intervene when another state or states is engaged in immoral or inhuman activity, as was the case in, for instance, the former Yugoslavia and Rwanda, doing so does not make sense unless those critical interests are threatened. As Fromkin put it for Kosovo,

> A realist American policy would have been non-intervention in Kosovo, on the grounds that the United States has no interests in the former Yugoslavia that would justify involving itself in the region. (Fromkin, 1999:183)

Pluralism

The mainstream critics of realism also stress the difficulties in forging win-win agreements to end conflict, albeit for markedly different reasons. As noted earlier, these theorists have a number of labels. I have chosen to use pluralism because it reflects their major contribution to international conflict resolution by drawing our attention to the complexities of domestic political life, which make rationality and the associated pursuit of interests difficult, if not impossible, to achieve.

Values

That is the case, first of all, because values and beliefs always have an important role in the way international conflict is addressed (Moravcsik, 1997). To see that, start with a statement by Kevin Toolis, a not unsympathetic observer of Irish republican politics, if not the Irish Republican Army (IRA).

> In their hearts, the IRA's Volunteers saw themselves as defenders. It did not matter that there could never be a military victory. 'Standing up to the British,' standing up to the Protestants by bombing and killing, served its own purpose by maintaining the spirit, the very possibility, of resistance in the face of an overwhelming enemy. (Toolis, 1995:82)

People who take part in the kinds of conflict considered in this book believe very strongly in the justice of their cause. Their commitment is not likely to waver, for example, if the possibility of a compromise to end the fighting is proposed. More generally, goals other than the rational pursuit of either a win-win or win-lose outcome may matter the most to them. For the working-class Catholics Toolis studied, standing up to the British and to the Protestants was a worthy end in and of itself, even if there was next to no chance of actually winning.

Participants in at least the weaker side of intense conflicts have deep feelings of injustice and persecution. Many have suffered and made tremendous sacrifices against other groups as well as the state, which they hold jointly responsible for their oppression. Thus, the Rev. Frank Chikane

> endured far more hardship than most mortals can conceive of. Since 1977, he has survived six rounds of detention, countless hours and unspeakable methods of torture, a year of hiding during the 1986 state of emergency, and, finally, a 1989 assassination attempt that very nearly succeeded. Over the years, such abuse has left him at various times paranoid, confused, unable to walk, sleep, or speak. Yet every blow and epithet only seemed to fuel his determination to fight back with his whole being. The apartheid enforcers failed to break him, but it was not for lack of trying. (Goodman, 1999:31)

It would hardly be surprising if men like Frank Chikane became and remained embittered toward the South African state and Afrikaners who were responsible for apartheid and its abuses. However, as we saw in chapter 3, stable peace requires reconciliation and the coming together of former antagonists. Put simply, that is not easy to do, and all societies that have entered a 'peace process' have had to deal with men and women who are unwilling or unable to move beyond the anger and the hatred that brought them into the conflict in the first place.

Psychological Dynamics

The same holds for three overlapping psychological dynamics that tend to drive the parties to a dispute farther apart.

The first is the image of the enemy, which also was discussed in chapter 4 (White, 1984; Keen, 1986; Frank and Melville, 1988). While there is now impressive evidence that such attitudes can be overcome, there is equally impressive evidence that when they exist, they make it hard for adversaries to deal with each other in any sort of constructive way. Under conditions of anarchy and scarce resources, people often think of conflict in 'we versus they' terms. We attribute 'good' motivations to ourselves. More important for our purposes here, we tend to see our opponents as wholly evil or at least wholly responsible for the problem. Leaders use rhetoric about 'the focus of evil in the world,' 'the Great Satan,' or 'the next Hitler.' As we use stereotypes and assume the worst of our opponents, it becomes harder and harder to sit down and talk, let alone act rationally in the realists' terms or reach the kind of sweeping agreements discussed in chapter 4.

Second, political leaders are like the rest of us – they make mistakes of judgment and interpretation. At times, their political vision is clouded by biases introduced by the kind of stereotypical thinking discussed above. At others, they simply make mistakes based on limited or faulty information about the other side's capabilities or intentions (Jervis, 1968). Such misperceptions are especially likely to occur and have serious consequences at the height of a crisis, when leaders have to make momentous decisions and, often, do so quite quickly. The most obvious recent example came during the Gulf crisis of 1990–91. United States intelligence agencies simply did not have clear enough information to provide the Bush administration with an unambiguous estimate of Iraqi intentions during the days before the invasion of Kuwait. Similarly, both before and after it moved in, the Iraqi leadership frequently misread the resolve of the U.S.-led coalition and its commitment to forcing Baghdad's forces out of Kuwait.

Third is group think, or the tendency on the part of small and relatively isolated groups to make a decision and then never consider evidence that might lead them to question that initial choice (Janis, 1983). The classic example comes from the Johnson administration's internal discussions on the Vietnam War. Advisers such as George Ball who voiced doubts about the administration's policies were shunted into the background. Others who began to question the conduct of the war, including Secretary of Defense Robert McNamara, were reluctant to air them for a variety of reasons, ranging from loyalty to the president to fear of losing their jobs and influence.

These three psychological dynamics can pose particularly difficult obstacles to successful negotiations (let alone reconciliation) when cultural differences among the countries are involved (Cohen, 1997; Avruch, 1998). A country's culture consists of the general and often unspoken values and assumptions that 'set the political stage.' Raymond Cohen, in particular, has demonstrated that the greater the cultural differences between parties to a negotiation, the harder it is for them to reach agreement. Americans, for instance, have a legalistic approach that leads them to focus on 'making a deal,' whereas many people in Asia and the Middle East focus instead on the relationship that emerges in the discussions, saving face, and obtaining respect. At the very least, it behooves negotiators to know as much about the culture and values of the people they are dealing with as possible, something that all too rarely happens in practice. Indeed, cultural differences can be a problem within societies as well, something we'll see in how little direct experience Whites had of Black living conditions in South Africa or Protestants of Catholics in Northern Ireland at the time serious discussions about ending those conflicts began.

Values and psychological dynamics are part of a much broader phenomenon – domestic politics – that almost always comes into play in international conflict resolution. Realists are frequently criticized for treating the state as a 'black box,' the insides of which do not matter. Similarly, many advocates of win-win conflict resolution are so taken by their new approaches that they often fail to explore the 'real world' obstacles to their use. What the pluralists show us is that what happens 'on the ground' invariably makes political life more complicated and successful conflict resolution more difficult.

That is easiest to see in the United States, whose system based on the separation of powers makes any sort of rational decision-making difficult. Thus, in fall 1999, Senator Jesse Helms (R-North Carolina) finally allowed hearings on the nomination of Richard Holbrooke to be ambassador to the United Nations to proceed after holding it up for more than a year. Meanwhile, in the annual budgetary give and take, the

Table 5.2 Factors determining pressure on policymakers

	Nature of Institutions	
Political division	Democratic or otherwise open	Authoritarian or otherwise closed
Deep	U.S. during Vietnam War and failed states	Iraq in the aftermath of the Gulf war
Not very deep	Japan on trade issues	Soviet Union during the early years of the Cold War

Congress refused to appropriate funds the Clinton administration had pledged to help implement the Wye River Accord negotiated the previous autumn between Israel and the Palestinian Authority, although it did finally cave in during the final negotiations with the White House.

Not all states face the same amount or kinds of pressures from outside the foreign ministry. Nonetheless, all do to some extent. For our purposes, the degree to which they do is largely determined by the interplay of two main factors. (See table 5.2 and Kegley and Gregory, 1999:12–18 for a more detailed and nuanced account of the impact of domestic politics.)

- How divided is the society over foreign policy and other matters?
- How open are the governing institutions to such pressures?

Democratic states provide at least some vehicles through which individuals and interest groups can influence the making of foreign policy. Polls have shown that the average voter in most countries is more interested in domestic politics than international relations (Rielly, 1999). Nonetheless, there have been periods when public opinion has had a major impact on the way a conflict was settled, as we will see in Israel following the elections of 1996 and 1999. There are other states in which pressures from below are extremely powerful, most notably the failed states that have all but collapsed in large part because of them.

Authoritarian regimes offer fewer opportunities for public participation. In Iraq, for instance, it has been not just illegal but downright dangerous to oppose the Baath regime since Saddam Hussein came to power in 1979. Nonetheless, there have been times when the alienation of the minority Kurds and Shiite Arabs was so intense that they defied the authorities in Baghdad and rose in revolt.

In short, we need to consider the second dimension captured by the rows of table 5.2. Whatever type of regime a country has, the state will face the most pressure if it is deeply divided as the United States was at the height of the Vietnam War. There will be less at times when the divisions are not very intense. That has been the case for most of the postwar years in Japan, especially regarding trade policy. It also was true of the United States during the early Cold War years, when Senator Arthur Vandenberg made his famous statement that 'politics stops at the water's edge.'

Most states involved in an intense international conflict are going to face significant pressures from their own societies. For example, protests from the Protestant community delayed implementation of parts of the 1998 Good Friday Agreement in Northern Ireland until November 1999. Similarly, many observers worry that sooner rather than later the African National Congress government will have to provide more jobs and services for Blacks, which, for now, can only come at the expense of the White minority.

Useful Web Sites

Here, the best web sites focus on international conflict through the lens of day-to-day politics.

The Conflict Processes Section of the American Political Science Association has a site with research papers presented at its sessions along with a series of links to home pages with other data and research findings. <http://wizard.ucr.edu/cps/cps.html>.

The Institute for Security and International Studies has one of the best general web sites among the think tanks.
<http://www.isis-online.org>.

The Carnegie Endowment for International Peace in Washington, D.C., has long sponsored high-quality research on a number of issues, especially nuclear nonproliferation. <http://www.ceip.org>.

The University of California's campuses cooperate in the Institute for Global Conflict and Cooperation. <http://www-igcc.ucsd.edu>.

The Canadian military provides an excellent site that, not surprisingly given Canada's history, emphasizes peacekeeping as well as conflicts themselves. <http://wps.cfc.dnd.ca>.

Professor Rudolph Rummel of the University of Hawaii has by far the most extensive site, with data and findings on the controversial theory linking democracy and peace.
<http://www2.hawaii.edu/powerkills>.

Those pressures can also affect countries that are third parties to a dispute. Thus, the general disinterest in African affairs went a long way toward explaining why the Clinton administration did not support a massive intervention during the genocide in Rwanda. Similarly, the power of the 'Jewish lobby' is such that all American administrations since 1947 have 'had' to tilt primarily toward Israel in their dealings with the Middle East.

Perhaps most important of all, it is domestic politics that leads to the lack of political will that 'orphans' so many peace settlements. As we saw in the last chapter, the problem is rarely a lack of potentially useful ideas for strengthening the peace. Instead, either the direct participants in the conflict or the third parties (or both) succumb to political pressures, especially impatience with the slow pace of change, the unwillingness to bear the cost of maintaining a peacekeeping force, or the desire to seek revenge.

The Democratic Peace

There is one finding from the pluralist literature that could provide some support for analysts or activists who believe in win-win conflict resolution and stable peace. There is now strong support for theories about the 'democratic peace' (Russett, 1993; Weart, 1998, but also see the withering critique in Gowa, 1999). Democracies rarely, if ever, go to war with each other. They fight other kinds of regimes, and many have been oppressive toward some of their own citizens, a point we will see in the Northern Irish and Israeli cases. Nonetheless, virtually every observer is convinced that there is some link between democracy and peace.

There is far less agreement about why the democratic peace exists or what its implications are for conflict resolution. One version holds that the tolerance and compromise that are a central part of domestic political life in a democracy carry over into international affairs (Muravchik, 1996). If that proves to be the case, it may well be that if democracies continue to take root in the former Soviet bloc and the third world, we will see a decline in the number of violent international conflicts.

EIGHT MORE FACTORS

As was the case with the theories discussed in chapter 4, we can cull specific factors that may well affect international conflict resolution from the abstraction of realist and pluralist thought. In this case, however, they fall into two categories. The first three focus on why win-win conflict resolution and stable peace are so difficult. The others involve opportunities to make progress in settling a dispute, though, reflecting the comparative pessimism of most of these theorists, doing so falls far short of the kind of conflict resolution discussed in the previous chapter.

Obstacles

1. Institutions of global governance may be more active now than they were twenty or thirty years ago. However, they are still rather ineffective when it comes to intense conflict because of their own weakness and the anarchy of the international system as a whole.

This point can be seen in the rise and decline of UN operations in the 1990s. In the first half of the decade, it was involved in more missions than in the first forty years of its history combined. What's more, some of those missions went well beyond traditional peacekeeping efforts.

By the middle of the decade, however, the limits of what the UN could accomplish had become clearer, and it had been forced to scale back many of those operations. In large part because the United States failed to pay its dues in a timely manner until late in 2000, the UN found itself without the funds to take on all the missions it might have wanted to. More important, because it lacked troops of its own and had an increasingly difficult time convincing all five of the permanent members of the Security Council to continue backing controversial and dangerous missions, the UN proved unable to act quickly or decisively. The most important international actions of the late 1990s in Bosnia and Kosovo were conducted by NATO largely because the UN proved unable to do so.

In short, the UN and other international organizations can have an impact, But they do so largely on the margins. They lack the resources, power, and authority to conduct the massive and forceful operations many observers believe are necessary to confront the complex emergencies that threaten international stability today.

2. Long-standing disputes are most often resolved only after they have reached a hurting stalemate, at which point the parties realize that the costs of continuing the fighting far outweigh any potential benefits, because victory has come to seem all but impossible. Not surprisingly, the parties to the dispute become more amenable to negotiations once a hurting stalemate has been reached.

However, the years of conflict and combat also leave the participants bitter. As we will see in Northern Ireland and the former Yugoslavia, they may agree to end the fighting, but that does not mean that they are open to reconciliation and the other parts of the peacebuilding process. In many cases, the end of the fighting by no means reduces the likelihood that they will take up arms again in the not-so-distant future.

3. Domestic politics will almost always make the search for win-win conflict resolution more difficult. There is no need to repeat the specific points made regarding table 5.2 other than to reinforce the pluralists' caution that the complexities of domestic political life render the pursuit of stable peace – and any other goal – extremely difficult in the short as well as the long run.

The only exception comes in those rare moments when the active members of a society reach what Daniel Yankelovich (1999) calls public judgments on new principles and agree to set off in a wholly new political direction. In his own work, Yankelovich sees public judgment developing largely at the grass roots as a result of the kind of track-two and grassroots work discussed in chapter 4.

Opportunities

1. The least intrusive of the policies that can reduce tensions is humanitarian intervention (Weiss and Collins, 1996) in which the international community provides aid to help civilians and refugees who have been caught up in the fighting. This kind of intervention is not new, having been formally begun with the creation of the International Committee of the Red Cross (ICRC) in 1864.

The ICRC's charter defines what humanitarian intervention has traditionally entailed, since it obliges the organization to be strictly neutral and to aid all sides in a conflict. That role is vitally important in today's complex emergencies, because the fighting leads to social, economic, demographic, and environmental problems as well as to bloodshed and physical destruction. Indeed, armies are often used to distribute the food, medicine, and other material and to protect aid workers who distribute it in the combat zone.

Most important for our purposes, the UN's various aid agencies and many nongovernmental organizations have begun to see humanitarian relief as part of a broader peace process (Eiliasson, 1998; Ogata, 1998). It can be a political 'carrot' they can use to try to get the antagonists into negotiation. And, they increasingly use aid to support one side of a conflict more than the other, as we will see was the case in Bosnia.

Therein also lies the potential problem with humanitarian relief. It can actually prolong a conflict, as may well have occurred in Bosnia. Even if it does not do so, the fact that the international community is perceived to be taking sides can stiffen resistance on the part of the group that feels it has been slighted, which almost certainly was the situation in Somalia.

2. There are two political 'sticks' to go along with the 'carrot' of humanitarian relief. States and alliances have long used the threat of force to get their adversaries to go along with their wishes, which Alexander George and his colleagues called coercive diplomacy (George, Hall, and Simons, 1971; George and Simons, 1994). As George defined it:

> Coercive diplomacy bears a close resemblance to the ultimatum. [It has] a specific demand on the opponent, a time limit for compliance, and a threat of punishment for noncompliance. (1994:2)

Until recently, coercive diplomacy had been used primarily for conventional foreign policy goals, not as part of a strategy for achieving stable peace. That has begun to change with, for instance, the growing imposition of sanctions by either ad hoc collections of states, the United Nations, or other international governmental organizations.

Sanctions typically take one of two forms:

- an arms embargo that blocks the transfer of weapons to either a state or all parties to a conflict, or
- broader bans on trade and other economic transactions, such as freezing the overseas bank accounts of individuals and/or organizations in the offending states.

Given their apparent failure to force Iraq to pull out of Kuwait in 1990 or rein in the Serbs later in the decade, the conventional wisdom is that sanctions and other forms of coercive diplomacy are not particularly effective. However, more systematic research has provided empirical support for United Nations secretary-general Kofi Annan's conclusion after sanctions and the threat of bombing forced Iraq to capitulate to the international community in 1998. Diplomacy coupled with the threat of force can work. To do so, sanctions must be enforced effectively, imposed on economic sectors that can truly harm the leaders who are being targeted, and given enough time to have an effect. If the South African case is any indication, that time period can run to years rather than merely a few weeks or months.

3. The second 'stick' is the actual use of armed force through what is euphemistically called peace imposition. Obviously, the use of force is not new. However, the international community rarely intervened in the domestic politics of states – even those that had been deemed to have violated international norms or law. Though anticipated by the UN Charter, the Cold War superpower rivalry made such intervention

difficult, if not impossible, between 1945 and 1990.

Now, however, it has become a far more frequently used device. As we saw in chapter 3, the UN and other international bodies have gone beyond traditional peacekeeping and taken a far more proactive stance regarding some particularly violent conflicts. In most of them, fighting is still occurring or could break out again at a moment's notice. In most recent cases, the international forces have intervened over the objections of at least one of the parties to the conflict.

Peace-imposition operations are different from traditional forms of international intervention in another way that is reflected in another term often used to describe them – peacemaking. As the NATO allies loudly proclaimed in the spring and summer of 1999, they did not launch the air war on Serbia just to stop the ethnic cleansing and other abuses in Kosovo. Rather, they viewed the fighting as the first step in a campaign to move toward something like stable peace.

There are, however, serious doubts about both the cost and potential effectiveness of peace imposition. The wars against Iraq and Serbia consumed vast amounts of American and other allied firepower before inflicting defeats on far-overmatched adversaries. But those defeats were limited at best. Saddam Hussein, Slobodan Milosevic (until his defeat at the polls in late 2000), and their regimes remained in power. In Iraq, at least, human rights abuses and violations of internationally imposed weapons bans continued. Even otherwise supportive observers have questioned the scale of the attacks, worrying that they may have violated the Geneva Conventions and the more general principles of 'just war' theory. Meanwhile, few efforts at reconciliation were made, since the allies had demonized their erstwhile opponents, whose own indignation toward the West only increased.

To make matters even more unsettling, conservative opponents of multilateral intervention after the Gulf war regularly pointed out that the 'international community' had opened up a Pandora's box. Iraq and Serbia were but two of many repressive states whose forces engaged in policies that smacked of genocide. Yet the international community was not prepared nor was it able to act in all of them. To use the words of the 1960s folk singer, Phil Ochs, the United States and their allies sometimes acted as if they were the 'cops of the world' without either fully taking on the role or considering the negative consequences for long-term peace and stability of their having done so.

Furthermore, it is not clear how easily the cooperative problem-solving techniques that lead to stable peace can be used once one of the parties to the conflict has been subjected to the use of force and develops the enduring anger that it typically leads to. In other words, stable peace is built in part because the parties to the conflict gradually develop more trust in each other as well as the ability to work with each other. We simply have too little experience with the use of force in those ways to know if and how it can be used in the longer-term process of building stable peace.

4. There has also been increased interest in holding the men and women responsible for genocide and other offenses legally accountable for their actions (Barker, 2000). Thus, in the aftermath of the carnage in the former Yugoslavia and Rwanda, the United Nations created international courts to prosecute those accused of war crimes, the first time it had done so since the trials of German and Japanese leaders at the end of World War II. As of this writing, indictments had been handed down as a result of the fighting in those countries, and some convictions had been obtained against middle-level Croatian and Serbian officials from the Bosnian war. More recently, the international court issued indictments against Slobodan Milosevic and four other top Yugoslav officials for crimes allegedly committed in Kosovo. Perhaps most promising of all, an agreement to create a permanent international criminal court was reached in 1998, though it still faces a number of obstacles, including likely opposition from the Bush administration, before it actually comes into existence.

But this is another area in which the realists and other mainstream international relations theorists point out the relative powerlessness of the United Nations and other transnational bodies. Few observers object to the strengthening of international criminal courts, but skeptics are quick to point out that they are still extremely weak. Virtually none of the senior officials indicted in Rwanda or the former Yugoslavia have been brought to trial. Thus, none of the key Serbian officials from either the Bosnian (for example, Radovan Karadzic and Ratko Mladic) or the Kosovo wars (other than Milosevic) has been apprehended, let alone tried or convicted.

5. Not surprisingly, the academic and political supporters of the 'democratic peace' argue strongly for democratization as a long-term strategy to prevent future conflicts. They point, for example, to the combination of Marshall Plan aid and democratization that helped create what Singer and Wildavsky (1996) call the zone of peace in western Europe. They similarly expect democratization in eastern Europe to further expand that zone as the former communist countries become eligible to join the European Union and NATO (which added the Czech Republic, Poland, and Hungary in 1999).

Critics, however, have pointed out two problems with democratization. First, as noted earlier, we really do not understand what makes the 'democratic peace' work. It may not involve democracy at all, but perhaps cultural norms common in western Europe and North America that cannot be readily exported whatever institutions a country adopts. Second and probably more important, building democracy is a lot like eroding the image of the enemy. It takes a decade or more of the smooth and proper functioning of elections and representative institutions before most political scientists are prepared to acknowledge that a country has a stable democratic regime. And, as we have seen time and time again in the last three chapters, the parties to a dispute who have reached a tentative peace agreement rarely have that kind of time.

CHAPTER 4 VERSUS CHAPTER 5

At first glance, the theories discussed here are quite different from those covered in chapter 4. (See table 5.3.) Both start with the assumption that resources are scarce, but after that, their world views diverge dramatically. The theories discussed in chapter 4 seek to identify the factors that make win-win conflict resolution and stable peace possible. Realism and pluralism focus more on why they have occurred so rarely throughout human history.

Table 5.3 Traditional (realism) and new theory (globalization) contrasted

Area of concern	Realism	Globalization
Availability of resources	Scarce	Scarce
Nature of relationships	Independent	Interdependent
Motivations	Self-interest	Good of whole
Time perspective	Short term	Long term
Nature of conflict	We v. they	We with they
Nature of power	Power over	Power with
Interpretation of conflict	Bad	Potentially good

The theories, however, are not wholly incompatible. Each purports to analyze one part of an international system in which both parts now feature prominently. In addition, the events of the 1990s have led people from both schools of thought to look for intellectual common ground.

Some observers and practitioners who use the new theories have tried to find common ground between the two schools of thought. Until recently, most of them ruled out even the threat of force, because it tends to deepen rather than reduce antagonisms. However, the tragedies of Somalia, Rwanda, Bosnia, and, especially, Kosovo have led at least some of them (including this author) to be more receptive to the limited use of force if it is part of an overall strategy for ending a conflict and moving toward stable peace.

From the other perspective, many practitioners, in particular, are more willing then ever before to intervene even if it to some degree undermines or even violates the sovereignty of the states involved. A smaller, but still significant number, are exploring many of the ideas considered in chapter 4, most notably in the work the Reagan administration's undersecretary of state for African affairs, Chester Crocker, has done for the United States Institute for Peace (Crocker, Hampson, and Aall, 1996).

We will not be able to do much more to blend them together in the rest of this book. Nonetheless, we will show ways in which both are helpful, with the newer theories providing the best insights for the first three cases in part 2 and the more traditional ones doing the same for the last two.

SELECT BIBLIOGRAPHY

Avruch, Kevin. *Culture and Conflict Resolution*. Washington, D.C.: United States Institute for Peace, 1998.

Buzan, Barry. *People, States, and Fear: An Agenda for International Security Studies in the Post-Cold War Era*. London: Harvester Wheatsheaf, 1991.

Cohen, Raymond. *Negotiating across Cultures: International Communication in an Interdependent World*. Rev. ed. Washington, D.C.: United States Institute for Peace, 1997.

Eiliasson, Jan. 'Humanitarian Action and Peacekeeping.' In *Peacemaking and Peacekeeping for the New Century*, edited by Olara A. Otunnu and Michael W. Doyle, 203–14. Lanham, MD: Rowman and Littlefield, 1998.

Frank, Jerome, and Andrei Melville. 'The Image of the Enemy and the Process of Change.' In *Breakthrough/Proriv*, edited by Anatoly Gromyko and Martin Hellman, 199–208. New York: Walker, 1988.

Fromkin, David. *Kosovo Crossing: American Ideals Meet Reality on the Balkan Battlefields*. New York: Free Press, 1999.

George, Alexander L., and William E. Simons, eds. *The Limits of Coercive Diplomacy*. Boulder, CO: Westview, 1994.

George, Alexander L., David K. Hall, and William E. Simons. *The Limits of Coercive Diplomacy*. Boston: Little Brown, 1971.

Goodman, David. *Fault Lines: Journeys into the New South Africa*. Berkeley: University of California Press, 1999.

Gowa, Joanne. *Between Ballots and Bullets*. Princeton, NJ: Princeton University Press, 1999.

Janis, Irving. *Groupthink*. Boston: Houghton-Mifflin, 1983.

Jervis, Robert. 'Hypotheses on Misperception.' *World Politics* 20 (1968): 454–79.

Keen, Sam. *Faces of the Enemy: Reflections on the Hostile Imagination*. New York: Harper and Row, 1986.

Kegley, Charles, and Gregory Raymond. *How Nations Make Peace*. New York: Worth, 1999.

Kolodziej, Edward. 'Modeling International Security.' In *Resolving Regional Conflicts*, edited by Roger E. Kanet, 11–42. Urbana: University of Illinois Press, 1998.

Moravcsik, Andrew. 'Taking Preferences Seriously: A Liberal Theory of International Politics.' *International Organization* 51 (Autumn 1997): 513–44.

Muravchik, Joshua. 'Promoting Peace through Democracy.' In *Managing Global Chaos: Sources of and Responses to International Conflict*, edited by Chester Crocker, et al., 573–86. Washington, D.C.: United States Institute for Peace, 1996.

Nye, Joseph. *Understanding International Conflict: An Introduction to Theory and History*. New York: Longman, 2000.

Ogata, Sadako. 'Humanitarian Responses to International Emergencies.' In *Peacemaking and Peacekeeping for the New Century*, edited by Olara A. Otunnu and Michael W. Doyle, 215–31. Lanham, MD: Rowman and Littlefield, 1998.

Rielly, John. 'Americans and the World: A Survey at Century's End,' *Foreign Policy* no. 114 (Spring 1999): 97–117.

Rose, William. 'The Security Dilemma and Ethnic Conflict,' *Security Studies* 9, no. 4 (Autumn 2000): 1–55.

Russett, Bruce. *Grasping the Democratic Peace: Principles for a Post-Cold War World*. Princeton, NJ: Princeton University Press, 1993.

Singer, Max, and Aaron Wildavsky. *The Real World Order*. 2d ed. Chatham NJ: Chatham House, 1996.

Toolis, Kevin. *Rebel Hearts: Journeys within the IRA's Soul*. New York: St. Martin's, 1995.

Waltz, Kenneth. *Man, the State, and War*. New York: Columbia University Press, 1959.

Weart, Spencer R. *Never at War: Why Democracies Will Not Fight One Another*. New Haven: Yale University Press, 1998.

Weiss, Thomas and Cindy Collins. *Humanitarian Challenges and*

Intervention: World Politics and the Dilemmas of Help. Boulder, CO: Westview, 1996.

White, Ralph. *Fearful Warrior: A Psychological Profile of U.S.-Soviet Relations.* New York: Free Press, 1984.

Yankelovich, Daniel. *The Magic of Dialogue: Transforming Conflict into Cooperation.* New York: Simon and Schuster, 1999.

Zartman, I. William. *Ripe for Resolution.* 2d ed. New York: Oxford University Press, 1989.

Part 2

CASE STUDIES

6

SOUTH AFRICA

This easy talk about a 'rainbow nation,' reconciliation, and nation-building – I think one must be very realistic about it. Given the inequalities, it's a lifelong process of trying to get a situation where we can live peacefully together – not necessarily be big friends – but somehow not use violence as a way of dealing with our conflicts. Perhaps that's what reconciliation is about at a national level – peaceful coexistence.
                                                              –Wilhelm Verwoerd (Goodman, 1999:175)

The five case studies in part 2 start with South Africa, because it – along with El Salvador, Cambodia, and a handful of other examples – can be used to illustrate the conditions under which the new theories of conflict resolution are the most accurate empirically. We will end with Iraq, which does the same for realism and other traditional approaches to international relations. The remaining three cases – Israel and the Palestinians, Northern Ireland, and the former Yugoslavia – fall in between.

South Africa deserves to be considered first here. As recently as 1990, it was ruled by a tiny White minority, which cruelly oppressed the Black majority. A decade later, it had held its second all-race democratic election, was governed by a Black-dominated political party, whose recently retired leader was the most respected leader in the world, and was one of the few functioning democracies in Africa.

The transition to peaceful, democratic rule is by no means complete. South Africa remains a violent country; for example, it may well have the highest rape and murder rates in the world. Much of the violence has political overtones, especially in the intertribal 'Black on Black' attacks that have characterized all elections campaigns so far. Also, there is still plenty of tension between Blacks and Whites, which seems certain to continue as long as the economic chasm between the two communities is not closed.

Nonetheless, South Africa has done what most observers thought was the unthinkable a few short years ago. Its leaders were able to reach a sweeping agreement to end a struggle that antedated the arrival of the National Party to power in 1948 and the formal adoption of apartheid. Even more important for our purposes, the new regime led by the ANC (African National Congress) has gone further than any other covered in this book to try to forge reconciliation between racial groups that had been in conflict since the Whites first arrived in 1652. Most notable here is the work of the TRC (Truth and Reconciliation Commission), which has tried to do what its name implies – discover what really happened under apartheid and use that information to build bridges across racial and political lines.

The hopes and fears regarding the South African transition are encapsulated in the statement that begins this chapter. Wilhelm Verwoerd is undoubtedly right. Reconciliation does not mean we have to become best friends with those we disagree with. Rather, stable peace 'simply' requires finding ways of settling the disputes that will inevitably arise in our lives nonviolently. And, he is no doubt right that it will take time and may not, in the end, work out.

At that level, there is nothing unusual about his statement. Just about every prominent leader in the new South Africa has said more or less the same thing.

What makes it remarkable is the fact that Verwoerd is the grandson of H. F. Verwoerd, the National Party prime minister who was the main architect of apartheid. The fact that Wilhelm joined the ANC and worked on the staff of the TRC was a symbol of how far some Whites had traveled in the last few years. But, as Verwoerd's family shows us, that political journey is by no means over. His father, also Wilhelm Verwoerd, no longer speaks to him. So, the younger Verwoerd knows from firsthand experience that reconciliation will be a long, difficult, and not purely political process. Indeed, full reconciliation may never be achieved. But, more than other political leaders around the world, Verwoerd and his colleagues have taken important first steps in that direction both as apartheid collapsed in the first half of the 1990s and since then under the governments of Presidents Nelson Mandela and Thabo Mbeki.

THEORETICAL FOCUS

Not surprisingly, the South African case provides the most clear-cut support for the theories that stress win-win conflict resolution. However, for the reasons noted in the discussion of the case study method in chapter 2 (also see box), I will not stress those theoretical concerns at the beginning of this chapter and the four that follow. Instead, I will offer a brief list of issues to guide your reading, which we will return to at the conclusion of each chapter:

- the degree to which the changing nature of international relations contributed to the transition in South Africa
- the emergence of a hurting stalemate in which the major parties to the conflict concluded both that they could not win and could not afford to continue the struggle in its current form
- the role leaders on both sides of the dispute played from the start of negotiations onward
- the way the post-apartheid government in general and the TRC, in particular, have tried to weaken the image of the enemy and other psychological barriers to reconciliation
- the attempt to address the social and economic inequalities that could imperil the entire transition

---

Reading a Case

To move from the facts to theory, you need to know how to 'read' a case so that you can go through something like the interactive experience you would have had in a classroom with an instructor who uses the technique. Therefore, as you read, consider the following set of questions and guidelines.

- Get the story right. Be sure you can answer the journalist's five key questions. Who did what, where, when, and how?
- Put the case in its historical context, which is not the one we live in today. See how the events leading up to the case helped predispose people to act and think as they did at the time.
- Don't focus too much on the details. Concentrate instead on the general issues of international relations that are addressed in the case.
- Ask why the case turned out as it did. Obviously, we cannot invent a time machine and 'rerun history.' Nonetheless, consider how decisions during the case narrowed the options available to the people involved. And, try to figure out what it would have taken for the case to have had a different outcome, including those you would have preferred and those you think would have been worse than what actually happened.
- Ask Rosenau and Durfee's question: 'Of what is this case an instance?' In other words, what general conclusions does it lead you to? How might they apply to other examples of conflict?

Table 6.1 The racial composition of South Africa

Race	Percentage of the population	Percentage of personal income (1988)
Blacks/African	75.2	34
Coloured	8.6	9
Indian/Asian	2.6	4
White	13.6	54

SOUTH AFRICA: THE BASICS

South Africa is a large country by African standards. More than twice the size of Texas, it has nearly 43 million people.

It is also one of the most diverse countries in the world. It has eleven official languages – English and Afrikaans along with nine indigenous African languages. More than two thirds of its population is Christian. Most of the rest follow one of the traditional African religions, though there is a sprinkling of Muslims, Hindus, and Jews.

The most important aspect of the South African population is race. Most South Africans still use the racial categories developed by the apartheid authorities. (See table 6.1.) About three quarters of the population is Black. As the table also shows, Blacks, however, earned only about a third of the country's total income during the latter years of apartheid. Whites, by contrast, make up 13.6 percent of the population but account for more than half of the income. About 60 percent of the Whites are Afrikaners, descendents of Dutch, German, and French immigrants and speak Afrikaans. The rest are either of English origin or have assimilated into that culture. Slightly less than 3 percent of the population are Indians who were brought to work in South Africa in the late nineteenth century. The rest are Coloureds, who are the mixed-race descendants of settlers and the *khoi* people, who lived near today's Cape Town on the south coast. Although Indians and Coloureds have done reasonably well economically, they were almost as severely discriminated against in other areas of life as Blacks.

ROOTS OF THE CONFLICT

The roots of the conflict stretch all the way back to 1652, when a handful of Dutch settlers arrived at what is now Cape Town to set up a refueling station for ships sailing from Europe to Asia (Thompson, 1995). The area was sparsely populated. The few Dutch settlers, however, established a harsh regime, which included slavery for the natives. They also gradually expanded their control outward into today's Western Cape province.

The Afrikaners lost control when the British seized the Cape from the Dutch during the Napoleonic wars. Shortly thereafter, English settlers began to arrive, and London soon abolished slavery.

These actions infuriated the conservative Dutch (or Boers as they became known). To make a long story short, most of them left the Cape region in 1835 and set off on what they today call the Great Trek. As they moved northeastward, they fought pitched battles with the Africans they encountered, the most important of which occurred at Bloemfontein in 1838. What they took to be a miraculous victory reinforced the Afrikaners' sense of their own superiority and Black inferiority to the point that Bloemfontein remains the most important symbol of Afrikaner resistance and solidarity to this day.

Although the Afrikaners had settled on land far removed from the British, the peace between them did not last. Following the discovery of diamonds (1867) and gold (1886) in the republics the Boers had created, the British set their sights on the rest of what is now South Africa. Tensions reached a peak in the mid-1890s when Cecil Rhodes (whose estate funds the Rhodes scholarships) called on the English settlers in the Afrikaner republics to rebel. Finally, in 1899, the Boer republic declared

Table 6.2 The evolution of South Africa

Date	Event
1652	Dutch arrive
1806	Final British takeover of the Cape
1835–40	Great Trek
1867	Diamond mining begins
1886	Gold mining begins
1899–1902	Boer War
1910	Union of South Africa created
1912	ANC formed
1948	National Party elected; formal apartheid begins

war on the British, setting off one of the fiercest struggles the world had seen up to that point.

The two sides signed a peace treaty in 1902. In 1906 and 1907, the Transvaal and Orange Free States passed under British control. In 1910 the various South African colonies merged, becoming the Union of South Africa, which was a largely self-governing entity inside the British empire (and later, the Commonwealth of Nations).

Although the apartheid laws, per se, were not put on the books until the late 1940s, the Union was always run by the tiny White minority. Only a handful of Africans and Coloureds had the right to vote. Successive governments enacted laws limiting the political and economic freedoms of Africans, such as one passed in 1913 that restricted their right to buy land outside of 'reserves,' which were not terribly different from Indian reservations in the United States.

Opposition to those racist policies began as soon as the Union was created. In 1912 a largely middle-class, multiracial group formed the ANC, which was modeled on its Indian equivalent, the Indian National Congress, and was thus committed to nonviolent change. The ANC and other opposition groups, however, had little impact before the 1950s.

At the time, there were more serious tensions between the English and the Afrikaners. The latter were particularly frustrated by their lack of economic and political power even though they outnumbered the English. Frustrated Afrikaners turned to the National Party and the even more militant Broederbond (literally, band of brothers) to maintain the purity and power of what they, like the Germans, called the *volk*.

World War II proved to be the major turning point for the Afrikaners. Many refused to support South African participation on the Allied (British) side. A minority actively supported the Nazis, whose racist and anti-Semitic policies they found appealing.

After the war, the Afrikaner community came together as never before, and the National Party won the 1948 election (as it did every subsequent election until 1994). Immediately, it began introducing apartheid legislation.

APARTHEID

Apartheid produced the all-but-total separation of the races as part of a regime in which the minority White population brutalized everyone else. Among other things, apartheid

- denied the few Africans, Asians, and Coloureds who were still on the rolls the right to vote;

- banned mixed marriages and sexual relations across racial lines;
- limited where Africans could live outside of 'homelands' and required them to carry passbooks or internal passports;
- segregated all public facilities.

Especially under the third National Party prime minister, H. F. Verwoerd, an elaborate justification for apartheid was developed. In it, the Afrikaners drew on their belief that they were God's chosen people and were thus superior to the Africans. That led them to the 'need' to develop their culture and society separately from inferior groups.

Most scholars, however, also emphasize the fear that Afrikaners felt toward the Blacks and even the English. After all, they were a tiny minority and had, themselves, lived under British rule for the better part of a century (Sparks, 1990).

Apartheid was enforced by one of the most repressive regimes of the second half of the twentieth century. The best estimates are that over 40,000 people were killed by a police force that used everything from random arrests to torture to try to keep Africans and other opponents 'in their place.'

We should also note something that was to prove critical in the negotiations in the early 1990s. The National Party used its forty years in power to transform the South African economy. Before World War II, most Afrikaners were poor, because they lived on small, inefficient farms or lacked the skills to get good jobs in the English-dominated urban, industrial economy. The National Party used the patronage powers of the state to shift contracts to Afrikaner-dominated banks and industrial firms, give a disproportionate number of jobs to their own people, create state-owned enterprises run by Afrikaners, and create living conditions for the White population that were nearly equal to those in Europe or North America.

RESISTANCE

Opposition to apartheid began before the first laws were enacted. A handful of White liberals (mostly English) openly opposed apartheid. So, too, did the South African Communist Party. But its influence was limited because it was banned as early as 1950. (See table 6.3.)

The most effective internal resistance came from the ANC. For its first forty years, it emulated the nonviolent and nonconfrontational tactics of its Indian namesake. Under the influence of its Youth League (including Mandela, Walter Sisulu, Oliver Tambo, and Govan Mbeki, father of the current president), the ANC moved leftward in the 1950s. Most notably,

Table 6.3 Resistance to apartheid in South Africa

Date	Event
1955	ANC issues the Freedom Charter
1960	Sharpeville massacre
1962	Umkhonto we Sizwe, armed struggle begins
1964	Mandela arrested and imprisoned
1976	Soweto uprising
1977	UN arms embargo imposed
1977	Death of Steve Biko
1984	UN declares apartheid a crime against humanity
1986	EC and United States impose sanctions

it adopted a more militant Freedom Charter (1955) and launched a Defiance Campaign reminiscent of the U.S. civil rights movement of the same period.

The government failed to yield. As a result, many younger leaders began to question nonviolence, especially following the 1960 Sharpeville Massacre in which at least sixty-nine peaceful demonstrators were killed. That led Mandela and many of his colleagues to endorse violent resistance against the regime and led to the creation of its armed wing, Umkhonto we Sizwe, or MK (Spear of the Nation), two years later.

Over the next quarter century, MK launched attacks from its bases outside South Africa. In practice, it was not very effective. It never had many members, and most of the guerrillas it sent into the country were captured; many were killed.

The regime was also able to neutralize the ANC leadership. One group of leaders, including Mandela, was arrested on treason charges and sentenced to long terms or life in prison. Most ended up on the infamous Robben Island off the coast at Cape Town, where they lived under grueling if not inhuman conditions. The leaders who were able to escape arrest, including Tambo and Joe Slovo, fled the country and ran the ANC and MK from exile in Britain and, later, friendly African countries.

The National Party's repressive apparatus and propaganda machine were relentless. As noted earlier, 40,000 Blacks and other opponents were killed and perhaps ten times that number were arrested. Even more remarkable in this media age, the regime was able to keep all pictures and any mention of Mandela and his fellow prisoners out of the press from their imprisonment until the eve of their release.

Nonetheless, from the mid-1970s on, protest against the regime stiffened. The ANC continued to organize and orchestrate much of the domestic opposition from underground. However, other groups that shared goals and had some organizational ties with the ANC but that had not been banned took center stage. In particular, the churches and, later, the Black trade unions helped build opposition against the regime at home and abroad.

In 1976 Soweto and other townships erupted with protests by young people, whose anger was sparked by a government decision to require teaching in Afrikaans in Black schools. The Black Consciousness Movement was able to focus much of that anger until its leader, Steve Biko, was arrested, tortured, and executed by the police in 1977.

In the 1980s the state cracked down ever harder. Despite the repression, protestors effectively disrupted the educational, township, and industrial systems in an attempt to make the country ungovernable.

There were also developments on the more conventional political front. Most notably, the ANC was the driving force behind the United Democratic Front (UDF) in 1983. It eventually numbered 600 groups and went a long way toward solidifying the ANC's organization at the grass roots, especially among the young people who knew little or nothing about Mandela or the ANC, since the censored media were not allowed to mention either of them.

There was also mounting opposition from abroad. As early as the 1940s, foreign activists such as Britain's Father Trevor Huddleston opposed South Africa's racist policies and helped organize resistance inside the country. The first General Assembly of the United Nations took note of the South African situation when India objected to the way people from the subcontinent were treated there.

By the 1960s and 1970s, apartheid sparked an extensive and, eventually, effective series of sanctions and other diplomatic efforts (Klotz, 1995; Crawford and Klotz, 1999). The Soviet Union and its allies gave the ANC substantial money and training (remember, the South African Communist Party was an ANC ally). However, because the Soviet Union was about to collapse at the same time apartheid did, it had little to do with resolving the conflict, and we will therefore focus our attention on the West and the rest of Africa here. Although the impact and enforcement of the policies discussed below was always limited, the opposition to apartheid did mark the first time that so many states, international organizations, and nongovernmental organizations (NGOs) made as concerted an effort to end a domestic dispute.

The United Nations was often the focus of the antiapartheid movement, though its actions were stymied by the British and/or American desire to continue working with the South African regime, which they saw as a Cold War ally. The General Assembly had begun criticizing South Africa in the late 1940s. However, the General Assembly has no real power, and its resolutions therefore had next to no impact. Attention therefore shifted to the Security Council, where British and American reticence was more important because of their ability to cast a veto and thereby block any action. Still, the Security Council passed a mandatory embargo (Resolution 418) on all sales of arms and related technologies to South Africa in 1977. Later it banned the sale of spare parts and police equipment to South Africa and the purchase of arms made in South Africa.

Meanwhile, the General Assembly continued taking symbolic steps that helped crystallize public opinion against apartheid. South Africa was expelled from the General Assembly and then from the UN's affiliated organizations whenever a simple majority of the member states was enough. In 1984 the General Assembly declared apartheid a crime against humanity.

The UN was often criticized for its failure to take tougher stands on South Africa. Nonetheless, it channeled hundreds of millions of dollars in humanitarian aid into the country and consistently kept the opposition and Mandela on international central stage.

The UN was not the only international organization involved. Because it had been a British colony, South Africa was a member of the Commonwealth of Nations. As more and more former British colonies in the third world gained their independence, apartheid became an important and divisive issue within the Commonwealth. Despite the regular opposition of the British government, the Commonwealth took ever stronger stands against South Africa and the breakaway White-dominated government of Rhodesia (now Zimbabwe). The Commonwealth passed sanctions against South Africa and sent an Eminent Persons Group, which met Mandela and found the ANC open to a dialog with the regime.

The final significant international organization was the Organization of African States, many of whose members also belonged to the Commonwealth. It, too, took stands against apartheid but lacked the economic clout to pass sanctions that would have much of an impact on Pretoria. Instead, its member states did what they could to raise global awareness about apartheid. South Africa's neighbors did what they could to reduce their economic dependency on South Africa. Most, too, became frontline states, which were willing to house and otherwise support the ANC and other guerrilla forces.

Individual states were far less consistent in their opposition to apartheid. None was more disappointing than Britain, whose less-than-constructive involvement in the region before 1912 has already been discussed.

Britain had major cultural and economic ties to South Africa. On the one hand, that sparked opposition to apartheid, especially from the unions, left of center political parties, and liberal interest groups. On the other hand, the antiapartheid movement was not able to build strong enough bridges to the British movement for racial equality. It also failed to get a place near the top of the Labour Party's foreign policy agenda, which meant that it did little for South Africa when in office from 1964 to 1970 and 1974 to 1979. The Conservatives under Margaret Thatcher (in office 1979-90) opposed any strong steps against the South African regime. They rationalized their position as an attempt to save jobs in Britain, stop the spread of communism, and keep the situation in South Africa from getting any worse. As we saw earlier, the British government resisted proposals for more sweeping action from the Commonwealth in the end by turning the issue over to the European Community (now the European Union). When that body enacted partial sanctions in 1986, London had no choice but to go along, although recently revealed scandals suggest it often honored them in the breach.

The United States played a similar, though in the end, slightly more assertive role in opposing apartheid. The United States did not have as extensive cultural or economic ties to South Africa as Britain did; nonetheless, the two were major trading partners, and successive American administrations saw South Africa as a bulwark against the spread of communism in an otherwise volatile region. That said, given its own civil rights problems, South Africa was bound to become an issue in U.S. domestic politics. Indeed, as early as 1960, the Rev. Martin Luther King Jr. took a strong stand, denouncing apartheid as worse than segregation in the United States.

Momentum against apartheid grew during the Carter administration, which made human rights in general an important foreign policy priority. Unlike the case in Britain, American activists were able to bring the civil rights community and the traditional left on board in its antiapartheid activities, which included educational efforts, sit-ins and other protests, and the disinvestment movement to be discussed in the next paragraph.

It was only in the 1980s, however, that enough opposition had built to force a change in U.S. policy. The decade did not start out auspiciously. The new Reagan administration adopted constructive engagement, or a policy of staying involved in South Africa while pressuring its government to reform. Critics were incensed by the administration's failure to apply all levers possible against Pretoria and by the president's frequent misstatements (for example, praising National Party leaders for their role as World War II allies, when many of them spent time in prison as Nazi collaborators). By the middle of the decade, liberals and moderate Republicans had come to reject constructive engagement as ineffective. And, whether as a matter of principle or a desire to get more votes from Blacks, a broad coalition of most Democrats and Republicans passed the Anti-Apartheid Act. It was vetoed by President Reagan, but the House and Senate overrode the veto. The act called for Mandela's release, imposed restrictions on most areas of trade between the two countries, and required American firms to use a version of the Sullivan principles that banned them from discriminating if they remained active in South Africa.

Finally, NGOs and businesses played a major role in the antiapartheid movement during the 1970s and 1980s. American activists, universities, and interest groups, for example, led the pressure for disinvestment and the Sullivan principles. In 1985, for example, Chase Manhattan led a consortium of banks that denied a cash-strapped South Africa $24 billion in short-term loans. These moves were not just American initiatives. Corporations around the world either pulled out of South Africa altogether or, along Sullivan lines, ended the racist policies practiced by their subsidiaries in South Africa. Indeed, the most important blow came when the British-based Barclay's Bank stopped dealing with South Africa as a result of business losses there and pressure from its customers at home. Some international NGOs were able to establish conflict resolution, and educational and development operations in the Black community. Events ranging from the publicity given such figures as Desmond Tutu in winning the Nobel Peace Prize to that given the late Steve Biko in the popular film, *Cry Freedom*, all added to the opposition to apartheid. Though it might seem trivial to outsiders, South Africa's expulsion from international athletic competition was actually a tough blow for the sports-mad country.

ANATOMY OF A MIRACLE

Most South Africans first heard about the momentous changes that were about to sweep their country when de Klerk made his surprise announcement to the National Assembly on 2 February 1990:

> The prohibition of the African National Congress, the Pan Africanist Congress, the South African Communist Party, and a number of subsidiary organizations is being rescinded. The government has taken a firm decision to release Mr. Nelson Mandela unconditionally. (Waldmeier, 1997:142)

The negotiations that led to that statement had occurred on two tracks.

The first was between the still-imprisoned Mandela and the top leadership in South Africa. The second involved informal discussions between the ANC and White private citizens who sometimes acted with, and sometimes without, the approval of the government.

Useful Web Sites

The most obvious and important web site for our purposes is run by the Truth and Reconciliation Commission. It documents all its activities and has a link to the government site that has all five volumes of the report users can download.
`<http://www.truth.org.za>`.

There are also lots of sites dedicated to South African politics. The South African Political Information Exchange is one of the best, though not one of the most active `<http://sapolitics.co.za>`. The South African Web-Chart is a Yahoo- or LookSmart-like site that organizes home pages in South Africa into categories, including politics `<http://sa.web-chart.com>`. Both of these sites have links to the leading parties, newspapers, interest groups, and so on.

SANGONet is a clearing house for the leading NGOs working in the country. `<http://sn.apc.org>`.

In his meetings with foreign visitors and the White authorities, Mandela consistently demanded that any agreement had to include three main points:

- elections in which everyone could vote
- a government determined on the basis of one person, one vote
- Whites belonging in South Africa, since they were Africans, too

The second half of the 1980s proved to be a tough time for the South African government, and the regime's difficulties undoubtedly contributed to its willingness to find a negotiated solution. The ungovernability campaign had forced President P. W. Botha to impose a state of emergency. Meanwhile, as the sanctions began to take hold, economic conditions deteriorated to the point that the White standard of living was threatened.

In response, Botha offered limited reform. Some of the more noxious symbols of apartheid, such as segregated beaches, were removed. Botha also privately offered to release Mandela if the ANC renounced the armed struggle. Mandela refused. Nonetheless, he had Mandela moved from Robben Island to a less austere prison and allowed him to have regular contact with the ANC leaders in exile.

The available evidence suggests that the government thought it would outsmart Mandela and split the ANC. In fact, the opposite happened.

Between 1988 and 1990, Mandela held forty-seven meetings with the authorities. Few of his colleagues knew the details of what has happening, prompting some tensions within both the prison community and the ANC as a whole.

In those meetings, Mandela routinely spoke Afrikaans and, in many cases, charmed his adversaries with his dignity and graciousness. Some of the stories from that period are truly remarkable. Mandela was once taken for a drive by a prison warden who went into a store to buy a soda, leaving the keys in the car. Mandela made no attempt to escape. Mandela liked one of his guards, James Gregory, so much that he invited him to his inauguration. Gregory had voted for the ANC in the election. Most remarkable of all, Mandela built an exact replica of his final prison house to serve as his retirement home.

Then on 5 July 1989 Botha invited Mandela to his office outside of Cape Town for tea and an informal meeting. They treated each other with dignity and respect and surprised each other by how well they got along, though no progress was made on either Mandela's release or broader issues.

At that point, the situation seemed to take a step backward. Botha was too rigid and too worried about appearing weak to find a way to release Mandela and deal with the broader issues raised in the negotiations. Then, in one of those 'accidents of history' that often play a vital role in political life, Botha resigned. He had suffered a stroke in January, yet tried to hold onto power. However, once word of the meeting with Mandela leaked, pressure on him to resign intensified. Six weeks later, he did so and was replaced by F. W. de Klerk, who was widely viewed as a hard-liner.

Track-two discussion began at about the same time as those between Mandela and his captors. In September 1985, Gavin Relly, chair of the immensely influential Anglo-American Corporation, met (illegally, given South African law) with Oliver Tambo and other ANC leaders in Zambia. The fact that it was a business leader of English origin who began this set of contacts was not surprising. English speakers had always been somewhat more liberal than most Afrikaners. More important, the business community was deeply worried about the state of the economy, which they were convinced would continue to deteriorate as long as apartheid was in force.

There were rumblings of change within the Afrikaner community as well. In 1986 Pieter de Lange, the new head of the Broederbond, met Thabo Mbeki at a Ford Foundation-sponsored meeting on Long Island. Lange stated flatly that South Africa would have to change; Mbeki was skeptical. Groups of Afrikaner clergymen violated South African law by meeting ANC and other opposition figures in neighboring countries. A British politician who was also an executive of Consolidated Goldfields facilitated twelve meetings in which middle-level ANC and Afrikaner leaders met at country homes in the United Kingdom.

As was the case in the secret negotiations that led to the Oslo agreement between Israel and the Palestine Liberation Organization, the informal side of these meetings (often leavened with alcohol) may have accomplished more than the negotiations themselves. Thus, at one of the first meetings, ANC and Afrikaner representatives alike watched a cricket match and bemoaned the fact that apartheid deprived them of the opportunity to watch their mutually beloved cricket, soccer, and rugby teams play in international competition.

Many key Afrikaners emerged from those meetings convinced of the need for fundamental reform. Included among them was de Klerk's younger brother. Though the two de Klerk's did not agree politically, Wilhelm joined the other well-connected Afrikaner participants in reporting what they were doing to the South African security forces. In an ironic twist of fate, the political leaders of the security apparatus – who of course understood how bleak the situation was – ended up spearheading support for a negotiated settlement in the National Party and the Broederbund.

Everything came to a head in the six months following Botha's resignation. Before taking office, de Klerk had not been 'in the loop' about the secret discussions. At his first State Security Council meeting, he routinely approved one of those initiatives without fully under-standing the importance of his actions. When informed that two of his top intelligence officials had met with Thabo Mbeki and others in Switzerland, de Klerk was furious. When he was fully briefed, he realized how badly the situation had deteriorated at home and how far negotiations with the ANC had proceeded. As one of the government participants in those meetings put it, 'from that moment on, he took the ball and ran with it' (Sparks, 1995:114).

He then allowed the first legal ANC demonstration in nearly thirty years. In December 1989 he met with Mandela. Though the two did not hit it off well personally, it was clear to both of them that they could work together. So, on 2 February he made his famous speech. Mandela was informed he would be released on the eleventh. Later that day, he spoke to a crowd of over 100,000, most of whom had not even seen a picture of a man who not been mentioned in the South African media for more than a quarter century.

TRANSITION TO DEMOCRATIC RULE

Freeing Mandela and unbanning those organizations by no means ended the conflict. In fact, it seems that de Klerk acted quickly so that he might catch the ANC unprepared and take the political initiative back, thereby limiting the changes the Whites would have to accept. As was the case throughout the transition, that is not what happened.

Table 6.4 Transition to majority rule

Date	Event
1985	Mandela meets with Commonwealth Eminent Persons Group
1987	Mandela begins meeting with government officials
1989	Botha and Mandela meet, de Klerk replaces Botha
1990	Mandela released, ANC and other groups unbanned
1991	CODESA formed
1993	Interim constitution adopted
1994	First all-race elections, Mandela and ANC elected
1996	Permanent constitution adopted
1999	Second election, Mbeki and ANC elected

It took weeks, for instance, simply to arrange the legal indemnifications that allowed ANC exiles to return home and not face prosecution. More important, it was well over a year before the Conference on a Democratic South Africa (CODESA) was named, and another two years passed before it reached an agreement on an interim constitution. Eighteen parties were represented, but in the end, the differences involving the ANC, National Party, and the Inkatha Freedom Party proved to be the biggest obstacles.

It took so long because the differences between the ANC and the government were still vast and because the overall situation remained tense and often violent. Not surprisingly, the ANC wanted a system of one person, one vote that would all but certainly bring Black (and ANC) rule. The National Party insisted on provisions that would guarantee minority representation in the cabinet and limit the redistribution of income and wealth.

In August 1990 the ANC called off the armed struggle, though it maintained a small underground organization just in case it was needed and called on the international community to maintain sanctions. The government realized it would have to accept Black participation but hoped to find ways to limit its impact so that the National Party could stay in power at least for the short term. De Klerk also wanted to avoid an election to choose an assembly that would draft a new constitution, something that Mandela at first demanded. To make matters more complicated, the personal relationship between the two leaders deteriorated considerably.

The difficulties did not only exist at the bargaining table. At least partially political violence swept the Black townships. Although the evidence is still incomplete, there is good reason to believe that a shadowy 'third force,' operating through the security services, helped organize and fund the more conservative Inkatha to try to blunt the strength of the ANC.

The security services also probably instigated fighting that pitted Inkatha-supporting Zulus against ANC-supporting Xhosas, which threatened to add a second ethnic dimension to South Africa's conflict. In the worst single incident, Zulus hacked thirty-seven workers to death in a hostel in Boipatong outside of Johannesberg on 16 June 1992. Indeed, the violence continued until the eve of the first election, when a group of right-wing fanatics tried to seize power and set up a new apartheid state in rural Bophuthatswana, one of the apartheid-era sham homelands.

Finally, the ANC agreed to an all-party constituent assembly as long as elections would be held shortly after it concluded its deliberations. On 21 December 228 delegates from 18 parties assembled for the first meeting of CODESA. The parties agreed that they would move forward once the chair decided they had reached 'sufficient consensus' (a term also used in Northern Ireland).

The desire for consensus masked a game of political hardball played by the ANC and National Party. Both took more intransigent positions on such issues as minority representation. After Boipatong, Mandela issued a list of fourteen demands the government would have to meet for negotiations to resume, including an end to violence against ANC organizers and increasing security in the townships.

Mandela began to back down as the violence escalated. In September 1992 police in the homeland of Ciskei killed twenty-eight demonstrators at a rally held by the ANC. Indeed, the possibility that violence could derail the entire transition seems to have jolted both sides, especially the people one level below Mandela and de Klerk in their respective hierarchies. Roelf Meyer led a group of younger National Party officials who argued that holding out would even further jeopardize the political and economic status of Whites. To the surprise of many, the communist leader, Joe Slovo, convinced the ANC that it needed Whites not just to run the economy but the state as well, because the government-in-waiting did not have anywhere near enough qualified people to staff the state apparatus. Slovo also convinced Mandela to go along with some form of power sharing with the National Party for a limited period.

Negotiations began again after Mandela and de Klerk signed a memorandum of understanding in late September 1993. Ironically, their task was aided by the obstructionist tactics followed by the Inkatha's leader, Mangosuthu Buthelezi, which drove the ANC and National Party closer together. However, in yet another tragic irony, it may have taken two more bursts of violence – the attempted coup in Bophuthatswana mentioned earlier and the assassination of Chris Hani, secretary-general of the Communist Party – to convince the negotiators to close a deal.

In the predawn hours of 18 November 1993, the negotiators agreed to the final clause of a 142-page interim constitution. Much of the document was written to reassure Whites by:

- institutionalizing minority representation in the cabinet for five years;
- guaranteeing property rights, although also holding open the possibility of reparations for people whose property had been illegally seized;
- providing for a degree of decentralization and an upper house that would represent the provinces.

The country's attention then turned to what many expected to be a tumultuous election campaign. While there was some violence and Buthelezi did what he could to disrupt the elections until he decided to run a slate of candidates at the last moment, the elections occurred remarkably smoothly.

As expected, the ANC won handily, with 62 percent of the vote. The National Party, Inkatha, and a number of minor parties trailed far behind. On 10 May 1994 Mandela was sworn in as president with, in perhaps the most remarkable irony of all, de Klerk as his first deputy president.

The impossible had happened.

TOMORROW IS ANOTHER COUNTRY

As we will see in the next section and the rest of the book, there are many reasons why conflict resolution in South Africa has been smoother than in most other countries. At the top of any such list is the fact that parties to the negotiations paid more attention to what happened after the beginning of majority rule. While we will see what South Africa has done on this score here, the importance of those efforts may not be clear until you read about the more 'orphaned' agreements in Northern Ireland and the Middle East in the chapters that follow.

The Truth and Reconciliation Commission has received the lion's share of the publicity in that respect (Tutu, 1999). However, it is but part of a larger effort to heal the wounds brought on by forty-five years of apartheid and centuries of other racist policies before that (Marks, 1990a).

The new government, however, took three broad initiatives that sought to heal the wounds that had built up over the decades. All were controversial, especially among some of the ANC's supporters at home and abroad, because they flew in the face of what most 'winners' expect to do when they prevail after an intense conflict.

First, the ANC has sought to govern with members of the old regime as much as possible. That started with the inclusion of de Klerk and the National Party in the cabinet after the transition. No one expected that to last indefinitely, and de Klerk and his colleagues resigned in 1996, once the permanent constitution was adopted without provisions guaranteeing minority representation. Perhaps more important for the long term, the government has taken Slovo's concerns to heart and kept on most of the White civil servants, only firing those who had been most deeply implicated in defining and enforcing apartheid policies. The federal component of the constitution also allowed the National Party to stay in power in its regional bastion around Cape Town and for Inkatha to do the same in KwaZulu Natal.

Second, the ANC has pursued surprisingly market-oriented economic policies. Before taking office, the ANC was committed to democratic socialism and was affiliated with the South African Communist Party. That past led many observers to assume that it would expropriate White-owned resources that remained in private hands and pass tax laws that would redistribute income and wealth to the poor.

The pressures to do so were overwhelming. Some 40 percent of Blacks were unemployed. Only 2 percent of all Whites but over half of the Blacks lived in poverty, earning less than $200 a month. Mandela's government started out with policies in keeping with its socialist past. It did not have to nationalize many industries, since the National Party had set up state-owned companies in most key industrial sectors. It did, however, commit itself to fulfilling the 'basic needs of the people' by adding new jobs, building a million houses by 2000, expanding access to running water and electricity, improving health care in the townships and rural areas, and more. At first, it seemed as if the strategy might work. With the lifting of the last sanctions in 1994 and the general goodwill shown the government, growth rebounded to 3 percent a year in 1994 and 1995.

But the government changed course for two main reasons. First, the economy as a whole was in a tailspin, largely because of sanctions and other costs of apartheid. Second, the global economic powers-that-be had turned their backs on socialism and were increasingly concentrating aid, loans, and investment in third world countries that did the same.

Most notably, in 1996, the government realized it would need a growth rate of at least 6 or 7 percent a year to reach its ambitious social goals. Indeed, at current rates of growth, unemployment among Blacks would actually increase by 5 percent by the end of the decade. And, it could only hike its growth rate by accommodating itself to capitalism at home and abroad. In 1996, therefore, it adopted its Growth, Employment, and Redistribution Plan (GEAR), which is typical of the structural adjustment policies that are now used in most of the third world. It calls on the government to:

- reduce government debt to 3 percent of GNP
- Bring inflation under control by keeping wage and price increases below the rate of growth in productivity
- establish stable exchange rates
- privatize many of the companies nationalized or created by the National Party (for example, Swiss Air bought much of the South African airline in 1999)
- increase labor market flexibility

All of these policies were designed to improve the chances of luring back the foreign investment that left during the last years of apartheid.

Despite what many critics on the left – including many in the ANC's own coalition – claimed, GEAR and related policies do not amount simply to a capitulation to international capitalism and the South African White community. Within this procapitalist framework, the government has added programs that it expects to benefit its core constituents as well in the early 2000s:

- Encouraging the small group of young Black entrepreneurs and other public-private joint ventures to succeed and then plow back some of what they make into the community (Goodman, 199:246–82).
- Using its own investment funds to create industrial development zones and other regional projects, especially in rural areas. These

funds will be used not only to expand employment but will also be concentrated in Black-owned firms. Thus, millions have already been invested in projects to encourage tourism and agricultural exports on the coast near the border with Mozambique and in building a world-class port near Port Elizabeth.

- Expanding the use of microcredit to create small businesses in poor Black, Asian, and Coloured communities as a vehicle for helping people pull themselves out of poverty. (On microcredit in general, see Yunus, 1999; Bornstein, 1997.) For instance, the Small Enterprise Foundation in the Northern Province (where two-thirds of the population is unemployed) has made nearly 20,000 loans of about $700 each, primarily to women for dressmaking, small grocery stores, and other businesses that employ an average of 2.5 full time workers each.

As with most structural adjustment programs, it is too early to tell if these policies will do much to improve the conditions of the half of the population that currently lives in poverty. For now, it is enough to note that these programs were adopted to encourage economic as well as political healing. Along those lines, leftist critics correctly point out that this was a political and not a social or economic revolution. The jury is still out, however, on whether the necessary steps toward social and economic equality can be made in this way or not.

Third, the best-known example of the efforts at lasting conflict resolution in post-apartheid South Africa is, of course, the Truth and Reconciliation Commission. It started as a compromise between the ANC, which wanted to reveal the crimes of the apartheid era and the National Party, which hoped to limit the legal retribution that could be taken against its own supporters.

Quickly, however, the idea of truth *and reconciliation* became something bigger than and different from what either party had anticipated. The 1993 interim constitution ended with a call for a commitment to human rights and peaceful coexistence among all South Africans. To that end, on 19 July 1995 the parliament passed a law creating the Truth and Reconciliation Commission to be headed by Desmond Tutu.

It was by no means the only institution of its type. In recent years, more than fifteen other countries have created similar bodies to uncover the truth about the human rights violations under a previous, authoritarian regime. The TRC was different in that it also explicitly sought reconciliation between Blacks and their former oppressors.

The TRC was, thus, based on a different vision of justice than one normally finds in political life that revolve around such values as retribution and punishment for wrongdoers. Instead, the TRC has had two main goals – first, to learn as much of the truth as possible in order, second, to speed up the healing across racial lines in what Martha Minow calls restorative justice (Minow, 1998: ch. 4; also see Tutu, 1999). Countries that have endured genocide and mass violence suffer from a societywide equivalent of post-traumatic stress disorder, for which a kind of collective therapy is needed. Indeed, if the perpetrators cooperate, truth and reconciliation commissions can both get more information out in public and help old enemies put at least some of the past to rest. The traumatic story can be 'transformed through testimony about shame and humiliation to a portrayal of dignity and virtue, regaining lost selves and lost world' (Minow, 1998:66). Prosecutions, confiscatory economic policies, and the like, by contrast, tend to reinforce the anger of the former rulers but rarely provide many tangible benefits for the people they oppress.

The TRC was actually three separate bodies, two of which were still functioning when these lines were written. The best known of the three held hearings around the country (most of which were also televised) in which victims and perpetrators alike were encouraged to tell their stories. A second and separate committee determined if amnesty would be granted to violators of human rights who asked for it. The third will determine how much – if any – reparations are to be paid to the victims.

The hearings often marked the first time that people were able to talk about what they and other family members had suffered or what crimes they had perpetrated. The results were mind numbing; even Tutu and the other commissioners were often seen weeping.

In three years the commission heard from 20,000 witnesses. In October 1998 it published a 3,500-page document that minced no words about crimes committed by the apartheid state. It also criticized the more limited violations of human rights perpetrated by the opposition, including those orchestrated by Mandela's former wife, Winnie Madikizela-Mandela.

There is one common misperception about the TRC. It could not grant amnesty unconditionally. Rather, a perpetrator had to formally ask for it, the crime had to be explicitly political, and the applicant had to demonstrate contrition. When the initial report was released, the TRC had dealt with almost 5,000 of the 7,000 pending applications. To the surprise of many, it had only granted amnesty to about 125 people. It is not clear how many of the others will ever be prosecuted. Nonetheless, the low rate at which amnesty was given suggests that the TRC was not simply freeing abusers of human rights.

It is too early to tell how much of a positive impact the TRC has had.

Its shortcomings, however, are already apparent. Some people – including Steve Biko's family – denounced it for not obtaining justice in the traditional sense of the term. Botha, de Klerk, and some other prominent National Party leaders either refused to cooperate or did so halfheartedly. Similarly, one of the first public opinion polls suggests that a desire for revenge may be as common as a hope for reconciliation, though this evidence is sketchy at best (Gibson and Gouws, 1999)

Still, there are signs that many of the victims who testified regained some of their lost dignity. And there is some evidence that the TRC's procedures allowed many of the perpetrators of those crimes who did feel remorse to come forward and become partners in the building of the new South Africa.

There have been other attempts at reconciliation outside of the formal political world. For example, during the violence that marked the transition between Mandela's release and the first elections, a Dutch Reformed minister who had begun meeting with the ANC in the late 1980s organized the National Business Institute. His assumption was that the 'space' where Blacks and Whites came together had to be expanded if South Africa were to avoid catastrophe. And since South Africa would have to be peaceful in order to be prosperous, the business community had a powerful incentive to bring the communities closer together. Similarly, the lifting of sanctions allowed South African teams to participate in international competition again. The world rugby federation decided to hold its 1995 World Cup in South Africa. Rugby had long been the favorite sport of most Afrikaners and thus was detested by most Blacks. In fact, ANC activists put considerable pressure on Mandela to outlaw the sport. However, the president not only attended the 1995 final, but handed the victorious South African team its trophy while he was wearing a copy of the uniform worn by its Afrikaner captain, François Pienaar.

No one would argue that reconciliation alone will solve all of South Africa's problems, let alone do so quickly. Nonetheless, it is an increasingly widely used mechanism that states and the international community have turned to, which Tutu perhaps summed up best in the introduction to the 1998 report:

> Reconciliation is not about being cosy; it is not about pretending that things were other than they were. Reconciliation based on falsehood, on not facing up to reality, is not reconciliation at all.
>
> We believe we have provided enough of the truth about our past for there to be a consensus about it. We should accept that truth has emerged even though it has initially alienated people from one another. The truth can be, and often is, divisive. However, it is only on the basis of

truth that true reconciliation can take place. True reconciliation is not easy; it is not cheap. (Accessed at <http://www.truth.org.za> on 1 August 2000)

WHAT HAPPENS NEXT?

There is little doubt that South Africans have made tremendous strides toward peace and reconciliation. Thus, in one of the few comparative studies on conflict resolution, Daniel Lieberfeld argues that most Whites have realized that their worst fears of an ANC victory were unfounded and that they can survive (if not necessarily prosper) under majority rule (Lieberfeld, 1999). The second national election and the transfer of power from the highly charismatic Nelson Mandela to the much more 'normal' leader, Thabo Mbeki, went as smoothly as one could have hoped for.

Nonetheless, several problems remain on the horizon, any or all of which could seriously harm – if not destroy – the South African miracle (O'Flaherty and Freeman, 1999; Friedman, 1999). The most important of these include:

- The wrenching poverty that most Black South Africans endure. The economic policies described above may work in the long term, especially if more direct foreign investment and aid are forthcoming. However, the results so far are not encouraging. Meanwhile, new social problems loom on the horizon, such as an HIV infection rate that may be as high as 25 percent among young people.
- There is still no evidence that the government can dramatically improve the living conditions of its Black constituents without eroding those of the White population.
- Especially if those social and economic problems are not effectively addressed, there is serious danger of what Steven Friedman of Johannesberg's Centre for Policy Studies calls the 're-racialization' of South African politics (1999). In 1999 the various parties' electorates broke down even more clearly along racial lines than they had in 1994. Only the new United Democratic Movement drew considerable support across racial lines, but it won less than 5 percent of the total vote. Instead, there are signs that successful parties may turn out to be those that are capable of what he calls 'racial outbidding,' playing on racial prejudices, hatreds, and fears to maximize their votes.
- There is no viable alternative to ANC rule. Democratization theorists stress the importance of regular and routine alternation between incumbent and opposition parties as evidence of a stable and

successful democracy. That is simply not on the horizon in South Africa. The ANC fell just short of the two-thirds majority it would have needed to amend the constitution on its own in the 1999 elections. However, no other party has given any indication that it will pose a serious threat to the ANC. Inkatha and the UDM have only done well in a single province. The New National Party did poorly in 1999, losing votes to the Democratic Party in large part because the latter played the racial outbidding game extremely effectively among Whites.

THEORETICAL PERSPECTIVES

Since this is the first of five cases we will consider comparatively, it is hard to draw any firm conclusions at this point. Nonetheless, six of the factors discussed in chapters 4 and 5 had a major impact on the way the South African transition has evolved so far. In particular, the first two – shifts in the international balance of power and the emergence of a hurting stalemate – which play a central role in the academic literature, seem less vital here. There probably could not have been a transition to majority rule without them. Nonetheless, they are, as the cliché puts it, necessary but by no means sufficient causes. They 'set the political stage' that made accommodation possible, but it took the other four factors to make the shift away from apartheid possible.

1. The international environment. This came into play in two ways. First, sanctions undoubtedly took a toll on the White population. Although it is hard to reach definitive conclusions about the South African (and most other) sanctions, they almost certainly indirectly led to an erosion of support for hard-line apartheid policies. As Tutu likes to put it, if the sanctions weren't having an impact, why did the South African government lobby so hard for their removal? Second, the end of the Cold War stripped the ANC of a major source of funds for its armed insurrection and the National Party of what it called the communist threat that it used to rationalize much of apartheid.

2. The hurting stalemate. There is little doubt, too, that leaders on both sides of the racial divide understood that the country had reached a hurting stalemate by the late 1980s in two senses of the term. First, each understood it could not win a definitive and decisive victory. Second, they both also realized that the continued conflict was imposing unacceptable costs on their own supporters, something that was magnified by the changing geopolitical and economic conditions that accompanied the end of the Cold War. No one put it better than Mandela.

It was clear to me that a military victory was a distant if not impossible dream. It simply did not make sense for both sides to lose thousands if not millions of lives in a conflict that was unnecessary. It was time to talk. (Waldmeier, 1997:94)

3. Domestic leadership. The compromise reached between the government and the ANC held open the possibility of real benefits for both sides. But that, too, would not have been possible without the amazing leadership in both the ANC and the National Party. Mandela truly was a remarkable leader for shunning the revenge he might well have sought and pushing instead for a multiracial democracy. Perhaps even more surprising is de Klerk, whose family and whose own career until 1989 offered no signs that he was willing to even question apartheid. Nonetheless, he, too, overcame his past and helped forge the agreement that led to the transition of 1994 and the Nobel Peace Prize he shared with Mandela. There were other visible leaders, including Tutu, who helped spearhead opposition to apartheid and Joe Slovo, who, to the surprise of many, pushed his comrades toward reconciliation rather than revenge.

4. The image of the enemy. The same, too, is true of the commitment to getting beyond the image of the enemy and other debilitating values and assumptions. Such stereotypes abounded as in the Afrikaners' use of the term *kaffir* (roughly equivalent to the American nigger) to describe black Africans. This is not just a question of language. Post-apartheid South Africa saw two major efforts. It is here that the TRC and other attempts at reconciliation are most important and, comparatively speaking, rare, though it remains to be seen if they will succeed.

5. Social and economic change. As noted in the preceding section, social and economic difficulties could well be the transition's Achilles heel in the first years of the twenty-first century. Despite that fact, one cannot help but be impressed by the seriousness of the government's plans to integrate social and economic change into its broader strategies for achieving reconciliation and stable peace. At first glance, that might seem an obvious conclusion for the ANC and other leaders to have reached. But, as we will see especially in chapter 9 on Bosnia, domestic leaders as well as the international community have rarely done so, even when the conflicts caused far more physical damage than in South Africa.

6. Third parties. The one thing missing from a 'classic' version of win-win conflict resolution is the extensive use of outside third parties. To be sure, the Commonwealth Eminent Persons Group gave the antiapartheid movement new momentum when it was allowed to meet with Mandela in 1985. Similarly, British business leaders and others helped bring ANC officials and Whites together in the track-two diplomacy of the late 1980s and early 1990s. Nonetheless, the agreement that led to the ANC's election in 1994 was for all practical purposes achieved by South Africans acting on their own. As such, it may be the exception that proves the rule. None of the other cases we will consider (or any of the others not included in this book) had the kind of leadership we saw in South Africa.

SELECT BIBLIOGRAPHY

Bornstein, David. *The Price of a Dream: The Story of the Grameen Bank*. Chicago: University of Chicago Press, 1997.

Crawford Neta, and Audie Klotz, eds. *How Sanctions Work: Lessons from South Africa*. London: St. Martin's, 1999.

Friedman, Steven. 'South Africa: Entering the Post-Mandela Era.' *Journal of Democracy* 10 (October 1999): 4, 3–18.

Gibson, James, and Amanda Gouws. 'Truth and Reconciliation in South Africa: Attribution of Blame and the Struggle over Apartheid.' *American Political Science Review* 99 (September 1999): 501–17.

Goodman, David. *Fault Lines: Journeys into the New South Africa*. Berkeley: University of California Press, 1999.

Klotz, Audie. *Norms in International Relations: The Struggle against Apartheid*. Ithaca N.Y.: Cornell University Press, 1995.

Lieberfeld, Daniel. 'Post-Handshake Politics: Israel/Palestine and South Africa Compared.' *Middle East Policy* 9 (February 1999): 131–40.

Mandela, Nelson. *Long Walk to Freedom*. Boston: Little-Brown, 1994.

Meredith, Martin. *Nelson Mandela: A Biography*. London: Hamish Hamilton, 1997.

Minow, Martha. *Between Vengeance and Forgiveness: Facing History after Genocide and Mass Violence*. Boston: Beacon Press, 1998.

O'Flaherty, J. Daniel, and Constance J. Freeman. 'Stability in South Africa: Will It Hold?' *The Washington Quarterly* 22 (Autumn, 1999): 151–60.

Sparks, Allister. *The Mind of South Africa*. New York: Ballantine, 1990.

––––––––. *Tomorrow is Another Country: The Inside Story of South Africa's Negotiated Revolution*. London: Arrow Books, 1997.

Thompson, Leonard. *A History of South Africa*. Rev. ed. New Haven: Yale University Press, 1995.

––––––––. 'Mbeki's Uphill Challenge.' *Foreign Affairs* 78 (November–December 1999): 83–9.

Tutu, Desmond. *No Future without Forgiveness*. New York: Doubleday, 1999.

Waldmeier, Patti. *Anatomy of a Miracle*. New York: Penguin, 1997.

Yunus, Muhammad. *Banker to the Poor: Micro-Lending and the Battle against World Poverty*. New York: Public Affairs Press, 1999.

7

NORTHERN IRELAND

If you took the word 'no' out of the English language, there'd be a lot of speechless people in there.

– John Hume

On Good Friday 1998, the British and Irish governments made a momentous announcement. A team of international mediators led by former U.S. senator George Mitchell had succeeded in brokering an agreement between themselves and the leading political parties in Northern Ireland (or Ulster as it is called, mostly by Protestants) to end the thirty years of the Troubles between Catholics and Protestants in that disturbed province.

Like the Oslo Accord that marked the first breakthrough between Israelis and Palestinians (see chapter 8), the Good Friday Agreement was a classic example of a partial agreement that marked a major step toward peace but left many issues still to be addressed.

On the one hand, it ushered in 'a level of peace, a promise of prosperity, and a climate of cross-community cooperation [Northern Ireland] has not known for most of [the twentieth] century' (Hoge, 1999:7). The agreement laid out plans to hand control over much of the province's internal affairs to a new parliament and cabinet in which all the major parties – Catholic and Protestant alike – would share power. It would also create 'cross-border' institutions through which the British and Irish governments could help assure the peace. And most important of all, the paramilitaries all but completely stopped the violence that had wreaked havoc both in Northern Ireland and the British 'mainland' since the late 1960s.

On the other hand, the deal was what Fen Osler Hampson calls an 'orphaned' agreement (Hampson, 1997). While it certainly was a major breakthrough, it failed to address many critical issues. It did little, in particular, to promote reconciliation, which was so vital in the South Africa settlement. Even more important for the short run, it postponed the critical question (especially to Protestants) about how the IRA (Irish

Republican Army) and other paramilitaries would hand in their weapons.

The problems surged to the surface almost immediately. The IRA made it clear that it would not start decommissioning its weapons before the new government was formed. In response, the leading Protestant or Unionist Party and its leader, David Trimble, refused to participate in a cabinet with Sinn Fein, which is commonly viewed as the political wing of the IRA, until the paramilitaries started handing in their bombs and guns.

After months of haggling, the British and Irish governments gave the parties in Northern Ireland a 30 June 1999 deadline. It came and went without any progress toward forming the new government, leading the moderate Catholic John Hume to make the statement that begins this chapter.

The British and Irish governments then tried to impose a take-it-or-leave-it plan in which a new government would be formed on 15 July and decommissioning would begin within a matter of days. However, Trimble stuck to his position linking Unionist participation in the cabinet with decommissioning.

Pessimists were convinced that the bombing, shooting, and rioting would soon begin anew. Instead, London and Dublin called Mitchell back in, and in mid-November, the parties agreed to a plan whereby the IRA promised to turn over the first portion of its weapons as soon as the new cabinet was created, which duly happened on 2 December.

The peace process was dealt another serious blow in February 2000. Jean de Chastelain, a retired Canadian general who was part of the team of international mediators, issued a report that confirmed that the IRA had not begun to hand in its weapons. The IRA then issued an announcement that it would not do so on either the British or the Unionists' terms. On 6 February, a splinter republican group that rejected the peace process out of hand exploded the first bomb in nearly two years. The Unionists threatened to quit the new government. Instead, the British government suspended the new institutions on 12 February.

Once the IRA agreed to 'completely and verifiably' put its arms beyond use and the international team inspected the first two arms caches, the British put the provincial institutions back in operation. Nonetheless, the rest of 2000 went anything but smoothly. Both sides were dissatisfied with the decommissioning process, and Catholics were upset at the failure of London to implement recommendations for sweeping change in the police force. In short, Northern Ireland is still far from anything approaching stable peace. Nonetheless, it is hard to deny how far the province has come in the last few years.

To that end, consider these words by Fintan O'Toole, a columnist for the *Irish Times*:

In the resolution of bloody conflicts, the difficult can be achieved quickly but the impossible takes a little longer. ... It is well to remember how recently any kind of deal on the future of Northern Ireland seemed a pipe dream.

   The very frustration of the recent inconclusive talks at Stormont is a mark of the astonishing success of the peace process. We are frustrated not because there is no solution to the Northern Ireland problem, but because a settlement that once seemed like a madly optimistic fantasy is now so tantalizingly close to becoming reality. (O'Toole, 1999:B4)

THEORETICAL FOCUS

In short, along with the Palestinians and the Israelis, Northern Ireland offers us an intermediate case. It inspires less confidence than the remarkable transition in South Africa. However, the parties have made enough progress that it is hard to see them returning to the bloodshed of earlier years, something we will not be able to claim for the former Yugoslavia or Iraq.

   In the pages that follow, we will be concentrating on nine theoretical issues.

- The conflict itself is more complicated than the one in South Africa. It is much more than a conflict over religion, but one with strong cultural and economic roots as well. What's more, unlike South Africa, it has more important and wider international implications for politics in Great Britain and the Republic of Ireland as well as Northern Ireland itself.
- We will not, however, see that changes in the international system surrounding the end of the Cold War had much of an impact in Northern Ireland.
- Most observers still view the conflict in Northern Ireland more in zero-sum terms than they do in South Africa. That is especially true given the asymmetrical nature of the power relations between Protestants and Catholics over the years.
- This is the first case in which we will clearly see the indispensable role a third party can play as a mediator facilitating a peace process.
- As was also the case in the Middle East, the Good Friday Agreement and the November 1999 creation of the new government in Ulster only produced incremental change. Still, this sort of less-than-total agreement can have a lasting impact, as O'Toole's comment suggests.

- That said, we will see that there is a marked absence of steps taken to promote reconciliation.
- The negotiations and institutions created by the Good Friday Agreement may offer a model that can be used in settling other disputes that cross national borders. This entails what Jonathan Stevenson (1998) calls the partial 'dilution' of sovereignty with the growing power of the European Union, which made the creation of the cross-border institutions in 1998 and 1999 easier than it would have been earlier.

THE TROUBLES

English political domination of Ireland began when the pope granted King Henry II legal control of the island. English influence ebbed and flowed over the next several centuries. For most of the time, it only dominated the so-called English Pale along the coast near Dublin. Despite the English influence and Henry VIII's imposition of Anglicanism during the Reformation, Ireland remained overwhelmingly Catholic.

A rebellion broke out in the early 1640s, but it was resolved when most of its leaders agreed to support the Royalists during England's civil war. They were defeated by Cromwell's forces in 1651, who then gave more than two-thirds of the island to the Protestants, pushing the Catholics to the south and west (O'Leary and McGarry, 1996).

Table 7.1 The evolution of the conflict in Northern Ireland

1690	Battle of the Boyne
1801	Act of Union
1840s	Potato famine
1916	Easter Rising
1921	Partition
1969	Start of the Troubles
1972	Bloody Sunday
	Imposition of direct rule
	Massive deployment of British army

The fighting continued after the monarchy was restored. On 12 July 1690, Protestant troops under King William III crushed Catholic resistance at the Battle of the Boyne, It was at that time that Protestants came to be known as Orangemen because of their support of William, who had come to England from the Dutch state of Orange. It was another year before the English took Limerick and, with it, control over the entire island. At that point, the king negotiated reasonably generous terms, which would have granted the Catholics a degree of religious freedom, and returned most of their land to them. However, the Parliament rejected the plan and imposed a regime that for all intents and purposes banned Catholicism and the Irish language.

Most Catholics worked the land as virtual slaves of English-based landlords. The small urban economy was dominated by Protestant immigrants from Scotland and England. The Scottish Presbyterians, however, were not allowed to vote, and most of them ended up supporting the American and French revolutions. To quell the budding rebellion, British prime minister William Pitt had the Act of Union passed in 1801, which joined the two islands politically. He also had planned to emancipate all Catholics, but that initiative was blocked by King George III.

The nineteenth century made a bad situation worse for most Catholics. Economic conditions deteriorated, especially during the potato famine of the 1840s, which killed hundreds of thousands and forced an even larger number to emigrate. Political uprisings broke out early in the century and, again, toward its end as more and more people demanded either Home Rule or outright independence.

In the late 1890s, the journalist Arthur Griffith founded Sinn Fein to support independence. It, and other groups, fomented the Easter Rising of 1916, which took Dublin but was soon brutally crushed by the British. In 1919, the revolutionaries regrouped, formed a parliament, declared Irish independence, and formed a guerrilla army, which later became known as the IRA.

In 1921 the British agreed to partition Ireland. The twenty-six counties in the south became the Irish Free State, with dominion status equivalent to that of Canada. (It became a fully independent country in 1949.) The six counties in the north (Ulster) remained part of the United Kingdom. Partition also split Sinn Fein. A small faction demanding a united Ireland continued to fight. Though the IRA was defeated before the 1920s were out, support for unification never disappeared either in the south or in Ulster.

Britain gave Ulster its own provincial government based at Stormont. Like everything else in the province, it was dominated by the Protestant Unionists.

From Civil Rights to Civil War

Protestants have been fiercely attached to the union with Britain, because they see it as the only way to protect their religion and culture. I could provide all sorts of statistical data on that score, but just as revealing is the chorus from one of the Loyalists' most popular songs, sung to the tune of 'Home on the Range.'

No, no Pope of Rome,
No chapels to sadden my eyes.
No nuns and no priests and no rosary beads,
And every day is the Twelfth of July. (McKittrick, 1996: 39)

The Players

Because this case is complicated, it is useful to lay out who the main players have been.

- Most Unionists are Protestants who want to remain a part of Great Britain. The main Unionist parties operate through the constitutional system.
- Loyalists claim they are loyal to Great Britain, but through their paramilitaries, they have been as willing as the IRA to attack the British.
- Most nationalists are Catholics who favor the unification of Ireland but only through constitutional means.
- Republicans have been willing to resort to violence in the pursuit of unification.
- The British government has, until recently, viewed Northern Ireland through a largely Unionist lens. In the 1980s, however, it acknowledged that the Republic of Ireland had to be involved and began to act in a more evenhanded way toward both Catholics and Protestants in Ulster.
- Until 1999 Articles 2 and 3 of the Irish constitution called for unification. And, the two main parties have their roots in the civil war of the 1920s that was fought in large part over the fate of the north. In most of the period covered here, however, Irish priorities lay elsewhere and the Republic did not have much of an impact on the north until quite late in the peace process. If anything, southerners of almost all political stripes found the Troubles in general and the IRA in particular objectionable.

Protestant domination of all aspects of life in Ulster approached that of Whites in the segregated American South. To be sure, there were no Jim Crow laws that denied the Catholics basic human rights. Nonetheless, the Protestants succeeded in gerrymandering districts for local councils, the provincial assembly at Stormont, and its seats in the House of Commons in London, which reduced Catholic representation to a minimum. To cite but the most glaring example, the overwhelmingly Catholic city of Derry (Londonderry to the Protestants) was always run by a Protestant-Unionist administration. Protestants ran the economy, preventing Catholics from getting good jobs to the point that unemployment among Catholics frequently topped 40 percent. Perhaps most galling of all to the Catholics, Protestants dominated the police force (the most recent version being the RUC, or Royal Ulster Constabulary), which was often accused of treating Catholics brutally and arbitrarily.

The IRA reconstituted itself in the 1950s and carried out a series of attacks. However, by the 1960s it had lost most of its support and had degenerated into little more than a sect that spent most of its time trying to blend Marxism with Irish nationalism.

Then, inspired in part by protests sweeping the rest of the Western world, a Catholic civil rights movement emerged in the late 1960s. Unlike the case in most other countries, it quickly turned violent, though much of the early fighting was instigated by Protestants. For instance, several hundred Catholic families had their homes in mixed neighborhoods burned; the same thing happened to a far smaller number of Protestants. Not surprisingly, the IRA reconstituted itself again.

The situation worsened in 1971 when the British introduced a policy of internment. Suspected terrorists could be arrested and held without trial and without the usual judicial provisions regarding the rights of the accused. Hundreds of IRA activists were interned or imprisoned without trial; no Protestants were.

The violence culminated with Blood Sunday on 30 January 1972, when British paratroops opened fire on a demonstration, killing at least fourteen people. By that point, young militants led by the likes of Gerry Adams and Martin McGuinness took over from the older generation and created the new, Provisional IRA.

The British government had already sent troops to Northern Ireland in 1969 at Stormont's (that is the Unionists') request. The authorities in London hoped to bolster the moderate Unionists in what they expected would be a brief stay. They were initially welcomed by many Catholics, who hoped that their presence would reduce Protestant violence and aid in their struggle for civil rights.

In practice, the British biases toward the Unionists and the status quo made them anything but an ideal third party or peacekeeper. For example, the British troops largely turned a blind eye as Protestant mobs forced more Catholics to flee their homes.

After Bloody Sunday, the British presence and power both grew dramatically. The government of Prime Minister Edward Heath dissolved Stormont and imposed direct rule by London. British authority was buttressed by the deployment of thousands of British troops, making Northern Ireland the only example covered in this book in which a government had to send peacekeeping forces to control its own citizens. The army has remained in Northern Ireland ever since. Almost 1,000 soldiers have died, 100 of them in 1972 alone.

The army's role has always been controversial. In the early years, it was widely – and probably accurately – perceived as supporting the Protestants. Even as it became more impartial, the best that could be said was that it was partially effective at keeping the peace, since there were neighborhoods in which the soldiers had next to no impact.

To their credit, the British soldiers and their political leaders did at least try to stop the fighting. They were not, however, terribly effective in doing so. Indeed, one of their most lasting achievements is also one of the most powerful metaphors for the level of hatred and violence in the province. They built a thirty-mile long Peace Line to separate Catholic and Protestant areas in the Belfast metropolitan area that reminded everyone of the infamous Berlin Wall.

Northern Ireland became a very violent place indeed. More than 3,300 people were killed in wave after wave of shootings and bombings that stretched beyond Ulster to the Irish Republic, the British 'mainland,' and as far as Gibraltar. Bombings in English train stations were so frequent that the government removed all trash receptacles. A bomb planted at the Grand Hotel in Brighton during the Conservative Party conference in 1984 nearly killed Prime Minister Margaret Thatcher and most of her cabinet colleagues. Sometimes, British soldiers and Irish paramilitary members were targeted. At other times, the victims were civilians who were in the wrong place at the wrong time when a bomb went off.

The conventional wisdom is that the IRA was largely responsible for the violence. It did carry out the most spectacular attacks, especially in England. In later years, however, Loyalist paramilitaries were responsible for as many deaths. Indeed, they killed more people than the IRA from the mid-1980s onward.

By 1995 there were more than 120,000 legally held firearms, or more than one for every ten adults. No one knows how many more illegal weapons there were.

When the Berlin Wall fell in 1989, there was little sense that the Peace Line would follow in its wake. Indeed, the area was as divided and as violent as ever. Typical of sentiment at the time was this statement by an IRA member given in an interview with David McKittrick, who is by most accounts the best journalist writing about politics in Ulster.

> We can state absolutely, on the record, that there will be no ceasefire, no truce, no 'cessation of violence,' short of a British withdrawal. That, as blunt as that, is our position. (McKittrick, 1996:5)

TOWARD GOOD FRIDAY

As is almost always the case with international conflict resolution, it is hard to define the exact date when the peace process began. In Northern Ireland, the first steps to end the fighting were taken shortly after the start of the troubles. From the beginning, they included what would prove to be the components of the Good Friday Agreement reached nearly thirty years later – relations between Catholics and Protestants, the internal workings of the two communities, cooperation of the British and Irish governments and, occasionally, outsiders (Tonge, 1997).

Between 1969 and the mid-1990s, none of those steps seemed to get anywhere. In retrospect, some of them did have an impact. Little of the anger subsided, and none of the parties backed away from their long-term goals. Nonetheless, more and more of the participants in the Troubles saw both the need for and the possibility of taking steps that would make the province more peaceful.

Under Conservative and Labour governments alike, the British supported direct rule and a hard line toward the IRA. They were anything but neutral, because everything from the Royal Ulster Constabulary to the leading private businesses were in Protestant hands. Thus, the British tended to deepen the Catholics' sense of injustice and the divide between themselves and the Catholics.

To its credit, the Conservative government of Prime Minister Edward Heath did try to find a solution to the Troubles. However, for most of the last quarter century, the British focused on what David Bloomfield (1997, 1998) calls a 'structural' outcome negotiated by governments and party leaders and did not address the 'cultural' divisions between the two communities 'on the ground.' In 1973 the Secretary of State for Northern Ireland, William Whitelaw, brokered the Sunningdale Agreement, which created a new government in which 'constitutional parties' (that is not terrorist organizations) would share power. It also created a Council of

Table 7.2 The Irish peace process

1974	Sunningdale Agreement collapses
1985	Anglo-Irish Agreement
1993	Downing Street Declaration
1994	IRA cease-fire
1995	Initial appointment of George Mitchell and other mediators
1996	Canary Wharf bombing
1997	Elections in Britain and the Republic of Ireland
1998	Good Friday Agreement
1999	Northern Ireland government takes office

Ireland in which representatives of the new assembly would meet regularly with their counterparts in the southern Dail. Grassroots unionists rejected the cross-border arrangements and launched a series of crippling strikes that destroyed the new institutions within a matter of weeks.

Useful Web Sites

The BBC (British Broadcasting Corporation) has a vast site that includes text of its stories and now 'streams' many of its television and radio broadcasts. <http://news.bbc.co.uk>.

The *Independent* has the best coverage of Northern Ireland in the mainstream British press. <http://www.independent.co.uk>.

The Northern Ireland Office of the British government has most official documents, including the Good Friday Agreement. <http://www.nio.gov.uk>.

CAIN (Conflict Archive on the Net) is a project on 'the Troubles' based at the University of Ulster. <http://cain.ulst.ac.uk/index.html>.

INCORE (Initiative on Conflict Resolution and Ethnicity), also based at the University of Ulster, is one of the world's best sources of information on ethnic conflict in general and Northern Ireland in particular. <http://www.incore.ulst.ac.uk>.

The main Northern Ireland political groups include Sinn Fein <http://sinnfein.ie/index.html> and the Ulster Unionist Party <http://www.uup.org>.

Corrymeela has an extensive site on its activities and philosophy. <http://www.corrymeela.org.uk>.

Little progress was made in the next decade. Some observers do stress Pope John Paul's criticism of violence during his 1979 visit as an important first step toward convincing the IRA and Sinn Fein to seek peace. However, the first truly critical events occurred in the 1980s.

The Irish Taoiseach (prime minister), Garrett Fitzgerald, again proposed a Council of Ireland in another effort to unravel the North-South strand of the problem. Publicly, that initiative collapsed before it got off the ground when Prime Minister Margaret Thatcher rejected it out of hand shortly before an IRA bomb almost killed her and many of her cabinet colleagues. Behind the scenes, however, the British and Irish governments inched toward the 1985 Anglo-Irish Agreement. The agreement made the Dublin government a permanent participant in the peace process in exchange for its de facto acceptance that Ulster would remain in the United Kingdom as long as a majority of its population wished to do so. The Unionists reacted against it far more vehemently than Thatcher had expected. Nonetheless, it marked the beginning of what has been reasonably successful cooperation between London and Dublin ever since.

Between 1987 and 1991, London initiated a set of prenegotiations with the various constitutional parties that became known as the talks about talks. They accomplished little largely because the parties representing the paramilitaries were excluded. Meanwhile, John Hume of the 'constitutional' Social Democratic and Labour Party (SDLP) began a series of unsuccessful (at the time) negotiations with Gerry Adams following Sinn Fein's decision to end its policy of abstention from elections in the republic. Many observers took that move as a first sign that the IRA was prepared to accept some sort of 'two Ireland' solution.

In the end, it took new leadership in Dublin, London, and Washington to spur the negotiations toward a successful conclusion. In 1990 Thatcher's Conservative colleagues forced her into retirement and replaced her with John Major. Though he was Thatcher's protégé, Major was more flexible and a better negotiator than the 'iron lady.' Two years later, Albert Reynolds became Taoiseach. He moved his formerly prounification Fianna Fail Party toward acceptance of a permanent partition of the island. He also began a series of meetings with the SDLP and Sinn Fein leaders, who were also meeting secretly with British civil servants.

Those discussions produced the Downing Street Declaration of 15 December 1993. It reiterated the two governments' commitment to a British Ulster as long as a majority of its people wished to stay in the United Kingdom. Moreover, it anticipated that political parties that represented the Catholic and Protestant paramilitaries could join negotiations toward a permanent settlement if they rejected violence and started decommissioning their weapons. Significantly, the British cabinet declared that it had 'no selfish strategic or economic interest in Northern Ireland,' while the Irish government stated that 'it would be wrong to impose a united Ireland, in the absence of the freely given consent of a majority of the people of Northern Ireland.'

Although it is hard to document with any precision, most average citizens had begun to tire of the violence. It wasn't just the fear of death. Everyday life was filled with difficulties. Simple trips to the store were delayed by searches by security officers looking for weapons. The ever-present armed patrols and the euphemistically named Peace Line were among the many, constant reminders of just how troubling the Troubles were.

While the details still are not clear, it seems that a growing number of the 'hard men' in the paramilitaries were also moving toward the conclusion that they had to put down the gun. We may never know exactly why that happened. To some degree, it reflected a genuine rejection of violence by men and women who had spent years in the Maze and other prisons and seen dozens of their friends and relatives killed. To some degree, too, it was the result of pragmatic decisions by politicians who realized that it was highly unlikely to get what they wanted through violence. The IRA in particular came to see that it could turn to the ballot box and the negotiating table because Sinn Fein was building a strong base of support in the Catholic community.

Whatever the mix of causes, in 1993 and early 1994, leaders from both communities began issuing more hopeful statements, such as the following one by David Ervine, who had been a member of the Ulster Volunteer Force and a prisoner in the Maze:

> The politics of division has seen thousands of people dead, most of them working class, and headstones on the graves of young men. We have been fools: let's not be fools any longer. All elements must be comfortable within Northern Ireland. We have got to extend the hand of friendship, we have to take the peacelines down brick by brick, and somehow or other we have got to introduce class politics. You can't eat a flag. (McKittrick, 1996:39–40)

Similarly, instead of referring to the Unionists as little more than pawns of British colonial rule, Adams and his colleagues started talking about the need for both communities to coexist in dignity. As that happened, the political wing of the IRA moved ever closer to the leadership in the South and to Hume and the SDLP, the one northern politician and party that have worked steadfastly for a peaceful resolution to the conflict from the onset of the Troubles.

At about this time, the IRA and Sinn Fein apparently decided that talking was not tantamount to defeat. Its supporters in the United States as well as the new Clinton administration had convinced it that considerable economic development funds would stream into Ulster if peace were to break out.

Then, the most dramatic and, to some, the most unexpected event in this long saga occurred. On 30 August 1994 the IRA announced 'a complete cessation of all military activity.' The main Protestant paramilitaries followed suit within a week. While people outside Ulster saw the IRA decision as the key, in some ways the Protestant one was at least as important, because their paramilitaries had been far less disciplined and had been responsible for more killings in the 1980s and 1990s.

For the first time, there was real hope that the Troubles could end. In the short term, the British were able to scale back their activities in Ulster, and life there returned to something approaching normal.

Still, there were three major obstacles to overcome, which made the situation in Ireland quite different from that in South Africa.

- The IRA and other Republicans were still unwilling to give up their weapons until major political steps had been taken, because they remained convinced that the authorities were still biased toward the Protestants and that they would leave themselves defenseless by disarming.
- The Unionists left themselves with very little room for maneuver in the negotiations. Even the moderate Unionists feared that any significant change on any of the strands of the talks would erode the union and thus endanger their position on the social, economic, political, and security fronts.
- Progress toward peace was hampered by politics in the United Kingdom and, to a lesser degree, in Ireland. In London, John Major's majority all but disappeared, and he needed the support of the nine Unionist MPs to stay in office and get any major legislation passed. Moreover, by mid-1995 almost all attention was focused on the upcoming 1997 parliamentary elections. Consequently, Prime Minister Major was unable to take any major risks as far as Northern Ireland was concerned. Meanwhile, the Republic of Ireland careened through a number of scandals that had nothing to do with policy toward Ulster, but which did lead to three different Taoiseachs in the same three-year period.

In the meantime, Sinn Fein gained considerable credibility. Adams,

McGuinness, and its other leaders were frequent visitors to London and Dublin and seemed always to be on radio and television. Sinn Fein now regularly won about a third of the Catholic vote (or over 10 percent of the total), and its leadership insisted that it had become a conventional political party that had no formal ties to the IRA.

Still, Sinn Fein did not get what it wanted – entry into the negotiations. The Unionists refused to participate in talks with Sinn Fein as long as the IRA refused to decommission its weapons. Adams's and McGuinness's frustrations mounted.

On 22 February 1995 the British and Irish governments threw a political monkey wrench in the works when they issued a new document, *Frameworks for the Future*, which was designed to be the basis for all-party talks. It anticipates much of the Good Friday Agreement, including the creation of North-South bodies and a new parliament in which all parties in Northern Ireland would share power. The Framework Document was seen as a step forward by many Catholics. However, it confirmed the worst fears of many Unionists and Loyalists that Britain was prepared to sell them out and had already started Ulster on the slippery slope toward unification with the South.

In early 1995 the British finally decided to ask for outside help. Until then, the British government had viewed Northern Ireland as a domestic political issue and rejected any outside intervention as a violation of its sovereignty.

That year, Major's government reversed that long-standing position in large part because the United States was willing to weigh into the negotiations. In January, George Mitchell, who had recently retired from the U.S. Senate, agreed to serve as a special adviser in the State Department on Irish issues for a brief period, primarily to organize the White House Conference on Trade and Investment in Northern Ireland. After it was held, Mitchell agreed to stay on until the end of the year to do some follow-up work and help out on President Clinton's planned trip to Belfast. During Clinton's visit on 30 November 1995, the British and Irish governments agreed to appoint an international team to head negotiations, including George Mitchell, former Finnish prime minister Harri Holkeri, and retired Canadian general Jean de Chastelain. Mitchell agreed to London and Dublin's offer to chair the negotiations. Because he coordinated the political talks and has written on the process, I will focus on Mitchell here.

George Mitchell

George Mitchell provides us with the best example in this book of a 'third party' mediator.

Mitchell was born in 1932 in Waterville, Maine. He was the adopted son of a Lebanese-American family, and that is the cultural and religious tradition that most shaped him as a young man. Mitchell graduated from Bowdoin College and Boston University law school and, after a number of political false starts, was appointed to the Senate when Edmund Muskie joined the Carter administration. Mitchell quickly developed a reputation as one of the most effective coalition builders in the Senate, which propelled him to the post of majority leader. Mitchell prides himself for his skills as a listener and for his ability to 'leave his ego at the door.' And by the time he left the Senate, he was no longer particularly ambitious, having turned down an appointment to the Supreme Court and the job of commissioner of baseball.

In the end, it is probably that set of skills of listening to all sides, respecting all participants, and building bridges between them that makes a Mitchell, a Jimmy Carter, or a Terje Larsen (see chapter 8) so effective in facilitating this kind of tense and difficult negotiation.

Their initial brief only dealt with decommissioning, which was then holding up the negotiations. In early 1995 the British secretary of state for Northern Ireland, Sir Patrick Mayhew, had made decommissioning a precondition for entry into the talks, a position Sinn Fein rejected.

Mitchell and his colleagues understood that decommissioning before the start of all-party negotiations was a nonstarter. Gradually, the mediators convinced themselves and then the British government that the parties should be allowed to participate in the talks if they

- openly accepted nonviolence and democracy;
- made a commitment to hand over weapons as part of any agreement.

The Mitchell team presented that report on 23 January 1996 and assumed their work was over. The next day the British government threw the process off track by seizing on a minor portion of the report and calling for elections in Northern Ireland that would yield a new governing body for the province. This proved to be the last straw for the IRA and Sinn Fein. On 9 February a huge explosion ripped through the new, upscale Canary Wharf neighborhood, where many of the newspapers and financial corporations are located. The IRA cease-fire was over. There was no return to the widespread violence of earlier decades. Still, a number of bombs went off in England and Ulster, while more numerous bomb threats periodically disrupted road and rail traffic.

The British went ahead with elections to a new assembly. Parties that accepted the Mitchell principles and won seats would then be eligible to take part in talks to begin on 10 June. Although the elections threw the negotiations off even further, they did provide the Unionists with one of their key demands, and it gave Sinn Fein more credibility when it came in a strong fourth with almost 16 percent of the vote.

Mitchell and his colleagues returned for what he expected to be a few more months of talks. They, in fact, took almost two years. The negotiations started poorly. Sinn Fein was not present, because the IRA had not yet reinstituted its cease-fire. Ian Paisley's Democratic Unionists and another small loyalist party rejected Mitchell as chair and walked out.

The two governments and the seven Northern Irish parties that were left did agree to the Mitchell principles committing themselves to democracy and nonviolence. Despite that one step forward, the prospects for peace did not look bright.

The following Monday, the IRA set off a bomb that destroyed a new shopping mall in downtown Manchester, England. Rioting broke out when the RUC banned the Protestant Orange Order from taking its annual march through a Catholic neighborhood in Drumcree. The head of the RUC then drew the wrath of the Catholics as well when he changed his mind and let the march go ahead.

Mitchell and his colleagues persevered. By early fall, they had reached agreement on sufficient consensus. A proposal would be considered adopted if it gained the support of a majority of the representatives of each community. That meant, in particular, that Paisley and his supporters could not block an agreement on their own.

The election of Tony Blair and his Labour Party gave the peace process some needed new momentum. The Conservatives, who had been in power for eighteen years, had made their share of contributions toward peace in Northern Ireland. However, they were also seen as too pro-Unionist and risk averse. Labour brought more energy and a more positive attitude to the talks. Like Blair, the new secretary of state for Northern Ireland, Mo Mowlam, was young and enthusiastic, unlike the most recent Conservative ministers. Also, with its massive majority, Labour had the freedom to maneuver in Northern Ireland that John Major never had and Margaret Thatcher never wanted. Shortly after taking office, Blair began talking of a May 1998 deadline for the talks, since the elected forum, which did little other than provide the personnel for the talks, would go out of existence at that time.

Meanwhile, the Irish Republic also held an election. While the victory by Bertie Ahern at the head of a coalition led by his Fianna Fail party did not mark as major a change as the one across the Irish Sea, the new Taoiseach was more willing to try new approaches to the negotiations than his predecessor, John Bruton, had been.

Then, on 20 July, the IRA declared another cease-fire. This second end to the hostilities marked a truly dramatic transformation for the likes of Adams and McGuinness, who had begun their careers as IRA soldiers, spent time in jail, and been treated as ruthless terrorists by their opponents. And it brought Sinn Fein into the negotiations for the first time.

Not everyone approved of the cease-fire and Sinn Fein's participation in the talks. Paisley's Democratic Unionist Party and the tiny United Kingdom Unionist Party quit the negotiations.

The violence did not end. Some Republican splinter groups continued the 'armed campaign,' and a bomb in Markethill almost derailed the talks. The murder of the Loyalist Billy Wright (better known as 'King Rat') inside the infamous Maze prison touched off a series of sectarian killings.

At this juncture, the mainstream Unionists in general and their leader, David Trimble, in particular, became the focus of attention. Throughout his career, Trimble had been a loyal and intransigent member of the Orange Order. Like most politically active Protestants, he doubted everything Sinn Fein said and did. Moreover, he agreed with the Unionists, who understandably felt they had the most to lose in any agreement, since whatever happened, they were not likely to retain their all-but-total control of the province.

At this juncture, too, the final push toward an agreement began, during which Mitchell's skills as a negotiator came to the fore. He gradually got the participants to stop – in his words – demonizing each other, because you cannot make peace while thinking the worst about your opponent. Despite his rather deadpan manner, Mitchell can effectively play on people's emotions. For instance, his wife gave birth to a son at a particularly tense point in the negotiations. Mitchell had his staff find out how many children were born in Northern Ireland that day and asked the participants why those babies shouldn't have the same opportunity to live in peace that his son Andrew would.

Gradually, the momentum began to shift toward an agreement. Political prisoners play an important role in Northern Ireland. Many of them began to support an agreement, especially following an unprecedented visit by Mowlam to the Loyalists in the Maze prison.

Ironically, the growing violence deepened the pressure for an agreement. Sinn Fein and one of the small Loyalist parties were suspended from the talks when their paramilitaries were shown to have participated in the ongoing violence. Both left, but made it abundantly clear that they were committed to returning as soon as the details could be worked out for doing so.

Finally, Mitchell set Thursday, 9 April, as the deadline for an agreement. That date was chosen so that there would be enough time to hold elections to the new assembly before the always-contentious marching season began in July. Privately, Mitchell warned the participants that 'they could not fail, because the alternative was unthinkable' (Mitchell, 1999:127). Publicly, the three independent commissioners issued a statement:

> The participants know what needs to be done. It's now up to them to do it.
>
> We are totally committed to this effort. We are not considering any alternative plan in the event of failure because we believe that failure is unacceptable. These next few weeks will be decisive. Those who are determined to wreck the process cannot be allowed to prevail. The success of these negotiations will require steady nerves and courageous leadership by the men and women in whose hands rests the future of Northern Ireland. (Mitchell, 1999:145)

The two weeks before the deadline were hectic. Draft agreements flew from fax machine to fax machine, meeting to meeting. Blair and Ahern spent the last days in the nonstop discussions that almost always occur in the hours before a deadline. This was particularly difficult in Ahern's case, since his mother had just died and he had to fly to Dublin for her funeral at a particularly tense moment in the talks.

The negotiations continued past the deadline into Good Friday itself. Finally, that afternoon, Trimble phoned Mitchell to say that the Unionists had accepted the agreement. Fifteen minutes later, Blair and Ahern announced it to the waiting world. It included the following provisions:

- an elected assembly and cabinet in which all parties that received at least 20 percent of the vote and accepted the Mitchell principles would participate
- decommissioning of weapons by May 2000
- new cross-border consultative bodies that would bring Northern Ireland and Republic of Ireland leaders together on questions of joint interest
- reinforcement of the British policy that Ulster would stay in the United Kingdom unless a majority of its people voted otherwise

- removal of clauses in the Republic of Ireland's constitution that call for the unification of the country

As most observers expected, the Good Friday Agreement was not implemented quickly or easily (Lloyd, 1998). In particular, the Unionists refused to take their seats in a government that included Sinn Fein until the IRA agreed to at least begin decommissioning its weapons. Sinn Fein countered that the agreement did not require them to hand over any weapons as a precondition for forming a government.

Decommissioning, thus, held up progress for the rest of 1998 and most of 1999. As noted at the beginning of the chapter, it was the primary cause of the July 1999 breakdown in the negotiations that led to Mitchell's return the following September.

Just before he returned to the province in 1999, Senator Mitchell ended an interview on the Public Broadcasting System's *NewsHour* by stating that people in Northern Ireland now agreed on two, contradictory, things:

- Almost all of them want peace and cannot face the possibility of a return to the Troubles.
- All groups want to see the peace made on their own terms.

Eleven more weeks of tough talks followed. On 12 November it seemed as if the negotiations were about to collapse once and for all when the Unionists refused to accept a new plan put forth by Mitchell. The senator recessed the talks for the weekend. As he had done in the days and hours before Good Friday, he asked the parties to give serious thought to what would happen should they fail to reach an agreement.

Over the weekend, the IRA reached an agreement with de Chastelain, who still headed the decommissioning negotiations. It would begin the process of turning in weapons the day a government was formed and committed itself to meeting the May 2000 deadline for complete disarmament. On 16 November the Unionists agreed to the new deal.

It took another two weeks for all the details to be worked out. Nonetheless, on 2 December 1999, the British and Irish parliaments enacted the legislation that put the Good Friday Agreement into effect. On 3 December the new cabinet met for the first time, though the two members from Paisley's Democratic Unionist Party refused to attend. On 4 December an as yet unnamed official of the IRA began meeting with de Chastelain's commission, and all sides reported that substantial progress had been made at that first encounter.

To see how far Northern Irish politicians had come, contrast the statements from three of the leading participants in the 1999 talks with the remark from the anonymous IRA member quoted near the beginning of the chapter (unless otherwise noted, all are from Hoge, 1999b).

Gerry Adams:

> [Violence] is now a thing of the past, over, done with and gone.
> [Sinn Fein] wishes to work with, not against, the Unionists.

David Trimble:

> It is our belief that the establishment of new political institutions and the disarmament of all paramilitary organizations will herald a new beginning for all sections of our people – a new peaceful, democratic society where political objectives are pursued solely through democratic means, free from the use or threat of force. (<http://cnn.com>, accessed 16 November 1999)
>
> For too long, much of the unrest in our community has been caused by a failure to accept the differing expressions of cultural identity. [We need] mutual respect and tolerance rather than division and alienation.

Monica McWilliams of the small Women's Coalition, which played an active role both before and after Good Friday:

> These are the kinds of statements we thought were never possible in Northern Ireland.

WHAT STILL HAS TO BE DONE: RECONCILIATION AND SOCIAL CHANGE

In short, the 1998 and 1999 agreements are like many recent pacts. They marked a major step forward, made violence less likely, and opened the door to further negotiations. However, there are still dozens of issues that divide Catholics and Protestants in Northern Ireland and that therefore make peace anything but a certainty.

To achieve reconciliation and stable peace, its politicians and citizens will have to address what Bloomfield calls the 'cultural' side of conflict resolution. Reconciliation may be a term used frequently by participants in most conflict-ridden societies these days. It is, however, rarely uttered – even as empty rhetoric – by political leaders in Northern Ireland. And that is the main reason why most observers are less optimistic about the prospects for lasting peace in Northern Ireland than in South Africa.

Before the talks leading to the Good Friday Agreement, the Unionist and Sinn Fein leaders had never met. They have sat together in occasional official meetings since then, but as far as I know, Gerry Adams and David Trimble never exchanged a civil word before the eve of the

1999 agreement. As George Mitchell put it when he returned to the negotiations in July 1999, 'each side works on the assumption that the other side won't keep its promises' (PBS *NewsHour*, 29 July 1999).

It's not just the leaders. Just as important is the weakness of grassroots movements aimed at reconciliation. There have been some reconciliation projects whose efforts are documented in research by David Bloomfield (1997) and Mervyn Love (1995). However, they pale in comparison with those in South Africa and are now more extensive than similar initiatives involving Israelis and Palestinians.

The two communities in Northern Ireland remain amazingly isolated from each other. Housing is more segregated than it was before the Troubles began, because thousands of people were forced to move into now-homogeneous neighborhoods in the 1960s and 1970s. Protestants and Catholics do work with each other more, and more often as peers. More and more of them attend universities together. However, the all-important elementary and secondary education, social organizations, and, of course, the churches are still all but exclusively Catholic or Protestant.

And when they do come together, mistrust often gets in the way of making progress. Thus, Queen's University in Belfast now has almost as many Catholic as Protestant students. Catholics objected to the playing of 'God Save the Queen' at graduation ceremonies. Since the national anthem is rarely played at British graduation exercises, university officials agreed and proposed Beethoven's 'Ode to Joy' as an alternative. Protestants objected, saying that 'God Save the Queen' is a symbol of Northern Ireland's status as an integral part of the United Kingdom. Debates over anthems themselves do not spark violence, but such disputes are a sign of the still-deep mistrust and, therefore, of how far away they are from stable peace.

There are some grassroots efforts toward reconciliation that deserve at least a brief mention. Two political parties – Alliance and the Women's Coalition – explicitly try to reach voters from both communities. Together, they have never won even 10 percent of the vote, although the Alliance's Lord John Alderdyce is the speaker of the new assembly.

All in all, Mervyn Love (1995:72) identified thirty-one such groups, a number that has undoubtedly grown a bit since he wrote. They fell into five main categories of five to seven groups each, trying to work through:

- the schools
- the churches
- youth and sports organizations
- cross-community initiatives in a specific neighborhood or profession
- research projects

The best-known and largest of them is the Corrymeela community, which was established in 1966 to bring Catholics and Protestants together for spiritual rather than political purposes. Once the Troubles began, Corrymeela members decided that the community had to use its contacts to help stop the fighting.

Corrymeela itself is not very big. Not even 200 people formally belong to it, and its full-time staff has fewer than twenty officers. It has a house and office in Belfast and a retreat center in rural Ballycastle, which can accommodate 120 people. However, it has a broader reach and impact than its numbers might suggest. In the 1970s it started by hosting rather formal conferences that brought academics, members of the clergy, and others from the two sides together. Since the early 1980s, it has broadened its efforts to bring people from all walks of life to Belfast and Ballycastle. Ballycastle typically hosts 9,000 people a year for weeklong seminars for families, single parents, victims of violence, families of prisoners, and the like. Corrymeela also has programs in most cities that try to bring young Catholics and Protestants together.

There is no doubt that Corrymeela and the other groups have done important work. However, in a survey of its members carried out in 1989–90, only 3.2 percent felt it had a 'large impact' on the situation in Northern Ireland (Love, 1995:147).

Prospects for reconciliation will also be limited if little or nothing is done to close the economic gap between Catholics and Protestants. To be fair, the British government understood the importance of this at least as early as 1990. John Major's Conservative government, for instance, introduced a Policy Appraisal and Fair Treatment procedure to try to ensure that its actions were no longer biased toward the Protestants and a Targeting Social Needs policy meant to send a disproportionate share of state resources to poor communities, most of which are predominantly Catholic.

Left-wing economists (who are the only scholars to have seriously studied this issue) are highly critical of these and other social and economic policies (O'Hearn, Porter, and Harpur, 1999). There has, in fact, been relatively little government investment in Northern Ireland, and the amount has actually declined along with the general cutbacks in state spending under the Conservatives and, now, Labour. There has been considerable foreign investment by such companies as Fujitsu, which opened a large factory in predominantly Catholic West Belfast. However, preliminary data suggest that these new factories and offices are still hiring more Protestants than Catholics. Moreover, Fujitsu may be the exception to the rule, since most companies are locating their operations in Protestant areas to which Catholics are still reluctant to commute.

THEORETICAL PERSPECTIVES

Our last task for this chapter is to tease the theoretical implications from the history of the Good Friday Agreement. Because this is the second case we have considered, the points that follow are more detailed and nuanced than those in chapter 6, and that will continue to be the case with the three remaining case studies.

1. The international system. This is the one case we will consider in which the momentous changes in the international system since the end of the Cold War have not mattered much. It is still the case that the international community has not been actively involved whenever the vital interests of one of the major powers are at stake. Thus, as in the two wars in Chechnya, there has never been any real possibility that the UN or any other international organization would intervene in Northern Ireland.

International forces have come into play here. There is no more obvious example of that than the impact of the Clinton administration in supporting the talks since 1995. Still, the impact of global forces has largely been on the margins with but one exception.

2. Third parties. That one exception is the role of third parties. As we saw above, Senator Mitchell and his colleagues deftly gained the trust of the leading politicians, which allowed them to gradually build bridges between the previously antagonistic parties. Indeed, it seems highly unlikely that the parties could have reached an agreement without outside help.

As will be clearer after the next two chapters, having a third party does not guarantee success. Much depends on two factors – the size of the chasm between the two sides and how effectively the third party use the combination of political 'carrots' and 'sticks' at his or her disposal. In the Bosnian case, for instance, we will see that Richard Holbrooke and his colleagues used the threat of massive NATO air strikes and the lifting of the arms embargo against the Bosnian government to help 'convince' the Milosevic regime to participate in the process that led to the Dayton Agreement. Mitchell had few levers to use in forcing the parties in Northern Ireland to accede to his wishes. Instead, he drew on all the skills he developed in his years in the U.S. Senate as a coalition builder.

And, though we lack the tools to measure this with any precision, his task was probably made a bit easier by the fact that the violence in Northern Ireland did not claim as many lives or cause as much destruction as the fighting in any of the other countries covered in this book. If nothing else, that probably made it possible for him to gradually 'build trust' as it is envisioned in the general literature on conflict resolution, international or otherwise.

3. *Asymmetry.* This case reinforces the mainstream international relations conclusion that a negotiated settlement is hard to reach when there is a sharp disparity in the resources the parties bring to the conflict. Individuals and groups on the weaker side feel particularly aggrieved and worry that negotiating from a position of weakness could only undermine their position. The stronger side, by contrast, sees no particular need to talk, because successful negotiations could well lead to compromises that would 'unnecessarily' erode their advantages.

During the course of the late 1980s and 1990s, the relationship between Catholics and Protestants became much more balanced. In part, that reflected the higher birth rate among Catholics and the emigration rate among Protestants, which has left the latter with a much smaller majority in the province's population. More important, as the example of the national anthem at Queen's University suggests, Catholics are getting a somewhat 'fairer share' of most resources, including professional and other lucrative jobs.

The more neutral attitude of the British government toward the two communities has also produced a more even distribution of political, if not economic, resources. In particular, the British army and the RUC now treat the two groups in a more evenhanded way. This trend seems bound to continue, especially if plans to replace the RUC with a new police force that explicitly tries to recruit Catholics come to fruition.

Finally, there has been a distinct change in public opinion. In the 1970s and 1980s, most people in Britain, the Irish Republic, and Northern Ireland blamed the IRA for the Troubles. As the bombings and fighting dragged on and the Protestant paramilitaries actually did more killing than the IRA and other Nationalist splinter groups, a growing number of people turned against all the perpetrators of the violence, whatever their religion or their goals. That was especially true of residents of Omagh, site of the last (August 1998) and most deadly bombing in the history of the Troubles. Journalists have repeatedly returned to the town as the negotiations progressed and have consistently found that family members of the victims, in particular, think there is next to no difference between the Catholic splinter group that carried out the attack and the Protestant paramilitaries.

4. *Hurting stalemate.* Our concrete evidence on the way political leaders think is never very extensive. Nonetheless, the limited interviews they have given and the analytical work that has been done on Northern Ireland both strongly suggest that leaders of the key political groups all came to the conclusion that the province had reached a hurting stalemate.

The conclusion was reached at various times and in various ways. John Hume and his colleagues in the SDLP reached it first. They always rejected the use of force in reaching nationalist goals. In the early and mid-1990s, most of the IRA leadership seems to have done the same. Critics point out that the IRA only dropped the 'armalite and the gun' because it knew it could not win a 'military' victory. That may well be true.

But, even if their decision to seek peace only occurred because they realized they could not win the war, it does little to undermine empirical support for arguments about the importance of hurting stalemates. From that perspective, the normative goal now should be to make certain that the IRA and other groups never again get the weapons that would allow them to launch another wave of violence should they change their mind about negotiations.

The last (and most important from a theoretical perspective) group to do so – and then only at the last moments of the negotiations – were the Unionists. Mainstream Unionists were never willing to resort to violence other than the fisticuffs that often followed Orange Order and other marches. However, they were convinced well into 1997 and 1998 that they dare not and that they need not make concessions on such critical issues as direct negotiations with Sinn Fein, let alone participating in a government with its representatives. In fact, as we are about to see, Trimble and his colleagues had a very hard time selling the idea of negotiations and power sharing to a large minority of their fellow Protestants on both tactical and ideological grounds.

5. *Political leadership and domestic politics.* Here, the difference between Northern Ireland and South Africa is easiest to see. As we saw in the last chapter, South Africa was blessed with a number of remarkable leaders who forsook vengeance and sought reconciliation instead. While Nelson Mandela gets most of the public credit for this, there were dozens of prominent leaders in all political camps working for peace and reconciliation. Northern Ireland has had its share of advocates for reconciliation. John Hume of the SDLP, the Northern Ireland Women's Committee, and the Alliance Party have long worked for a nonviolent solution to the Troubles. However, with the exception of John Hume, none of them have a significant following in either the Protestant or Catholic community.

Perhaps more important for the long run is the opposition that still exists to the Good Friday Agreement. That includes Ian Paisley's Democratic Unionist Party, which regularly wins close to 20 percent of the vote and whose two members have so far refused to participate in the new cabinet. Even more ominous are the Catholic and Protestant paramilitary groups that have announced their plans to continue the armed struggle. As of this writing, there have been no new attacks like the one at Omagh. However, if one of these small groups does launch a major bombing campaign, it could do irreparable damage to the gains made so far.

6. An international dimension. The Troubles have largely occurred inside the borders of a single country. What's more, as we saw above, Britain's power and the all-but-universal recognition of its state's legitimacy made outside intervention impossible. Nonetheless, there are important international aspects to the way the Good Friday Agreement was reached and implemented that could conceivably be adapted in some other long-standing religious and ethnic conflicts.

The Irish and American (because of the large Irish-American population) governments had ties to the Catholic community in the North. Therefore, they could persuade the SDLP and, later, the IRA and Sinn Fein, to take a more moderate and conciliatory line. The prospect of more foreign investment in a peaceful Northern Ireland also no doubt had an impact on the willingness of the parties to negotiate.

Perhaps more important in general terms is the way that the Good Friday Agreement, in Jonathan Stevenson's terms, 'dilutes' British sovereignty in Northern Ireland (Stevenson, 1998). The cross-border institutions will, in particular, make the Republic of Ireland an active participant in Northern Ireland's political affairs. Furthermore, if Stevenson is right, the growing power of the European Union made this agreement possible, precisely because it provides more opportunities for one member state to engage itself in a constructive manner in the internal affairs of another.

7. Slow and incremental progress. More than South Africa, Northern Ireland supports a pair of overlapping conclusions rarely found in the literature on win-win conflict resolution. It typically takes a long time to reach an agreement, and the deal that is eventually concluded invariably only addresses some of the issues at stake in the conflict.

South Africa's transition to democracy occurred relatively quickly. Still, nearly a decade elapsed between the start of negotiations between Mandela and his jailers and the election of the African National Congress. Here, we have seen that the informal exploration of a peaceful settlement began almost as soon as the Troubles did, and nearly thirty years elapsed before the Good Friday Agreement was reached.

That it takes time should not be surprising. After all, the conflicts under consideration here are deep indeed. The years of violence and tension have driven crippling psychological wedges between the participants in all of them. In fact, as the Irish case shows, getting the leaders of the parties to the table can alone take years.

Under those circumstances, it should also not come as a surprise that negotiators have to settle for incremental progress. We academics may well be able to envision more sweeping changes, but it may not be practically possible to implement them, especially in a case like this one in which most of the participants in the talks faced opposition from within their own communities, a point we will return to in the next chapter.

8. Reconciliation (or the lack thereof). The preceding point should not be read as suggesting that participants in peace processes should settle for any agreement. Rather, it is important that an incremental agreement do at least two things above and beyond putting an end to the fighting.

First, it should be like the confidence-building measures in arms control through which an initial agreement established procedures that will make it easier to reach more sweeping ones later on. There is reason to believe that the implementation of the Good Friday Agreement in late 1999 can do that. As Britain's then secretary of state for Northern Ireland, Peter Mandelson, put it during a visit to the United States shortly after the government was formed, 'trust is creeping in' among the politicians who are part of the new institutions.

Second, moving from the tension that characterizes Northern Ireland today to anything approaching stable peace requires a concentrated effort at reconciliation. On that front, the Irish have done far less than the South Africans and, even, the Israelis and the Palestinians. As noted earlier in the chapter, there have been few formal attempts to bring the Catholic and Protestant communities together. If anything, they probably meet informally on the job or in their neighborhoods less than they did before the Troubles began. And, as John Lloyd (1999) put it in one of the first extended essays on the state of Northern Ireland after the government was formed, there is still a very volatile mix of violence and hatred throughout the province. He does cite the work of John Scott, who has led a team of unemployed young people that has covered over some of the most hateful and offensive graffiti in Dublin. But, as Lloyd also puts it in ending his articles,

> John Scott's story might show that the vast damage that civil society has suffered over the past three decades can be pushed back by courage and reassertion of what people really want. Yet it is not ordained: this is no happy ending. The Union Jacks and the tricolors [Republic of Ireland flags] still flutter on lampposts, and the gray walls of the estates scream hate and pride at each other. Peace has been proclaimed, but as attested to by the bitter experience of South Africa, Kosovo, Nicaragua, and many others in the last decade or so, it takes far more than a political pact and

good intentions to root out the pathologies of war and build a healthy society. (Lloyd, 1999:93)

SELECT BIBLIOGRAPHY

Bloomfield, David. *Peacemaking Strategies in Northern Ireland*. Basingstoke: Macmillan, 1997.

————. *Political Dialogue in Northern Ireland*. Basingstoke: Macmillan, 1998.

Coogan, Tim Pat. *The Troubles: Ireland's Ordeal 1966–1996 and the Search for Peace*. Boulder: Roberts Rinehart, 1996.

Hoge, Warren. 'Pledges by Ulster Rivals Break the Deadlock at Talks.' *New York Times*, Washington Edition, 17 November 1996b, A3.

————. 'Roadblock to a Peace Pact: Irish Mostly Say "No." ' *New York Times*, Washington Edition, 3 July 1999a, 7.

Holland, Jack. *Hope against History: The Course of Conflict in Northern Ireland*. New York: Henry Holt, 1999.

Lloyd, John. 'Ireland's Uncertain Peace.' *Foreign Affairs* (September–October 1999): 109–23.

————. 'The Troubles That Won't Go Away.' *New York Times Magazine*, 12 December 1999, 89–93.

McKittrick, David. *The Nervous Peace*. London: Blackstaff, 1996.

Mitchell, George. *Making Peace*. New York: Knopf, 1999.

O'Hearn, Denis, Sam Porter, and Alan Harpur. 'Turning Agreement to Process: Republicanism and Change in Ireland.' *Capital and Class* (Autumn 1999): 7–25.

O'Toole, Fintan. 'The Ulster Conundrum: The Words Used to Broker Peace Have Become Stumbling Blocks.' *Washington Post*, 11 July 1999, B4.

Stevenson, Jonathan. 'Peace in Northern Ireland: Why Now?' *Foreign Policy* (Fall 1998): 41–54.

Toolis, Kevin. *Rebel Hearts: Journeys within the IRA's Soul*. New York: St. Martin's, 1995.

8

ISRAEL AND THE PALESTINIANS

The Pope, according to a no doubt apocryphal story, maintained that there were two possible solutions to the Arab-Israeli conflict: the realistic and the miraculous. The realistic solution involve divine intervention; the miraculous solution, a voluntary agreement among the parties them-selves.

– Avi Shlaim

I sent my final draft of this book to the publisher shortly before the second Intifada *broke out in autumn 2000. Publication deadlines did not leave me with enough time to totally rewrite it, and it therefore remains largely as it was written in summer 2000. However, although I am only able to touch on the most recent outburst of fighting, the original chapter does suggest why it was at least as likely as a permanent settlement of the Israeli–Palestinian dispute was at the time I wrote.*

In September 1993 Israeli prime minister Yitzhak Rabin and Palestinian leader Yasir Arafat[1] signed the historic Oslo agreement on the lawn of the White House in Washington, D.C. It was dubbed the Oslo Accord, because the negotiations that produced it had been held in secret under the leadership of a team of Norwegian academics and diplomats. At the ceremony, Rabin spoke for many when he said:

Let me say to you, the Palestinians: We are destined to live together on the same soil in the same land. We, the soldiers who have returned from the battle stained with blood; we, who have seen our relatives and friends killed before our eyes; we, who have attended their funerals and

---

1. There are many ways of transliterating Arabic words and names. I have chosen to use the same transliterations one finds in the leading American news media such as the *New York Times* or *Washington Post*. They are not necessarily the best. They are, however, the ones readers of this book are most likely to be familiar with and/or encounter in further reading.

cannot look into the eyes of parents and orphans; we, who have come from a land where parents bury their children; we, who have fought against you, the Palestinians; we say to you in a loud and a clear voice – enough of blood and tears. Enough.

Rabin's hopes were similar to those we saw in South Africa and Northern Ireland. However, the Israeli-Palestinian peace process did not fulfill those hopes during the rest of the 1990s. After Rabin was assassinated by a right-wing Israeli, elections brought Binyamin Netanyahu to power in Israel. His conservative government was far more intransigent at the negotiating table than Robin's had been, and little progress was made on such critical issues as the transfer of the remainder of the West Bank land to the new Palestinian Authority.

Netanyahu and his Likud Party lost the 1999 election, bringing Labor back into office. The new prime minister, Ehud Barak, committed himself to reaching a definitive peace agreement not just with the Palestinians but with Syria and Lebanon as well. Late that year, final status talks on the future of Jerusalem finally began (even though the deadline for their resolution which was set out by Oslo, had already passed). Throughout 2000, U.S. Sponsored talks continued. Most notably, the two sides came closer than ever to an agreement on such divisive issues as the status of Jerusalem at talks held at the presidential retreat in Camp David, Maryland.

However, hopes for any lasting settlement ended when the second Intifada broke out. As of this writing, more than 300 people – mostly Palestinians – had been killed. Negotiations have continued throughout the new period of violence, and there have been reports of progress on some issues. Nonetheless, the continued violence, the end of the Clinton administration, and the likely election of a conservative government headed by Ariel Sharon in Israel all suggest that peace is a long way off.

A Complicated Conflict – and Some Analytic Limits

This chapter will focus on relations between Israel and the Palestinians. As should already be clear, that conflict is but a part of a larger cluster of disputes between Israel and all its Arab neighbors.

Unfortunately, we cannot do justice to the entire conflict here. Therefore, I will bring in material on the other Arab countries and their relations with Israel only when it is needed to see what remains the thorniest problem in the Middle East.

THEORETICAL FOCUS

As with Northern Ireland, we will concentrate on theoretical factors that help us understand why the Israelis and Palestinians have made some progress toward peace but also why major roadblocks in the peace process remain. At the end of the chapter, we will therefore return to the following issues:

- the changing structure of the international system after the end of the Cold War and the Gulf crisis of 1990–91
- the overall weakness of the international community in addressing conflicts in which one or more of the world's major parties believes it has a powerful interest
- the importance of third parties but also the difficulty in finding an effective one
- the role of informal or track-two diplomacy and grassroots citizens' initiatives in producing steps toward peace and reconciliation
- how the asymmetric nature of the relationship between Israel and the Palestinians has hindered progress toward peace since the beginning of the conflict
- the ways that domestic politics in general and leadership in particular can be both a source of progress and an obstacle to peace
- the continued role of 'rejectionist' groups and more widespread 'images of the enemy' among both Israelis and Palestinians
- a multistage peace process in which much will depend on the development of a stronger economy and civil society in the emerging Palestinian state

THE ORIGINS OF THE CONFLICT

The roots of the Israeli–Palestinian conflict are encapsulated in the titles of two books on it – *One Land, Two Peoples* (Gerner, 1994) and *Sharing the Promised Land* (Hiro 1999; also see Ciment, 1997; Shlaim, 2000). Both the Jewish Israelis and the primarily Muslim Palestinians have powerful claims to the same territory. To complicate things further, that land is also home to many of the most sacred sites in those two religious traditions – and in Christianity as well. Indeed, one of the most powerful symbols of how entangled the communities are is the al-Aqsa mosque, which is the third holiest place in Islam and which sits atop the ruins of the Second Temple and the Wailing Wall, the most sacred site in Judaism. It is also only a few hundred yards from the Church of the Holy Sepulchre, which many Christians believe is the spot from which Jesus rose to heaven.

The fact that these peoples can trace their origins in Israel/Palestine back thousands of years has led many observers to see this as a centuries-old conflict. That is not really the case. Until quite recently, the few Jews in Palestine got along reasonably with their Arab neighbors. In other words, the Arab–Israeli conflict is largely a product of twentieth-century political choices made by people both inside and outside of the region.

Israel began as the dream of Zionists in the 1890s. Those were tough years for Jews in Russia and the rest of eastern Europe, where they were subject to widespread discrimination and indiscriminate attacks known as pogroms. A relatively small number of Jews, led by Theodore Herzl (1860-1904), saw their future in the traditional homeland of the Jews.

The Jewish return (*aliyah*) began as a trickle. Only about 25,000 Jews lived in Palestine at the end of the nineteenth century, most of whom were descendants of people who had been allowed to move back to Jerusalem during the Crusades. A 1918 census registered 56,000 Jews, or about 8 percent of the total population of Palestine. The early Zionists were surprisingly uninterested in how they were received by the Palestinians. The few who did pay attention to the Palestinians treated them as inferior to the Jews.

By contrast, the 600,000 Palestinians had little real sense of national identity. That was not surprising, since Palestine had been under foreign rule for hundreds of years.

The political tide began to turn against the Palestinians during World War I. The British and French wanted to encourage local resistance against the Ottoman Empire, which had joined the war on the German and the Austro-Hungarian side. London and Paris sent mixed signals to the region. It told the Arabs that it would grant them independence if they supported the Allied effort. As we will see in more detail in chapter 10, they failed to live up to those promises.

More important for our purposes here, the British issued the Balfour Declaration, which many observers on all sides took as an endorsement for an eventual Jewish state despite its ambiguous wording:

> His Majesty's government view with favour the establishment in Palestine of a National Home for the Jewish people, and will use their best endeavors to facilitate the achievement of this object, it being clearly understood that nothing shall be done which may prejudice the civil and religious rights of the existing non-Jewish communities in Palestine.

Palestine was designated a British mandate in the Treaty of Versailles, and there is nothing in its administration of the region to suggest it planned to hand it over to either its Jewish or its Arab population.

Nonetheless, the Balfour Declaration was but one of many acts that convinced leading Palestinians that the Jews were at best a key element of British imperialism throughout the Middle East.

Meanwhile, the pace of Jewish migration stepped up, especially after Hitler came to power in Germany in 1933. By that point, the British were taking a more evenhanded approach toward the two communities and imposed stiff limits on the number of Jews who would be allowed to emigrate to Palestine.

Not surprisingly, the Palestinians came to resent the new settlers on 'their' land. The first protests broke out in 1921. In 1929 Jews attempted to make the Wailing Wall in the Arab-dominated Old City of Jerusalem accessible for prayer. Riots ensued in which 133 Jews were killed. A full-scale Arab revolt racked the mandate from 1936 to 1938; at least 5,000 people died.

The British established the Peel Commission to investigate the situation. Its 1937 report concluded that the Jews and Palestinians were unlikely to work out their differences and recommended partition and the creation of a small Jewish state. Most Zionists joined David Ben Gurion and other leaders in accepting the principle of partition if not the specifics of the Peel Report.

Table 8.1 The evolution of the Israeli–Palestinian conflict

Date	Event
1897	First Zionist conference
1917	Balfour Declaration
1933	Hitler comes to power in Germany
1947	UN Resolution on partition
	Arab–Israeli War starts
1948	Israel declares its statehood
1949	First war ends
1956	War starting with invasion of Suez
1967	Six-Day War
1969	Fateh and Arafat take control of PLO
1973	October/Yom Kippur War
1982	Invasion of Lebanon
1987	Start of the Intifada

Most Jews were willing to put the struggle for statehood on hold during World War II. But, as reports of the Holocaust streamed in, they became even more committed to creating the State of Israel than ever before – and more impatient with the British.

By the end of the war, the Jewish army was well armed as were small bands of terrorists that were part of the more militant Revisionist movement, which opposed partition. (See box.) The British cracked down, but the government in London had no desire to fight Jews a few short months after the horrid revelations about the Holocaust. It therefore announced plans to return its mandate to the United Nations.

On 29 November 1947 the UN General Assembly passed Resolution 181, which called for the creation of a Jewish state. The new state would also include 400,000 Palestinians. Needless to say, the Palestinians and other Arabs were adamantly opposed to this or any other arrangement that would have taken away what they saw as their land.

Fighting broke out again and consumed the region for more than a year. There is still considerable debate about who was responsible for what then occurred. In early 1948 there were intense battles between Jews and Palestinians. The Jews used both a regular army, the Israeli Defense Force (IDF), and less disciplined groups that today would be called terrorists. The latter carried out a series of attacks, the most important of which to their critics was at the village of Deir Yasin, where more than 200 civilians were killed.

On 14 May 1948 Prime Minister David Ben Gurion proclaimed the State of Israel. Immediately thereafter, the neighboring Arab states attacked in what would be the first of five full-scale wars. The outnumbered but better disciplined and motivated Israelis won the war. Although there was no formal treaty ending it, a series of negotiations led to the establishment of borders that would last until the 1967 war and could well become the frontiers of Israel again should the current peace process reach fruition.

The fighting intensified as the Arab states declared war on Israel. The Israelis finally won after months of intense fighting that cost over 6,000 Jewish lives. On 13 January 1949, the UN chief negotiator for Palestine, Ralph Bunche, led Israel and the various Arab states to an agreement on an armistice that ended the fighting. In some people's eyes, it marked a de facto acknowledgment on the part by the Arab states that Israel existed, though none of them would recognize it formally for another thirty years.

The establishment of a Jewish state brought tremendous joy to Jews around the world. That was anything but the case for Palestinians and the other Arabs.

The Iron Wall

The Zionist movement split in the 1920s. While the left-wing inheritors of the Herzl version remained dominant, the minority revisionist faction made one contribution that marked almost all Jewish Palestinians and then Israelis well into the 1980s.

In a 1923 essay, the revisionist leader, Rabbi Ze'ev Jabotinsky wrote of an iron wall that should separate Jews and Palestinians. He argued that it was impossible both to force all the Palestinians to leave and to reach a modus vivendi with them through which they could comfortably share the land. In fact, unlike many of the left-wing Zionists, he expected a struggle. Jabotinsky wrote:

> Every indigenous people will resist alien settlers as long as they see any hope of ridding themselves of the danger of foreign settlement. That is how the Arabs will behave and go on behaving so long as they possess a gleam of hope that they can prevent 'Palestine' from becoming the Land of Israel. (Shlaim, 2000, 13)

Instead, Jews had to create an 'iron wall of military force' to impose their will on the Palestinians that would result in some form of political autonomy for them inside a Jewish state.

The defeat was a dual tragedy for the Palestinians in what they call, *al-nakhba*, or the disaster. Not only did they lose control over most of their land, at least 800,000, or over 80 percent of the Palestinian population, fled, creating the refugee problem that still plagues the region to this day.

THE ARAB–ISRAELI CONFLICT

For the next twenty years, the conflict was centered not on the Palestinians but on Israel's relationship with the Arab states. The status of Palestinians at home and in the Diaspora was an all-important issue. However, virtually everyone – including most Palestinians – assumed that the Arab states would best represent Palestinian interests.

The failure of the other Arab states to redress Palestinian grievances set the stage for the violence of the Palestinian–Israeli conflict from the 1970s onward and much of the way the peace process evolved beginning in 1991. From that perspective, there were five crises (four of which turned into all-out wars) that deepened the tensions. For reasons of space, we can only note them in passing here.

- In 1956 Israel, France, and Great Britain launched a war against Egypt after it took over the Suez Canal under its new nationalist government headed by Gamal Abdel Nasser. The war was a catastrophe for the British and French, but the Israelis again demonstrated their military superiority over the Arab states.
- In 1967 Israel launched a preemptive attack, which became known as the Six-Day War. In a matter of hours, the IDF destroyed the various Arab forces and occupied the West Bank, the Gaza Strip, the Golan Heights, and the Sinai Peninsula.
- In 1973 the Israelis fought its last full-fledged war with the Arab States, known as the October War to most scholars but as the Yom Kippur War to many Israelis and Americans. This time, the Arab states gave the Israelis a stiffer fight but were eventually defeated, which meant that Israel retained control of the territories it occupied in 1967.
- In 1982 Israel invaded Lebanon and killed thousands of Palestinians in its raids on refugee camps dominated by the Palestine Liberation Organization (PLO), some of which were in Beirut. This was the only war during this period that did not involve all the major Arab states.

Palestinian Resistance

There was always some resistance against Israeli rule by Palestinians. From their perspective, Israel had taken their land and made hundreds of thousands of them into what turned out to be permanent refugees.

From the late 1940s onward, small groups of *fedayin* launched attacks from refugee camps, though these were as often attempts to reclaim lost property as political statements. Those raids only strengthened Israeli commitment to building a modern version of Zabotinsky's iron wall, even though the country was governed by men and women whose roots were in the original, left-wing Zionism. Everything from the development of the Israeli Defense Force to the creation of settlements along the borders was designed to protect the new state's security from attack by Arab armies and by the Palestinian guerrillas.

As noted earlier, the Palestinians initially deferred to the leaders of the Arab states. That changed after the Six-Day War for three main reasons. First, the war demonstrated that the Arab states were not likely to defeat Israel. Second, even more ominously for the Palestinians, it showed that the other Arabs were not all that committed to their cause. Third and most important, nearly a million Palestinians had all of a sudden come under Israeli rule in the Occupied Territories in the West Bank and Gaza.

Until then, there had been dozens of Palestinian organizations, some demanding the immediate return of their lands, others willing to follow a more gradual strategy. Among them was *Fateh*, organized by Yasir Arafat with the encouragement of Egyptian president Nasser. In 1964 Nasser organized a meeting in Cairo that created the PLO and its military wing, the Palestine Liberation Army. That May 422 delegates met in East Jerusalem (then still controlled by Jordan) and adopted the Palestinian Charter, which read in part:

> The partition of Palestine in 1947 and the establishment of the State of Israel, are entirely illegal regardless of the passage of time, because they were contrary to the will of the Palestinian people and to their natural right in their homeland, and inconsistent with the principles embodied in the Charter of the United Nations, particularly the right to self-determination.

Fateh was not one of the earliest or the most effective guerrilla groups. In fact, its first raid was a failed attempt to destroy a canal taking water from the River Jordan to the Negev desert. But because of its financial

---

Yasir Arafat and the PLO

Yasir Arafat has been the most visible and controversial figure in the Palestinian resistance against Israeli rule since he became leader of the PLO in 1969. Arafat was born in Gaza in 1929 and went into exile as soon as the State of Israel was formed. In the 1960s he formed Fateh, which became the leading guerrilla force and political movement in the Palestinian community after the Six-Day War in 1967.

Arafat has been an implacable foe of most Israeli policies regarding the occupied territories and backed the use of violence for most of his long political career. Despite his deserved radical reputation, Arafat has also been one of the more moderate PLO leaders, who always at least talked about negotiations even while leading its guerrilla campaign against Israel. In the 1980s, Arafat made the peace process possible on the Palestinian side by renouncing terrorism, accepting UN Resolution 242 as the basis for negotiation, and endorsing Israel's right to exist.

In 1989 he was named head of the Palestinian government in exile and six years later became president of the Palestinian National Authority, as the emerging Palestinian government is formally known.

Arafat is always seen in public with his kaffiya draped in a way that resembles the map of Palestine.

resources and the skills of Ararat and his colleagues, Fateh was able to take control of the PLO organization in 1969, after which it became the heart of Palestinian resistance.

The PLO has never been a unified organization. Its membership has always included moderates who favored negotiation and coexistence with Israel and radicals whose only goal was the destruction of the Jewish state and who were willing to use violence, including terrorism. For the bulk of the 1970s, the latter group was by far the most influential within the PLO.

The PLO initially hoped to form a regular army that could win back Palestine. However, it burst onto the world's political stage in the 1970s when it and other groups staged a series of dramatic terrorist attacks. Planes were hijacked. Israelis and other Jews were killed. In the most dramatic act of them all, Palestinian militants seized Israeli athletes at the 1972 Olympic Games in Munich, many of whom were killed in the shootout that ended the crisis. The PLO has never been responsible for all the acts of terrorism, a fact often lost on Americans and Israelis. Most of the incidents in recent years have been the work of other organizations, most notably Hamas and Hezbollah.

Indeed, as early as 1974, Arafat sent signals that the PLO was willing to entertain some sort of peaceful solution to the conflict. Thus, in his first address to the United Nations General Assembly, he stated:

> Today I have come bearing an olive branch and a freedom fighter's gun.
> Do not let the olive branch fall from my hands.

For the next twelve years, however, there was little of the olive branch. The PLO continued to attack Israel, which continued its often brutal administration of the Occupied Territories. The Israelis tried – and failed – to create Palestinian officials with whom they could work who were not part of the PLO. Meanwhile, the PLO's relations with the rest of the Arab world also deteriorated, especially following its forced departure from Jordan and then Lebanon.

The start of the Intifada made the prospects for peace seem ever more distant. On 8 December 1987 a vehicle carrying Israeli troops collided with a car in the Gaza Strip. Four Palestinians were killed. Rumors quickly spread that this was a deliberate Israeli attack. Whether it was or not, it touched off the most massive wave of protests yet seen in Israel proper and the Occupied Territories. Intifada can best be translated as 'shaking off,' and for many young Palestinians who joined in the demonstrations and threw stones at Israelis, they were literally trying to shake off the yoke of Israeli rule.

At first the Israelis tried to put the revolt down by using violence against the protesters and making wide-scale arrests, much of it planned by Yitzhak Rabin, who was then defense minister in the cabinet. In the first thirty months of the Intifada, over 800 Palestinians were killed, more than 200 of whom were under sixteen. Israeli repression, in short, only served to stiffen the resistance. It was only in early 2000 that Israel officially acknowledged that it had used torture on many of the Palestinians it arrested.

What's more, to the degree that the Intifada was a coordinated movement, its initial leadership was only loosely connected to the PLO. The PLO also was somewhat concerned about the Intifada because many of its veterans found their way to more militant groups like Hamas and Hezbollah in the 1990s.

THE ROAD TO OSLO

Israel and the Arabs

This case effectively illustrates two of the most important conclusions of this entire book. Negotiations usually take a long time, and they only reach fruition when leaders on both sides of the dispute can summon up the political will to make significant progress toward settling it.

In this case, Israel began discussions with the various Arab states almost as soon as the war surrounding its independence ended. However, for a variety of reasons we do not have the time to go into here, those talks accomplished little other than producing armistices to end the wars until the 1970s.

Indeed, the most important discussions (for example, those with King Hussein of Jordan and with Nasser shortly after he took power in Egypt) were conducted in secret because of the likely repercussions public disclosure would have had both in Israel and in the Arab world. Although Israel at least professed interest in living at peace with the Palestinians and the other Arabs, it was a long time before either side showed any serious interest in doing so.

Israel remained convinced that the Arabs were out to destroy the Jewish state, and therefore resisted making any concessions that would put the country's security in the slightest jeopardy. The Arab states publicly reinforced those fears. At the Khartoum summit following the 1967 war, they repeated their refusal to legally recognize the existence of Israel, let alone make peace with it.

In retrospect, however, we can see that the outcome of the 1967 war moved the sides closer to a hurting stalemate and opened the door to separate negotiations with individual Arab states as well as the

Palestinians. The 1973 war truly opened a door that ultimately led to a series of agreements starting with the Camp David Accords.

After the 1967 war, the United Nations adopted a series of resolutions on the Middle East. The most important of these was Resolution 242, which called in part for 'the withdrawal of Israeli armed forces from the territories occupied in the recent conflict' and stated the right of 'every state to live in peace within secure and recognized boundaries' (in Eisenberg and Caplan, 1998:157–58). It also deployed peacekeepers in the Sinai to monitor the tense standoff between Israel and Egypt. But, the blue helmets were withdrawn at the request of the Egyptians, an action that made the outbreak of fighting in 1973 easier.

Useful Web Sites

The University of Texas's Middle East Center maintains a list of groups supporting the peace process that have web sites.
<http://link.lanic.utexes.edu/menic>.

Neve Shalom/Wahat al-Salam, which will be described below, has an extensive site. <http://www.newas.com>.

PASSIA is one of the best nongovernmental organizations working on Palestinian-Israeli issues and also trains young Palestinian university graduates in conflict resolution, diplomacy, and the development of civil society. Its web site is filled with data. <http://www.passia.org>.

The first concerted effort by outsiders to defuse the tensions came with Henry Kissinger's shuttle diplomacy missions in the last few days of the 1973 war and in the months that followed. Despite the fact that the United States was so closely allied with Israel, Kissinger was able to get the sides to stop fighting and reach an informal agreement on subsequent relations. Kissinger was spurred on by the economic consequences of the OPEC oil embargo and the fears that many had that another crisis in the region could actually take the United States and Soviet Union to war. The United Nations did its part by passing Resolution 338, which called on all parties to start negotiations for a lasting settlement on the basis of 242. He was aided, as well, by a real sense of war weariness both in Israel and in many of the Arab states that had provoked it, most notably, Egypt. Meanwhile, Israeli and Egyptian military officers held a series of meetings, all of which culminated in the withdrawal of Israeli troops from Egyptian territory in early 1974.

Kissinger's initiative, however, did little to build a lasting peace. The first key steps in that direction came after two major political events occurred. In the United States, the Democratic administration of Jimmy Carter took office in 1977. That same year, Labor lost an election for the first time in Israel, bringing the more conservative Likud Party to power. Likud was a direct descendant of Revisionist Zionism. The new prime minister, Menachem Begin, had been the commander of the Irgun terrorist group after the war and had opposed partition, insisting that the new Israel had a legitimate claim to all of Palestine – if not more territory.

As has often been the case, the election of a conservative leader made new initiatives possible, because someone like Begin could take risks that would have been too politically costly for a Labor prime minister, few of whom were noticeably more dovish. At the time, most international attention was focused on convening a Geneva conference involving all the parties. Secretly, however, aides to Begin and Egyptian president Anwar Sadat began informal discussions that would lead to bilateral, not multilateral agreements. In a surprise to the world as a whole, Sadat told the Egyptian parliament that he was prepared to go to Jerusalem and speak to the Knesset if it would help the cause of peace. Ten days later, on 19 November 1977, Sadat arrived in Israel, where he and Begin apparently agreed on the outlines of a plan for Israeli withdrawal from the Sinai.

A flurry of further meetings occurred but accomplished little, contributing to growing frustrations on both sides. Finally, President Carter invited both sides to a summit he would host at the presidential retreat, Camp David. After ten hard days, the two sides agreed on 'A Framework for Peace in the Middle East,' which was followed by a formal treaty that was signed at the White House on 26 March 1979.

Israel agreed to withdraw its troops and settlers from the Sinai, which did not figure in Begin's hopes for a 'greater Israel.' Israel and Egypt also agreed to formally recognize each other and forego further wars. More important for our purposes, the treaty recognized the 'legitimate rights of the Palestinian people and their just requirements' and called for negotiations, beginning with the acceptance of 'Resolution 242 in all its parts.' Quickly, however, it became clear that Israel, Egypt, and the United States had made precious little progress in agreeing on what those terms meant, and negotiations on the status of Palestinians soon reached an impasse.

Israel and the Palestinians

The Israeli-Egyptian treaty had two, contradictory effects on the Palestinians. On the one hand, it reinforced the now widespread conviction that they could not rely on the Arab states to protect their interests. On the other hand, it showed that talks could actually get somewhere.

The next decade produced little or no progress. If anything, everything from the continued instances of terrorism to the construction of new settlements in the Occupied Territories made a negotiated settlement *less* likely.

The Intifada, however, marked a major turning point for many Israelis (especially in Labor) and for the PLO. Moderate Israelis, for instance, realized that they could not negotiate the fate of Palestinians with anyone but Palestinians and that the PLO might well be their best (or perhaps least bad) alternative.

Meanwhile, people close to Arafat worried about groups that were more militant than Fateh. As the Intifada raged, the Palestinian National Council met in Algiers in November 1988. Despite opposition from the radicals, it voted 253 to 46 (with 10 abstentions) to implicitly recognize Israel and agree that any peace settlement would have to begin with acceptance of UN resolutions 242 and 338, which both Israel and the United States had made a precondition for any serious talks.

The end of the Cold War also made a peace process easier to start by removing the Soviet Union as a major player in regional politics. It no longer had the resources to fund the PLO, other Palestinian groups, and Arab states. Even more important, the conflict between Israel and the Palestinians could be addressed on its own, without worrying about its broader implications for the superpower rivalry.

Similarly, in a curious way, the Gulf war also opened the door to the peace process. The PLO was weakened even further because of the reaction of other Arab states against its support for the Iraqi invasion of Kuwait. Ironically, too, the Iraqi attempt to link a proposed pullout from Kuwait in late 1990 to negotiations on the status of Israel actually built more momentum for peace once Operation Desert Storm defeated Baghdad.

The Bush administration, in particular, tried to seize the opportunity provided by the newly fluid regional relations and balance of power to hold regional peace talks. To that end, the United States and Soviet Union officially convened the Madrid Peace Conference in 1991 at which Israeli officials openly talked with Palestinians for the first time – though they still refused to negotiate with the PLO.

The Madrid process accomplished very little, because Israel would not budge on some of the key positions it had defended for years. Various governments in the late 1960s and 1970s proposed granting some autonomy to Palestinians in parts of the West Bank. However, these

Table 8.2 The peace process

Date	Event
1978–79	Camp David
1991	Madrid Conference opens
1992	Election of Labor
1993	Oslo Accord
1994	Israel and Jordan sign treaty
1995	Oslo II
	Assassination of Rabin
1996	Election of Netanyahu and Likud
1998	Wye River Agreement
1999	Election of Barak and Labor
2000	Start of the second Intifada
2001	Election of Ariel Sharon as prime minister of Israel

offers were made with preconditions that brought all but immediate rejection. In fact, Israel (and its American allies) would not deal with Palestinians linked to the PLO. A law passed in 1986 made it illegal for any Israeli official to even talk to a PLO member.

Although it did not seem so at the time, the 1992 Israeli election marked a momentous change. For the eight years before that, the country had been ruled by a coalition government of 'national unity' that included both Likud and Labor. The presence of Likud with its hard line toward the Palestinians made progress toward peace all but impossible. In 1992 Labor won, bringing the former general and prime minister Yitzhak Rabin back to office with Shimon Peres as foreign minister.

The Norway Channel

At first, no one expected a dramatic breakthrough, especially given the hard-line positions Rabin had taken against the Intifada in the national unity government. After the 1992 election, a BBC reporter asked an Arab janitor if he thought it would make a big difference.

> Do you see my left shoe? That is Yitzhak Rabin. Do you see my right shoe? That is Yitzhak Shamir. Two Yitzhaks, two shoes, so what's the difference? (Shlaim, 2000:502)

But the new Rabin government did prove far more flexible than its predecessor in the on-again, off-again negotiations taking place in Washington, opening talks with Syria, repealing the law banning contacts with PLO members, and releasing some Palestinian prisoners. It was not, however, prepared to make major concessions in those negotiations, and it continued to take a hard line on such issues as closing the borders with the Occupied Territories in retaliation against terrorist attacks.

The breakthrough did not occur, however, as a result of the formal talks, but of a surprisingly successful track-two initiative. We now know that several citizen diplomacy discussions had been secretly begun in the early 1990s.

The one that bore fruit came as a surprise. In fact, only about a hundred or so people in the world even knew the Norway channel existed until hours before the agreement was announced. Even the American, Palestinian, and Israeli negotiators meeting in the 'Madrid' talks in Washington were kept in the dark until the last possible moment.

In 1992 a Norwegian sociologist, Terje Larsen, informed the Israelis and the Palestinians that his research institute and the Norwegian government were willing to facilitate discussion between the two sides. Three days before the Israeli election, Larsen met with Yossi Beilin, Shimon Peres' closest adviser in the Labor Party, and Faisal Husseini, the most powerful Palestinian leader in Jerusalem. After the election, Beilin became deputy foreign minister, and two of his associates – Yair Hirschfeld and Ron Pundak – agreed to continue the discussions in their capacities as private citizens. In December Larsen helped arrange a meeting between Hirschfeld and the influential Palestinian, Abu Ala, in London. Then Hirschfeld apparently asked the Norwegians to organize a larger meeting in the guise of an academic seminar, which began on 20 January 1993, the day after Israel's parliament repealed the law banning any public or private meetings between Israelis and representatives of the PLO.

The Norway channel is a virtual 'how-to manual' for third-party-led track-two negotiations. The Norwegians were well suited for the role they ended playing brilliantly. To begin with, the Norwegian academic and diplomatic elite is quite small and interconnected. As a case in point, Larsen's wife was a diplomat specializing in Middle Eastern politics, while Johan Jorgen Holst's wife was on the staff of Larsen's institute and participated in the first session, though she did not realize that there were also negotiations going on.

Larsen, in particular, used his expertise in group dynamics to smooth the negotiations. Though he rarely participated in the talks themselves, he was prepared to step in when the parties wanted him to help clarify an issue or resolve a deadlock. Even more important, he and his colleagues created an atmosphere in which the Israelis and Palestinians got to know and like each other. By August, it is safe to say that the seven negotiators had become friends and that their personal friendship was critical to their being able to overcome many of the thorny issues they faced.

In each new session, the discussions got more specific and the deliberations more official. Thus, discussion of general issues led to agreement on more than a dozen specific points in the Declaration of Principles (DOP).

The DOP took one vital step; the two sides recognized each other. The PLO acknowledged Israel's right to exist. Israel accepted Palestinian authority first in Gaza and Jericho, an authority that would gradually spread to more of the West Bank, although the Israelis stopped far short of accepting a formal Palestinian state.

A timetable was set (but not met) for resolving 'final status' issues, including the future of Jerusalem. Side agreements called for a substantial infusion of aid and investment in the Gaza and the West Bank for social, economic, and political development, which included using the CIA to help train Palestinian security officers.

The Difficult Road since Oslo

Negotiations continued on a number of fronts. In February 1994 Israel and the PLO agreed to a redeployment rather than a full withdrawal of Israeli troops from Gaza and Jericho. The next year, they signed the Palestinian Interim Agreement on the West Bank and the Gaza Strip (dubbed Oslo II), which created the Palestinian National Authority (PNA) that would assume complete power in most of the urban areas in the Occupied Territories and share power with Israel in others, while Israel would retain control of sparsely settled areas it felt were vital to its interests. Oslo II and the 1997 agreement on Hebron also called for further transfers of land to 'area A' status under complete Palestinian control. 'Final status' talks on such issues as the future of Jerusalem were scheduled to start in May 1996 and be completed by May 1999. In April 1996 the PLO removed the clauses about the destruction of Israel from its charter.

Oslo also established new momentum for negotiations with other Arab states. Thus, Israel and Jordan signed a peace treaty in October 1994 and came close to doing so with Syria as well (Rabinovich, 1999; Feldman and Toukan, 1997).

There was by no means universal support for Oslo and the agreements it spawned. Skeptics were quick to point out that it failed to address such critical issues as the creation of a Palestinian state, the status of Jerusalem, or the fate of the more than 200,000 Jewish settlers who had moved into Gaza, the West Bank, and the parts of the Jerusalem metropolitan area that had been formally annexed by Israel in 1967.

The Likud, many settlers in the Occupied Territories, and some Jewish fundamentalists opposed the peace process from the beginning. Israeli and Jewish-American conservatives felt that Israel had conceded too much, including its historical 'right' to Judea and Samaria, as they called the West Bank. At the time, Netanyahu, for instance, said of Rabin:

> You are worse than Chamberlain. He imperiled another people, but you are doing it to your own people. (Shlaim, 2000:521)

Right-wing Jews committed a number of attacks, the bloodiest of which occurred at the al-Aqsa mosque in Jerusalem and at the Tomb of the Patriarchs in Hebron. Meanwhile, fundamentalist Jews built ever more settlements in the Occupied Territories in an attempt to make any land-for-peace deal more difficult.

Among the Palestinians, intellectuals such as Edward Said felt it gave too little to the Palestinians (Said, 1996; Guyatt, 1998). Organizations like Hamas and Hezbollah took those criticisms to the streets in a wave of bombings and other attacks that undermined Israeli support for the peace process.

The peace process almost came to a halt after Rabin was assassinated by a right-wing Israeli on 4 November 1995. He was replaced by his longtime colleague and rival in the Labor Party, Shimon Peres, who was, if anything, even more firmly committed to peace with the Palestinians. However, Peres was not as popular a leader as Rabin had been, and in an attempt to strengthen his personal and political mandate, called for early elections on 29 May 1996. A series of bombings by Hamas undermined what started out as a huge lead for Peres in the polls. When the Israelis actually voted, Peres lost to Netanyahu in the country's first direct election of its prime minister.

Officially, Netanyahu pledged to uphold Oslo and continue the peace process. In practice, his government took a number of steps that set the peace process back. Thus, in September 1996 it opened a tunnel under much of the Old City of Jerusalem that many Palestinians took to be an insult and that violated the Rabin government's agreement to settle disputes over Jerusalem through consultation. The next year, the Netanyahu government began building 30,000 homes in Har Homa/ Jabal Abu Ghneim despite protests from liberal Israelis, the Palestinians, and most foreign governments. It failed to pull its troops out of Hebron, which has a handful of Jews living in the center of the city. It failed to open a promised 'safe passage' linking Gaza and the West Bank. Netanyahu offered the Palestinians a settlement in which Israel would keep control of about 60 percent of the West Bank as well as all of Jerusalem. This offer, of course, was rejected out of hand. Negotiations with Syria were stopped. The Israeli government also tried to hold the PNA responsible for instances of terrorism and often implied that Arafat and the PLO were themselves still terrorists.

World leaders grew increasingly critical of Netanyahu. Finally, in October 1998, the United States brought the Israeli and Palestinian leaders to the Wye River Plantation in rural Maryland. President Clinton himself led one twenty-seven-hour negotiating marathon that culminated in a memorandum signed by Netanyahu and Arafat. The two sides agreed to a new schedule of Israeli withdrawals for 13 percent of the West Bank, while the Palestinians committed themselves to tracking down terrorists. The CIA would establish training programs and communications links for the Israeli and Palestinian intelligence services.

Meanwhile, Netanyahu's support dwindled, largely for domestic political reasons. In late 1998 it became clear that he could not continue to govern with the existing Knesset. Therefore, new elections were called for 17 May. Netanyahu and Likud were defeated by the new prime minister, Ehud Barak, who led a multiparty government in which Labor was the largest member.

Barak had been chief of staff of the Israeli army and was initially critical of aspects of Oslo. However, during the campaign, he pledged to withdraw all Israeli troops from Lebanon within a year, negotiate a treaty with Syria, and bring the final status talks to fruition by 2001. In his first six months in office, significant progress was made on all those fronts.

Israeli and Syrian negotiators came close to an agreement on the future of the Golan Heights, and Israelis and Palestinians feverishly tried to agree on a broad framework of final status issues before the deadline. However, Barak was a tough negotiator who made it clear that he did not intend to back down on key issues. In short, the peace process resumed, but the two sides failed to reach a final status agreement.

RECONCILIATION

The history of the Arab–Israeli conflict is primarily one of violence, hatred, and fear. However, there have also been important but ill-publicized attempts at reconciliation that have eclipsed efforts along those lines in Northern Ireland.

There are enough ongoing projects that *Newsweek International* printed a magazine-length ad from Benetton on them. Each picture, of course, showed Israelis and Palestinians wearing Benetton clothes. There are graduate courses in which Israeli and Palestinian students write joint dissertations. Palestinian and Israeli intellectuals have been meeting informally for years.

In short, reconciliation efforts can be found in almost all areas of life. None are more important – or better researched – than those involving young people. According to Abu-Nimer, there are at least forty such programs, some of which are funded by the Israeli government and others by private sources, including the Jewish and Palestinian diasporas, the foundation world, and various governments' development agencies.

One of the oldest and best known is Neve Shalom/Wahat al-Salam (Oasis of Peace), which was created in 1972 (Shipler, 1986:495–555). Much like Northern Ireland's Corrymeela, Neve Shalom/Wahat al-Salam began as a religious community and is located on 100 acres of land leased from a monastery. Initially established as a place where Arabs and Jews could live together, it has never had many more than thirty families living there at any one time.

Its outreach programs have had a much broader impact. Its School for Peace was founded in 1979 and runs 'encounters' that are designed to 'show the participants how their responses within the small group reflect the relationships and conceptions of the two national groups in the wider reality. In interpreting their responses, we attempt to pinpoint the underlying conceptions and the way these contribute to the conflict' (from <http://www.nswas.com>).

A full-time staff of twelve and more than twenty freelance facilitators run three-day sessions most of which are for teenagers, although some are now held for teachers and other adult groups. Each group has a Jewish and Arab facilitator. The teenagers' activities include a simulation in which they try to plan future relations between their two communities. Teachers are asked to develop new curriculum materials for their classrooms. In recent years, Neve Shalom/Wahat al-Salam has expanded further, setting up programs for women and ongoing courses at Israel's five main universities.

In the 1998–99 academic year, the community hosted twenty-two encounters for young people, with over 1,000 participants split evenly between Arabs and Jews. It also held its first programs in territory controlled by the Palestinian Authority. Its other activities included helping prepare a group of eighteen Jewish and Arab students who would be spending the summer studying together in Norway.

Not only are there a surprising number of programs attempting to forge reconciliation, but also six of them have been systematically and comparatively evaluated by Mohammed Abu-Nimer (1999), a former facilitator in one of them who has since become a conflict resolution analyst. In his introduction, Abu-Nimer evokes the power this work can have:

> Words fail to describe Palestinian teenagers or teachers when they truly, and for the first time, realize that Jewish participants who are associated with dominance and power, are sincerely scared of Arabs. Or the sudden awareness of a Jewish participant who must finish his or her first personal encounter with an Arab. (Abu-Nimer 1999:xx)

But Nimer's goal was to dig beyond these initial reactions and determine just how successful these programs are. Therefore, he studied six of the most prominent ones inside Israel that work with schools, including Neve Shalom/Wahat al-Salam. Note that he did not include groups that dealt with other issues or regularly included Palestinians living outside the 1967 borders.

His detailed findings are not as encouraging as the statement from his introduction might lead a reader to expect. Among other things, he found:

- Considerable resistance to participating on the part of the Jewish young people even though they were typically recruited from schools where the staff was sympathetic to the idea of reconciliation.
- Ignorance of the status of Arabs among Jewish students, many of whom denied there was a problem at all.
- Different goals. Arab teachers and administrators wanted their students to learn more about their oppression and become more assertive in their dealings with Israel, while Jews were more interested in breaking down stereotypes and changing other cultural values.
- Student participants often gave the encounters high marks not because of their political impact but because they got out of school, met people of the opposite gender, and had fun (most of them were, after all, between thirteen and seventeen years old).
- Language itself was often an issue. Very few Jews speak Arabic, while most Arabs speak some Hebrew, and some speak it quite well. However, many Arabs resented the fact that they had to use the oppressor's language.
- Rarely did the two sides reach the same conclusion about what the future should hold, especially regarding a Palestinian state.

Overall, Abu-Nimer reaches many of the same conclusions found in the general literature on conflict resolution. These kinds of programs can and sometimes do have a major impact on the people who participate in them, something I can attest to from my own work with recent Palestinian university graduates. However, there is no guarantee that they will 'work,' especially if, for instance, the facilitators are poorly trained or running the encounters because they can't find a more lucrative job.

Finally and perhaps most important, the impact of even the most successful programs diminishes the further one moves 'out' from the experiences of the individuals involved and toward the 'real world' of day-to-day politics. As noted in chapter 4, it may well be that 'people to people' workshops can lead to lasting political change. However, it always takes a long time, usually measured in years if not decades, and it probably requires even more widespread and better publicized efforts than are found in the Middle East today.

In short, the full accomplishments of programs like Neve Shalom/ Wahat al-Salam may not be seen until the generation of young people who have passed through their encounters reach positions of influence. And there probably are still more people in both communities who reject the very idea of peace and are willing to demonstrate that rejection violently than all the reconciliation groups combined have been able to reach.

A BALANCE SHEET

The bulk of this book was written between April 1999 and September 2000. It was thrown off course a number of times by unexpected shifts in the evolution of each of the five cases in part 2. None had more twists and turns than the Israeli-Palestinian peace process. As I was finishing the manuscript, the second intifada broke out, leading many pundits to despair of the peace process.

However, as with South Africa and Northern Ireland, it is important to cast our net back further historically in drawing up a balance sheet of what has – and has not been – accomplished. Laura Zittrain Eisenberg and Neil Caplan (1998) do so in their book on Arab-Israeli negotiations and focus on five main impediments that have stalled peace talks over the years:

- Zionist/Israeli failure to appreciate the legitimacy of Palestinian-Arab national sentiment and aspirations
- Arab failure to recognize the legitimacy of Jewish-Zionist national

sentiments and aspirations
- third-party pursuit of selfish interest and machinations that undermined chances for Zionist-Arab reconciliation
- the lack of direct contact and resulting misunderstandings between Arabs and Zionists/Israelis
- the persistence of passionately held but genuinely irreconcilable national goals (Eisenberg and Caplan, 1998:17)

If we take the last quarter century as a whole, tremendous progress has been made on all five of those fronts. There is now much that is routine and regular about Palestinian-Israeli relations. Important issues do remain unresolved, including the borders and nature of a Palestinian state, the status of Jerusalem, water rights, and the return of Palestinian refugees. However, the agreements and contacts discussed above have dramatically reduced the number and intensity of what they call 'passionately held but genuinely irreconcilable national goals' in their final impediment to peace.

The situation in the region could, of course, continue to deteriorate. In contrast, the Netanyahu years show that while the progress may not be wholly irreversible, it is hard to imagine a return to the days when Israel could or would try to brutally put down an uprising like the Intifada or the PLO could or would try to launch massive waves of attacks on Jewish targets around the world.

Or, as Eisenberg and Caplan put it in starting their book:

There has been something surreal about Arab-Israeli negotiations in the 1990s. ... It is unclear which is more stunning: that first public handshake in September 1993 ... on the White House lawn – or the rapidity with which Israeli-PLO meetings have become routine. We have become accustomed to the juxtaposition of two contradictory scenes: regular meetings between Arab and Israeli leaders, and continuing confrontations among the protagonists on the ground. (Eisenberg and Caplan, 1998:1)

THEORETICAL PERSPECTIVES

The Israeli/Palestinian example draws our attention to eight general implications. As befits an intermediary case, some help us understand why progress has been made; others shed light on the obstacles to peace.

1. There is no question that the changing nature of the international system brought on by the end of the Cold War and the Gulf crisis of 1990–91 made the peace process much easier. It may well have made it

possible. As we saw in the first half of the chapter, the superpower rivalry directly and indirectly magnified the tensions between Palestinians and Jews. The changes of the late 1980s and early 1990s made it harder for the Palestinians to maintain a hard line and also made it harder for countries like the United States and the members of the European Union to play a more constructive role.

2. That said, this case drives home a more pessimistic but no less vital conclusion. The international institutions cannot do much to help end a conflict if one of the five permanent members of the Security Council believes it has a vested interest in the outcome. For good or ill, the United States has consistently used its veto to stand in the way of major international involvement on issues involving Israel.

3. Even more than Northern Ireland, this case shows us the range of ways third parties can help. It took neutral outsiders to begin most of the informal citizen-to-citizen programs in the 1970s and 1980s. More important, it is hard to imagine how the Israelis and PLO could have even begun to talk to each other without the help of an outsider. And, it is highly unlikely that an American or someone from another country that had taken a strong stand on Middle Eastern issues could have done what the Norwegian team did. However, it has increasingly become clear since Oslo that only a third party with the power and prestige of the United States can do much to bring the two sides to close the gaps that separate them today. Indeed, almost every breakdown in talks has been accompanied by a plea from both the Israelis and Palestinians for Dennis Ross or some other diplomat to return to the region with new proposals.

4. Despite the reservations raised by Oslo's critics or in the research by scholars like Abu-Nimer, there is also no doubt that track-two and citizen-based efforts have made a major difference. The Oslo track did not appear out of thin air. Progressive Israelis and moderate PLO leaders had been meeting informally for years. In her powerful insider account of the Oslo process, Jane Corbin (1994) documents how the negotiators came to better understand and sometimes even like each other despite their political and cultural differences.

5. This is also a classic example of how important a hurting stalemate can be. Statements made by Arafat and Rabin in the early 1990s indicate a clear understanding that victory (for example, the elimination of Israel or the complete annexation of the West Bank and Gaza) was not possible. That realization certainly led both of them and their key advisers to pursue a negotiated settlement more seriously than they had in the past.

It is also a classic example of some difficulties with the concept. It took the Intifada and the end of the Cold War before mainstream leaders on both sides realized there was little chance of winning even though, objectively speaking, a mutually hurting stalemate probably existed as soon as Israel won the 1967 war. Intellectually and politically, the idea of a hurting stalemate gives us few guidelines for determining when and how the shift toward the negotiating table will actually occur.

6. Domestic politics is also vital in this – as in most – cases of conflict resolution. That is easiest to see in Israel, where the election of Labor in 1992, Likud in 1996, and Labor again in 1999 marked major turning points in the peace process. Palestinian critics are quick to point out that the two parties share many commitments and concerns. Nonetheless, there is no question that in recent years Labor has been much more flexible in its dealings with the Palestinians.

Palestinian politics is somewhat harder to fathom from the outside. Still, there have been two important dynamics here. First is the fact that the PLO has never been in total agreement about the best policy to pursue and Arafat has always had to balance his own relatively pragmatic goals against the more radical preferences of some of his colleagues, not to mention Palestinians in other organizations. Second, Arafat is old and not in particularly good health, which may have led him and his closest advisers to want to strike a deal that his successor would have a harder time getting accepted by the broader Palestinian community.

7. As David Lieberthal (1999) has argued, there is less tying Israelis to Palestinians than there is Whites to Blacks in South Africa. In South Africa, Blacks and Whites are almost completely dependent on each other economically. That is much less true in Israel, where, if anything, Israel relies less on Palestinian labor than it did a decade ago. The two communities will have to share certain resources, especially water, and find ways of sharing parts of the entire region, since Jews live in the Occupied Territories and Arabs in pre-1967 Israel. However, unlike South Africa, there are still precious few Arabs in key positions in Israeli corporations or even on its athletic teams.

That lack of integration may also contribute to the size of the 'rejectionist' groups in both communities. To be sure, organizations like Hamas and Hezbollah use violence more often than their Israeli counterparts. Nonetheless, it may well be the case that the Likud supporter, the settlers, and others who have profound objections to the peace process make up a larger proportion of the Israeli population.

8. Of the five examples covered in part 2, this case best illustrates the point that the creation of reconciliation and stable peace always takes time. Given the history of the region from the time that the first Zionists arrived, it is hardly surprising that the negotiators did not solve all their problems in a single agreement.

SELECT BIBLIOGRAPHY

Abu-Nimer, Mohammed. *Dialogue, Conflict Resolution, and Change: Arab-Jewish Encounters in Israel*. Albany: SUNY Press, 1999.

Ciment, James. *Palestine/Israel: The Long Conflict*. New York: Facts on File, 1997.

Corbin, Jane. *The Norway Channel*. New York: Atlantic Monthly Press, 1994.

Emmett, Ayala. *Our Sisters' Promised Land: Women, Politics, and Israeli-Palestinian Coexistence*. Ann Arbor: University of Michigan Press, 1996.

Feldman, Shai, and Abdeullah Toukan. *Bridging the Gap: A Future Security Architecture for the Middle East*. Lanham, MD: Rowman and Littlefield, 1997.

Gerner, Deborah. *One Land, Two Peoples*. Boulder, CO: Westview, 1994.

Guyatt, Nicholas. *The Absence of Peace: Understanding the Israeli-Palestinian Conflict*. London: Zed Books, 1998.

Hiro, Dilip. *Sharing the Promised Land: A Tale of Israelis and Palestinians*. New York: Olive Branch Books, 1999.

Lieberthal, David. 'Post-Handshake Politics: Israel/Palestine and South Africa Compared.' *Middle East Policy* 6, no. 3 (1999): 131–40.

Peters, Joel. *Pathways to Peace*. London: Royal Institute for International Affairs and the European Commission, 1996.

Rabinovich, Itamar. *Waging Peace: Israel and the Arabs at the End of the Century*. New York: Farrar, Strauss and Giroux, 1999.

Rosenwasser, Penny. *Voices from the Promised Land: Palestinian and Israeli Peace Activists Speak Their Mind*. Willimantic, CT: Curbstone, 1992.

Said, Edward. *Peace and Its Discontents*. New York: Vintage, 1996.

Shipler, David. *Arab and Jew: Wounded Spirits in a Promised Land*. New York: Random House, 1986.

Shlaim, Avi. *The Iron Wall*. New York: W. W. Norton, 2000.

9

BOSNIA

Why should I be a minority in your republic when you can be a minority in mine?

– Anonymous

I visited Yugoslavia as a high school exchange student in the mid-1960s. For someone who had lived his entire life under the cloud of the Cold War, Yugoslavia came as a surprise. The police and party did not seem to intrude much in people's lives. Everyone seemed to get along, even when they were discussing politics. A decade later, the French new left activists I was studying looked to Yugoslavia's self-managed market socialism as an alternative to the rigid, planned economy of Soviet-style communism.

Today, all that is history. Weakening economic performance, growing ethnic tensions, the death of Marshal Josip Tito, and the collapse of communism culminated in the splintering of Yugoslavia in the 1990s. Unlike the Soviet Union and Czechoslovakia, which split up relatively smoothly (Bunce, 1999), Yugoslavia imploded. Brutal wars killed hundreds of thousands of people, turned millions more into refugees, and introduced a new form of human rights violation into the international political lexicon – ethnic cleansing. Ethnic hatreds encapsulated in the quotation that begins this chapter split Yugoslavia into five new countries, and there may well soon be a sixth and even a seventh, if Kosovo and Montenegro gain their independence.

We cannot cover the entire Yugoslavian case in a chapter of this length. I will therefore focus on Bosnia, both because the fighting there was the most intense and because it lends itself better to general conclusions about conflict resolution than the wars in Croatia or Kosovo do.

The Bosnian case is also quite different from the first three we considered. We could realistically argue that dramatic progress has been made in South Africa, Northern Ireland, and Israel-Palestine.

That is not the case in Bosnia. To be sure, there has been next to no bloodshed since the Dayton Agreement was signed in November 1995.

However, there is at best a tense, armed standoff, and fighting could break out again at any time. Perhaps even more important for the long run, next to nothing has been done to bring the Muslim, Croatian, and Serbian communities together, while efforts to rebuild the Bosnian social and economic infrastructure have, so far at least, failed.

Therefore, we face a very different intellectual challenge here. While we will explore how and why the three parties agreed to the Dayton Agreement, our main focus will be on the failures not the successes of the 1990s.

The Bosnian case does not reflect abject failure. Stopping the fighting was by no means a trivial accomplishment. And albeit belatedly, the willingness of the international community to intervene with force to engage in peace imposition and, after Dayton, peacemaking, marked an important new direction in international relations. Indeed, it was adopted even more forcefully in 1999 when NATO launched an air attack on Serbia to stop ethnic cleansing in Kosovo. Nonetheless, on balance the Bosnian case forces us to consider why it is that international conflict resolution is so difficult to achieve.

THEORETICAL FOCUS

As a result, we will be focusing on the 'dangerous' aspects of the factors raised by theorists who have written on the new approaches to conflict resolution along with key themes from mainstream analyses of international relations (Rose, 2000). They include:

- how the changes of the post-Cold War world helped cause the conflict, initially delayed the international response, and finally made Dayton possible
- the difficulty of finding effective third parties
- the way the image of the enemy and other psychological factors can exacerbate a conflict
- how political leaders and domestic politics in general can intensify a dispute
- getting peace imposition and the use of force in conflict resolution onto the global political agenda
- the importance of patience while understanding that lasting, peaceful change in circumstances such as these cannot come quickly

THE COLLAPSE OF YUGOSLAVIA

This chapter requires more attention to the causes and nature of the conflict than the ones on South Africa, the Middle East, Northern Ireland, or Iraq. That is the case in part because the conflict itself is so complex and in part because there are so many critical misconceptions in popular accounts of it.

What Was Yugoslavia?

Yugoslavia was the least successful of the eastern and central European states created after World War I. It brought together people from a dozen ethnic groups, almost all of whom were ethnically Slavs (Yugoslavia literally means land of the southern Slavs) but who shared little else. True, most spoke a version of Serbo-Croatian and had no more trouble understanding each other than people in the United States and Canada do.

Where Stereotypes Come From

Throughout the book, I have stressed the way stereotypes and other aspects of the image of the enemy hinder effective conflict resolution.

Here, we need to see another aspect of the same problem – how the outside world can misread developments in a region because of misleading stereotypes, which in this case, can be largely attributed to a single author and a single book.

In the late 1930s, the British novelist and travel writer Rebecca West paid three brief visits to Yugoslavia. The country already was in deep trouble as a result of its own divisions and the looming threat of a second world war. Driven by a fear that her left-wing friends were not prepared to stand up to Hitler, West's account of Yugoslavia undoubtedly exaggerated the degree both of tensions within the Yugoslavia of her day and of the historic hatreds between its ethnic groups.

But, because *Black Lamb and Grey Falcon* was the most widely read and respected book on Yugoslavia for decades, her sense of a country riven by centuries-old vendettas has colored much of academic and journalistic coverage of the region ever since.

Table 9.1 Yugoslavia's ethnic groups: 1991

Republic or autonomous region	Total population (thousands)	Main ethnic group (percentage)	Significant minorities (percentage)
Bosnia-Herzegovina	4,155	Muslims (43.7)	Serbs (31.4) Croats (17.5)
Croatia	4,437	Croats (78.1)	Serbs (12.2)
Kosovo (autonomous region)	1,760	Albanians (90.0)	Serbs (10.0)
Macedonia	1,954	Macedonians (64.6)	Albanians (21.0)
Montenegro	604	Montenegrans (61.8)	Muslims (14.6) Serbs (9.3) Albanians (6.6)
Serbia proper	5,574	Serbs (87.3)	Others[a] (12.7)
Slovenia	1,871	Slovenes (87.6)	Croats (2.7) Serbs (2.4)
Vojvodina (autonomous region)	1,977	Serbs (57.2)	Hungarians (16.9) Croats (4.8)

[a] The 1991 census did not provide further breakdowns within Serbia proper (i.e., other than the two autonomous regions) other than for this generic category of others plus the 2.5 percent who called themselves Yugoslavians.

Source: 1991 census, adapted from Susan Woodward, *Balkan Tragedy: Chaos and Dissolution after the Cold War* (Washington, D.C.: Brookings, 1995), 33–35, and Branka Magas, *The Destruction of Yugoslavia: Tracking the Breakup 1980–92* (London: Verso, 1993), 191.

But, otherwise, Yugoslavia was an ethnic hodgepodge. As constituted in 1991, it consisted of six republics, of which Serbia also had two autonomous regions. (See table 9.1.) None were homogeneous. In fact, most people lived quite close to and interacted with fellow Yugoslavs from other ethnic groups on a regular basis.

The Serbs were the largest group. They made up, of course, the majority in Serbia (though not Kosovo), and there were also significant Serbian minorities in Bosnia and Croatia. Croatians were the second largest group. Most of them lived in 'their' republic, but there was also a substantial Croatian community in Bosnia. Serbs are Orthodox

Christians and Croats Roman Catholics. Serbs use the Cyrillic alphabet, Croats the Latin one. But, their languages are so similar that during the rough economic times of the 1980s, the main party newspaper published one page in Cyrillic and the next one in Latin script.

The other ethnic groups are noticeably smaller. Almost half of Bosnia's population consists of Muslims, Slavs whose ancestors converted to Islam under the Ottomans. Montenegrans are virtually indistinguishable from Serbs. Slovenes in the northwest were most Western in their orientation, since they shared lengthy borders with Italy and Austria. The Macedonian language is closer to Bulgarian than Serbo-Croatian, but they have no trouble understanding either Serbs or Croats. The only major non-Slavic groups in the former Yugoslavia were the Albanians, who speak a completely different language and made up close to 90 percent of the population of Kosovo, and ethnic Hungarians in the autonomous region of Vojvodina. (The tennis star, Monica Seles, is a Hungarian from Vojvodina.)

There were also important regional economic differences. The republics closer to the West (Slovenia and Croatia) were better off, and the gap between them and the poorer republics got wider in the 1960s and 1970s.

Origins of the Yugoslavian Conflict

The origins of the conflict in Yugoslavia stretch all the way back at least to 1389 and the battle of Kosovo Pole in modern-day Kosovo (Judeh, 1997; Malcolm, 1994). It paved the way for Ottoman (Turkish) control of much of the Balkans and is often portrayed as the first phase of the conflict between the mostly Muslim Albanians and the Serbs. In fact, the Kosovars were then Christians, and most fought with the Serbs against the invaders. Moreover, there were Serbs and Kosovars on the Ottoman side as well. With time, however, most Albanians converted to Islam, as did a significant number of Serbs and other Slavs, becoming what we now call Bosnian Muslims.

Over the centuries, there were massive population shifts, usually as the result of the wars that most frequently pitted the Ottomans against the Austro-Hungarian empire and, in the nineteenth century, southern Slavs trying to free themselves from foreign rule. Thus, the borders of places like Kosovo or Bosnia changed frequently. Relatively few Serbs lived in Kosovo until the late nineteenth century. Tens of thousands of Serbs were moved to the Krajina region of today's Croatia in the late seventeenth century to form a human buffer against the Ottomans (the word *Krajina* literally means frontier or border and is a linguistic cousin of Ukraine, which has similar geopolitical roots).

Until the nineteenth century, ethnicity was a fluid notion in most of the Balkans – as it was in most of the world. In other words, the kind of emotionally driven conflict we see today only dates to the late 1800s, when the Austro-Hungarian and Ottoman empires began to unravel and the various groups sought independence.

At that point, ethnicity and nationalism did produce the widespread violence that marked most of the twentieth century. World War I began as a result of the assassination of the Austrian Archduke Ferdinand by a Bosnian Serb in Sarajevo. The first Yugoslavian state never found a way to overcome the tensions among the major ethnic groups, especially Slovenian and Croatian fears that the leadership was really trying to create a greater Serbia rather than a truly multiethnic regime. There was major fighting in Yugoslavia during World War II, including the killing of hundreds of thousands of Serbs by the Croatian Ustase government that collaborated with the Nazis.

Nonetheless, there were periods of relative calm when ethnic tensions all but disappeared below the surface of political life. The most recent one occurred from the end of World War II until the death of Tito. Tito (1892–1980, born Josip Broz) led the communist party (later the League of Yugoslavian Communists – LCY) and its resistance against the Nazis, the Ustase, and other collaborators. Its partisans were the first major Yugoslavian political movement that organized among all the major ethnic groups and the first communist party to come to power in Eastern Europe in 1944, doing so without the active support of the Soviet Union.

For reasons too complicated to go into here, Stalin threw Yugoslavia out of the world communist movement in 1948. At that point, Tito and his colleagues had to chart a new course. They ended up creating a more open and decentralized regime than those in the rest of Eastern Europe. There was limited freedom of expression. Most economic and other decisions were made at the republic level, while committees of workers ran most factories and other enterprises. Atop it all sat Tito, who retained his nationwide support until his death.

I do not want to paint too idyllic a picture of Tito's rule. Manifestations of dissent in general and religious or ethnic feelings in particular were usually repressed. Thus, Bosnia's Alija Izetbegovic (1925–), who began his career as a writer on Islam, spent time in prison for his religious beliefs and activities. Similarly, Franjo Tudjman (1924–99) was sent to jail following the brief outbreak of nationalism during the 1974 'Croatian Spring.'

Table 9.2 The breakup of Yugoslavia and the war in Bosnia

Date	Event
1914–18	World War I
1919	Creation of first Yugoslavia
1939–45	World War II, occupation of Yugoslavia, victory of Tito's partisans
1949	Break with Soviet Union
1974	Croatian Spring
1980	Death of Tito
	Onset of economic decline
1987	Milosevic takes over Serbian LCY
1989	Collapse of communism in Eastern Europe
1991	Independence of Slovenia and Croatia
1992	Beginning of the Bosnian war
1993	Fighting between Muslims and Croats
	UN declares safe areas, arms embargo, NATO air strikes
1994	Sarajevo marketplace massacre
	Muslim-Croat federation created
	First NATO air strikes
1995	Croatian counteroffensive
	Mladic and Karadzic indicted as war criminals
	Dayton Agreement signed
1998	Ethnic cleansing begins in Kosovo
1999	Failure of Rambouillet negotiations
	Kosovo war

The Collapse of Yugoslavia

After Tito died, however, the situation deteriorated. There was no single person with a national appeal to replace him, so power was decentralized even further to a system of rotating leadership that left the central government all but impotent. Meanwhile, the bottom fell out of the economy, and the ensuing crisis hit people in the poorer republics particularly hard. Finally, as the 1980s wore on, it was becoming clear that communist regimes throughout Eastern Europe were weakening.

Here is where the stereotypes that grow out of West's and similar books are most misleading. Yugoslavia had had its share of ethnically based tensions. It was not, however, a political powder keg ready to explode the minute some spark touched it off.

Rather, in the new political world of the late 1980s, Yugoslav politicians had to curry public support to stay in office. Most chose to play the ethnic card in order to do so, thereby driving wedges between the country's main groups. In other words, the tensions that led to its collapse were manufactured by the politicians who rose to power, especially in Serbia and Croatia (Bunce, 1999). As Silber and Little put it in the book that accompanied their award-winning BBC documentary series:

> Yugoslavia did not die a natural death. Rather, it was deliberately and systematically killed off by men who had nothing to gain and everything to lose from a peaceful transition from state socialism and one-party rule to free-market democracy. (Silber and Little, 1997:25)

The most prominent and notorious example is Slobodan Milosevic (1941–). Milosevic did not start out as a nationalist and some observers still doubt his ethnic credentials, since he is widely seen as having 'sold out' the Serbs in Croatia and Bosnia. He began his political career as a loyal communist and by the mid-1980s had quietly risen to the top of the party hierarchy in Serbia. During the second half of the 1980s, he gradually reached the conclusion that he could best hold on to power by making nationalist appeals to Serbs both in Serbia itself and outside the republic. Thus, Milosevic burst onto the scene when he gave a speech to a group of Kosovan Serb demonstrators in which he shouted 'no one should dare to beat you' (Silber and Little, 1996:37). At that point, he began to use Serbian nationalism as a springboard to take control of the whole country and become the next Tito. Once that became impossible in 1990–91, he shifted gears and opted to try for a greater Serbia instead.

Kosovo was the key to his plans. Ever since the battle of Kosovo Pole, it has been central to Serbian tradition and identity, even though very few Serbs have actually lived there in recent centuries. As is often the case with members of an ethnic minority living outside its 'homeland,' Serbs in Kosovo were particularly receptive to nationalist demands and propaganda. For the next decade, the Serbian government removed any sense of autonomy enjoyed by the Albanian minority, including the use of their language in schools. They used the growing frustration of Kosovan Serbs to appeal, as well, to Serbian minorities in Croatia and Bosnia, who were also more nationalistic than their counterparts in Serbia itself.

In the other republics, nationalist sentiment built up largely outside of the LCY. And, as central rule continued to weaken, more and more opportunities to express that dissatisfaction were provided, culminating in free elections in all the republics by 1991. Noncommunist nationalists won in four of them, including Tudjman in Croatia and Izetbegovic in Bosnia-Herzegovina.

Meanwhile, during the first half of 1991, Slovenia and Croatia gradually created their own armies as the key step toward leaving Yugoslavia. Weeks of fruitless negotiations between them and what was left of the central government (now for all intents and purposes controlled by Milosevic) got nowhere. A late attempt by U.S. secretary of state James Baker to stop the descent into war also accomplished little. Finally, on 25 June 1991, both republics declared their independence.

Slobodan Milosevic

Slobodan Milosevic has been the central character in all the former Yugoslavia's wars in the 1990s. Since he is so often reviled in the Western press, it is worth presenting some basic information about him.

Born in 1941, Milosevic had a difficult childhood. His father committed suicide when young Slobodan was in elementary school; his mother took her own life a decade later. Though an excellent student, Milosevic made few friends; some claim his only friend was his future wife, Marjana Markovic, who became a prominent academic and politician in her own right.

Trained as a lawyer, Milosevic first made his mark as the head of Belgrade's leading bank in the late 1970s and early 1980s. In 1986 he became leader of the Serbian LCY, and in 1989 ousted his mentor to become president of Serbia, from which he later assumed the presidency of the FRY (Federal Republic of Yugoslavia).

Many outside observers place most of the blame for the former Yugoslavia's four wars in the 1990s on Milosevic, though he was also a key negotiator of the Dayton Agreement. He was indicted as a war criminal during the Kosovo war, but many thought he should have been indicated earlier for, at the very least, fomenting the nationalism that led to the wars in Croatia and Bosnia. Milosevic was defeated in presidential elections in late 2000.

Slovenia had little difficulty gaining its independence. Milosevic apparently decided he would have to go to war with Croatia to keep Slovenia in Yugoslavia, since his troops would have to cross the former in order to get to the latter. He decided that war with Slovenia was not worth the risk, because he and his colleagues had concluded that

Yugoslavia, as such, could not be held together and because there were virtually no Serbs in Slovenia.

Croatia, however, was a different matter. Fully an eighth of its population consisted of Serbs, which made it much more important to the authorities in Belgrade. Many of the Serbs lived in the Krajina region, which did not have a common border with Serbia. Not surprisingly, as support for independence grew in Croatia, Croatian Serbs grew worried and restive. Croatian Serbian police officers, for instance, refused to wear their new uniforms, because they had an insignia with the red and white checked symbol that the wartime Ustase government that had killed so many Serbs had used.

Militant groups gained control of most of the Serbian enclaves in Croatia and began arming themselves. Intense fighting broke out between the Croatian government and the Croatian Serbs in August. The Yugoslav army intervened. It professed neutrality, but in fact aided the Serbs. Hundreds and thousands of people who lived in the 'other sides' areas were killed or forced to move in the first instance of ethnic cleansing in the former Yugoslavia. Before the war, 295,000 Croats lived in the Krajina; afterward, there were barely 3,500. A cease-fire was declared in January. By that time, Croatia had its independence, but it had lost about a third of its territory (which it would regain at the end of the Bosnian war).

As terrible as the fighting was in Croatia, it would be Bosnia that riveted the world's attention on the former Yugoslavia. The Serbs and Croatians both regarded Bosnia-Herzegovina as an artificial entity, because it included substantial minorities of their people and because they thought of the Muslims as little more than Serbs or Croats who had converted to Islam.

In 1992 the Bosnian government held a referendum on independence, which the European Union required before it would grant diplomatic recognition. Virtually all the Muslims and Croats voted for independence; the Serbs boycotted the vote. That outcome served as a pretext for the Yugoslavian National Army (JNA) and the local Serbs to start fighting on behalf of a Serbian 'entity' (now the *Republika Srpska*) led by the psychiatrist, Radovan Karadzic. Milosevic soon agreed to withdraw JNA troops, but the best estimate is that 80,000 of them simply changed uniforms and took up arms with the entity's army led by Ratko Mladic, who had also played a major role in the uprising by the Krajina Serbs.

Bosnian president Izetbegovic asked the UN for peacekeeping troops. But, consistent with UN policies at the time, it refused to deploy them until a cease-fire was in place. It would take months (see below) before the UN reached the conclusion that it had to abandon that policy and send in troops anyway. By that time, tens of thousands were dead, and hundreds of thousands had been forced to flee.

Hatred and Victimization

Wars like the ones in the former Yugoslavia are so fierce in large part because of the emotions ethnicity, language, race, or religion evoke. Those emotions are particularly intense and conflict resolution most difficult when people reach the level of abject hatred toward and/or feel victimized by another group. Though no single statement from any one person can show that, consider this all too typical comment by a young Albanian living in Kosovo:

> You don't know what it is to kill with a hammer, with nails, with clubs, do you? Do you know why I don't like to drink plum brandy, why I drink beer always? Because the Chetniks used to do their killing after drinking plum brandy. Do you know what it is to throw a child in the air and catch it on a knife in front of its mother? To be tied to a burning log? To have your ass split with an ax? So you beg the Serbs, beg them, to shoot you in the head and they don't?
>
> And they go to church after. They go to their goddamn church. I have no words. There are things that are beyond evil, that you just can't speak about.

He went on shouting. Ismail was only twenty-six; he had no personal knowledge of the events he described. Rats infest his house, he told me. The Serbs were to blame. (Kaplan, 1993 : xvii)

Few regions of Bosnia were ethnically homogeneous. That prompted the Serbian forces to force Croatians and Muslims out of the areas they controlled in ethnic cleansing that surpassed the horrors in Croatia. The Serbs systematically killed men who might have served in the Bosnian army, built concentration camps, and raped thousands of Bosnian women – so many that rape is now considered a war crime. In all, about 250,000 people were killed and perhaps 2,000,000 became refugees in other parts of the former Yugoslavia and the rest of Europe.

In April 1992 the Serbs also laid siege to Sarajevo, cutting it off from the outside world. Their troops regularly fired on the town, turning its main street into 'sniper's alley,' which residents walked on at their peril. For three years, Sarajevo had no heat and very little electricity. As we will see shortly, the UN was able to get some supplies into the city, but Sarajevans teetered on the brink of survival, especially during the harsh winters. In one particularly symbolic and tragic act, the authorities had to turn the stadium in which the opening ceremonies for the 1984 Winter Olympics were held into a cemetery. In all, 10,615 people (including 1,601 children) were killed and another 50,000 wounded.

The fighting in Bosnia convinced much of the rest of the world that the Serbs were primarily to blame for the bloodshed. Atrocities were committed on all sides, something often overlooked by the Serbs' critics (Woodward, 1995; Judeh, 1997). Nonetheless, the Serbs both committed the lion's share of the human rights violations and did so in an open and often arrogant campaign to promote what they saw as Greater Serbia.

FAILED ATTEMPTS AT CONFLICT RESOLUTION

The international community reacted with shock and then outrage. What's more, the fighting occurred at a time when the talk of a new world order and international cooperation were at their peak.

However, international involvement did not come quickly or easily. The United States, in particular, was slow to respond. The Bush administration was too preoccupied with the lingering impact of the crisis in the Persian Gulf, the collapse of the Soviet Union, and its own reelection campaign to be willing to focus much of its attention on the situation in Yugoslavia.

Instead, the initial impetus for intervention came from the European Union. In 1991 and 1992, the EU had taken two major steps in its own evolution. The Single European Act, which created a truly integrated market had gone into effect, and the member states had signed the Treaty of Maastricht, which called for the establishment of a Common Foreign and Security Policy. What's more, the first serious warfare in Europe since 1945 was occurring along the border of one longstanding (Italy) and one new (Austria) EU country, while refugees from Yugoslavia were flocking to all fifteen member states.

Therefore, even while Yugoslavia was breaking up, the EU named former British foreign secretary Lord Peter Carrington to try to broker a peace plan. Carrington had left active politics during the war between Britain and Argentina over the Falkland Islands and was in semiretirement as chair of Christie's auction house. He took the Yugoslavian job only after he had been assured by EU officials that it could be done in two months. Quickly, he realized that such a timetable was hopelessly optimistic. Within six weeks, his plan for a more decentralized Yugoslavia in which each republic took essentially all the sovereignty it wanted failed. Serbia and Croatia rejected it, because they did not want to give up their designs on Bosnia.

Once the fighting began in Croatia, the United Nations entered the dispute when Secretary-General Javier Perez de Cuellar appointed former U.S. secretary of state Cyrus Vance as his special envoy. The UN and EU teams worked together for the next three years, but without much success. Their difficulties were magnified by the relative indifference of the United States and what many believe to be a premature recognition of Croatian independence by Germany against the wishes of most of its supposed European partners.

Finally, once the Serbs had made almost all the gains they could have expected on the battlefield, Vance was able to get the parties to agree to a cease-fire and a deployment of UN peacekeepers. On 14 February 1992 the Security Council passed Resolution 743, which authorized the second largest mission in UN history with a mandate covering all of the former Yugoslavia other than Slovenia. In a move that was seen as preposterous at the time (and proved even more absurd later on), the UN commander established his headquarters in Sarajevo.

UNPROFOR (United Nations Protection Force) would remain in place until the Dayton Agreement went into effect on 20 December 1995. At its peak, it would number nearly 40,000 soldiers from thirty-nine countries (United Nations, 1996). It was not, however, generally considered to be a success. Indeed, along with the mission in Somalia, UNPROFOR's difficulties set in motion the heightened criticisms of the UN's ability to undertake peacebuilding and peacekeeping missions that limited its impact.

As David Rieff (1995) in particular has argued, it could not or would not:

- stop the fighting from spreading to Bosnia
- guarantee the flow of humanitarian relief
- intervene to help the Muslims, Croatians, and other victims of Serbian crimes against humanity
- arrest war criminals after the ICTY (International Criminal Tribunal for Yugoslavia) was formed and handed down its initial indictments

UNPROFOR did little to heal the political wounds anywhere in the former Yugoslavia. In other words, it was a traditional peacekeeping operation whose principal mission was to see to it that an existing cease-fire held. But, as the dozens of cease-fires that were first negotiated and then broken between 1991 and 1995 attest, the challenge facing the international community was not one of keeping the peace but creating it in the first place.

For good or ill, neither the EU nor the UN was well prepared for such a task. Put simply, they lacked the troops and other human resources, financial backing, and political will of their members that any peace-making effort would require. That would require participation and probably leadership from the United States, which was not an option until late 1994.

The United Nations

The UN's peacekeeping role expanded dramatically during the first few years after the end of the Cold War. In 1994 it had 78,000 troops and civilians in the field at a cost of nearly $4 billion. Problems in Somalia as well as Bosnia and the reluctance of the United States and others to pay for UN operations have led to a sharp reduction in the size and scope of its missions. In mid-1999 there were only 12,360 peacekeepers working in sixteen operations that cost the UN under $1 billion even though new missions were deployed to East Timor, Sierra Leone, and the Democratic Republic of Congo. In Kosovo, the UN is responsible for all civil administration, while the NATO-led KFOR force's job will be to maintain security.

Most observers are also now convinced that, at this point, the UN cannot effectively mount the kind of massive military operations we saw in Iraq, Bosnia, Kosovo, and Sierra Leone. Those seem to work best when run by a regional security organization with more troops and firepower, which means NATO and the United States in European conflicts. Such bodies, too, find it easier to avoid the infighting and lack of coordination that have plagued UN operations in recent years.

The UN, by contrast, is better suited to (re)building civil society after the fighting has stopped, during which it can draw on its own development organizations and its links with nongovernmental organizations.

The EU-UN diplomatic initiative continued, though by this time another former British foreign secretary, Lord David Owen, had replaced Carrington. The envoys spent two years trying to obtain support for a plan that would create ten cantons, some of which would be controlled by Muslims and the rest by Croats and Serbs. Many in the West rejected the various versions of their proposal, because it would essentially mean the end of Bosnia. More important, it would legitimize the ethnic cleansing by, in essence, making the new homogeneous regions permanent and giving the Bosnian Serbs control of over half the territory.

All the parties did sign one version of the Vance–Owen plan on 30

January 1993. It would have kept little of what had been the republic of Bosnia-Herzegovina intact, but it might at least have stopped the fighting and would have led to the deployment of at least another 60,000 soldiers. However, on 5 May the Bosnian Serb parliament rejected the agreement that President Karadzic had signed. Meanwhile, as Bosnian Croats began institutionalizing their own republic, Herzeg-Bosna, fighting between the two communities intensified. It quickly became clear that the international community lacked the political will to go any farther in forcing the parties to an agreement.

By the middle of 1994, little or no progress had been made. At that point, the United States became more involved. The Clinton administration realized that the Europeans and the UN were not going to be able to stop the fighting, which led the president to appoint Richard Holbrooke (see box) to be assistant secretary of state for European and Canadian affairs in September 1994, with Bosnia as his primary mission.

Richard Holbrooke

Richard Holbrooke was born in New York in 1941. After graduating from Brown University in 1962, he joined the United States Foreign Service and was initially posted to Vietnam. He later served on President Lyndon Johnson's staff at the Paris peace talks that eventually ended the war.

In 1970 Holbrooke left the foreign service for a lucrative career in investment banking. He came back to government service during the Carter administration, only to return to the private sector after Reagan's election.

President Clinton first appointed Holbrooke to be ambassador to Germany, promoting him to assistant secretary of state for European and Canadian affairs, with the understanding that he would make Bosnia his highest priority. After the Dayton Agreement was signed, Holbrooke resigned to become vice president of investment banking at Crédit Suisse First Boston. President Clinton subsequently appointed him to be ambassador to the United Nations. After a lengthy confirmation fight, the nomination was finally approved in fall 1999.

Holbrooke is a tough negotiator and not a conciliator like George Mitchell, who played such a vital role in Northern Ireland. Indeed, his critics charge that he is something of an intellectual bully. Whatever his personality, there is little doubt that without his skills, dedication, and tenacity, there is little chance that the Dayton Agreement could have been reached.

As a private citizen, Holbrooke had visited Sarajevo early in the war (Holbrooke, 1998). That visit and subsequent events convinced him that the international community had to force the Serbs to stop their genocidal policies as a first step toward saving a unified Bosnia.

Over the next fifteen months, Holbrooke and his colleagues used a combination of force and diplomacy to bring the Muslims, Croats, and Serbs to the bargaining table. In practice, Holbrooke did not have much of an impact until the Serbs committed yet one more atrocity. In July 1995 Mladic's forces attacked Srebrenica and the other two Muslim 'safe havens' that were surrounded by Serbs in eastern Bosnia. After Srebrenica surrendered, the Serbs killed thousands of Muslims in cold blood, and Mladic announced that he was making a gift of the town to the Serbian people. The handful of UN peacekeepers in Srebrenica could do nothing to stop the carnage. The rest of the world looked on but did not act.

The attack on Srebrenica and other atrocities committed by the Serbs that summer finally convinced President Clinton that the United States had to take the lead. He had Holbrooke put together a team of diplomats and military officers and gave them the task of ending the war.

Meanwhile, the Croatians began an offensive that, to the surprise of many, led to major battlefield gains. Within a few months, they had regained all the territory lost to the Serbs in 1991-92. Similar gains were made by the Muslim–Croat federation forces in Bosnia.

Then one more atrocity occurred. On 28 August the Serbs launched a mortar attack on an open-air market in Sarajevo that killed thirty-five people. The Serbs later tried to claim that the Muslims had fired the shell in an attempt to make the Serbs look bad.

The attack on the market enabled Holbrooke to convince his superiors that only a strong show of force would bring Milosevic, if not the Bosnian Serbs, to the table. NATO's bombing campaign began two days later in what was also NATO's first actual use of force in its forty-five-year history.

While the fighting continued, Holbrooke's team embarked on a round of shuttle diplomacy that took them to thirty-one countries in fifteen days. Over the Labor Day weekend alone, they were in Belgrade (three times), Bonn, Brussels, Geneva, Zagreb, Athens, Skopje, and Ankara. They persuaded Milosevic that he would have to lead negotiations on behalf of the Republika Srpska, whose leaders had already been indicted for war crimes. In agreeing to attend a meeting of the foreign ministers of Yugoslavia (Serbia), Bosnia, and Croatia, Milosevic de facto acknowledged that Bosnia would remain a single country with its current,

Useful Web Sites

The Balkans Page is run through PeaceNet and has some of the most graphic material on the wars in the former Yugoslavia along with extensive coverage of grassroots organizations that opposed them. `<http://www.igc.apc.org/balkans/>`.

Bosnet is one of the few sources of news on Bosnia run by Bosnians in English. `<http://www.bosnet.org>`.

One of the most comprehensive research and analysis programs on the former Yugoslavia is based at the nonpartisan United States Institute for Peace. `<http://www.usip.org/oc/BIB/bibintro.html>`.

Columbia University's School of International and Public Affairs has the most extensive site on things Yugoslavian in general. `<http://sipa.columbia.edu/REGIONAL/ECE/bosnia.html>`.

The ICTY is not only the first war crimes tribunal since World War II, but also the first ever to have its own web site. `<http://www.un.org/icty>`.

The Office of the High Representative's site is filled with information on programs to rebuild Bosnia. `<http://www.ohr.int>`.

Similarly, the Organization for Security and Cooperation in Europe site documents its efforts in postwar reconstruction. `<http://www.oscebih.org>`.

internationally recognized borders. At the Geneva foreign ministers' summit in September, the Serbs formally agreed to the continued existence of Bosnia as a country. The Muslim–Croat federation would control 51 percent of its territory and the rest would be controlled by the Serbs. NATO would send in a massive force to keep the peace and begin rebuilding the country.

Much still had to be done. There was no letup in the fighting and bombing. Sarajevo remained under siege. Sanctions were still in effect. Most important of all, the parties could not agree on how Bosnia would be governed or even who would control which territory.

Next, Holbrooke met with Milosevic and, briefly, Mladic and Karadzic. At that point, the Serbs agreed to lift the siege of Sarajevo in exchange for an end to the bombing. The Holbrooke shuttle continued, though now its most difficult task was to get the Bosnian and Croatian governments to agree to a cease-fire since they had gained back so much lost territory in the fighting. That occurred on 5 October.

For most of September and October, Holbrooke's team continued to negotiate in the Balkans. At home, they prepared for a peace conference while building support for an agreement in Washington that would involve the deployment of thousands of American troops. Such a commitment was especially difficult at the time. Congress and the president were in the midst of the great budgetary 'train wreck' that paralyzed the U.S. government for much of late 1995 and early 1996.

It is still not clear why Milosevic made so many concessions. To some degree, he seems to have tired of the more fanatical Bosnian Serbs. To some degree, too, he understood that sanctions and bombings were taking a terrible toll on the Serbian population and that his own hold on power would be threatened if the fighting continued.

That decision made possible the full peace conference, which opened at Wright-Paterson Air Force Base in Dayton, Ohio, on 9 November. The conference was cochaired by the United States and the EU. Now Holbrooke and his teams shuttled between the three buildings on the base that had been outfitted for the three governments, whose leaders were rarely willing to talk to each other.

As was the case with the negotiations leading up to the Good Friday Agreement (see chapter 7), these talks seemed to drag on and on until the United State imposed a deadline. Holbrooke and his colleagues twisted arms until the three sides agreed to what became known as the Dayton Agreement on 21 November. They retain a unified Bosnia while giving considerable autonomy to the Republika Srpska. The peace would be enforced by the 60,000-strong, NATO-led IFOR (Implementation Force, now known as SFOR, for Stabilization Force). Elections would be held and monitored by the OSCE (Organization for Security and Cooperation in Europe). A high representative of the UN would be largely responsible for civil administration, including the creation of a new police force. Though they did not figure prominently in the negotiations themselves, the agreement contained provisions for a major effort to rebuild the Bosnian economy and begin creating a civil society.

DAYTON'S UNCERTAIN TRACK RECORD

The key to the Dayton Agreement lies in the eleven annexes to the agreement that specify goals and commitments for long-term peace-building. It maintained a single Bosnia and Herzegovina that was to consist of two separate entities, the Federation, dominated by Bosnian Muslims and Croatians, and the Republika Srpska, which would be run by the Serbs. A combined presidency would run the new national institutions. Unlike most peace agreements, it did far more than just stop the fighting. It imposed a massive peacekeeping force with a mandate to work with Bosnians to rebuild virtually the entire political system and economy (European Stability Institute, 1999; Sharp, 1997).

A consensus is now developing that Dayton accomplished only one of its three most important goals. To its credit, the fighting has all but completely ended. However, most observers agree that new fighting would break out if the SFOR troops were withdrawn. And most important for our purposes here, little or no progress has been made on its social, economic, and political goals.

As the International Crisis Group put it in their report on the agreement after four years:

> Today Bosnia and Herzegovina has three *de facto* mono-ethnic entities, three separate armies, three separate police forces, and a national government that exists mostly on paper and operates at the mercy of the entities. Indicted war criminals remain at large and political power is concentrated largely in the hands of hard line nationalists determined to obstruct international efforts to advance the peace process. In many areas, local political leaders have joined forces with police and local extremists to prevent refugees from returning to their pre-war homes. The effect has been to cement war-time ethnic cleansing and maintain ethnic cleansers in power within mono-ethnic political frameworks. The few successes of Dayton – the Central Bank, a common currency, common license plates, state symbols and customs reforms – are superficial and were imposed by the international community. Indeed, the only unqualified success has been the four year absence of armed conflict. (International Crisis Group, 1999:1)

The shortcomings are well documented, for instance, in a dense seventy-page report by the International Crisis Group. Among the most worrisome are:

- There has been a failure to arrest even half of the people indicted for war crimes, including Karadzic and Mladic. This is widely seen as a failure of political will on the part of NATO and its allies, not of logistical difficulties in tracking these men down.
- The three entities are far more ethnically homogeneous than they were before the war began.
- The entities are run by hard-liners in their respective communities. Indeed, the holding of elections has largely backfired on those who wanted to build a more peaceful Bosnia, since they have solidified the control of intransigents throughout what is now a country in name only. The borders of the two entities are peculiar at best and

will not be easy to maintain.

- All three leaderships have blocked people from voting in their pre-1991 cities, towns, and villages as called for in the agreement, which contributes to what the International Conflict Group calls the victory of the ethnic cleansers. Indeed, no more than 10 percent of the refugees have been able to return to their homes.

- The economy is in shambles. In late 1999, unemployment stood at about 40 percent in the Federation and almost half in the Republika Srpska. About a third of Bosnia's GNP came from foreign donors, but there will be far less aid in the next few years. And, given the corruption and continued economic uncertainty, there is every reason to believe that it will not be replaced by private sector, foreign investment.

There have been some successes. There is now a single Bosnian license plate, which means people can drive throughout the country without risking attack because they were, for instance, Serbs in a Croatian region. However, like everything else that has 'worked,' the new license plates were imposed on the three communities by the High Commissioner. By contrast, when the three groups have had to agree, next to nothing has been accomplished. And, the High Commissioner, whose staff numbers under 800, has limited power indeed.

Dayton has not, however, been an abject disaster even for those observers who are most committed to reconciliation and peacebuilding. By one count, there were 184 nongovernmental organizations (NGOs) operating in Sarajevo alone in 1999, each of which is contributing to the reconstruction of the country physically, economically, and psychologically. There have been some efforts to bring the communities together, often building on the new institutions currently being created (for example, integrating the police forces) or on the basis of contacts that existed before the war. To cite but one example, the Canadian military and an NGO with roots in the peace movement in the United States, Conflict Resolution Catalysts (Last, 1999), created the Neighborhood Facilitators Programme (NFP). It trained international and Bosnian facilitators to help people in the Banja Luka area deal with the physical and psychological aftermath of the fighting with the longer-term goal of promoting human rights, civil society, intercommunal trust, and democracy. During its five months in existence, the NFP handled cases for over 300 clients. The American-based National Democracy Institute has worked with OSCE to train facilitators in northwest Bosnia who work with displaced Croats and Muslims, women's groups, student's associations, and the like. Most of these efforts occur within only one of the entities. There are, however, scattered reports of facilitators helping smooth relations on those rare occasions when refugees actually do return to their former homes and have to deal with neighbors – and sometimes even former friends – who took part in their personal ethnic cleansing.

THEORETICAL IMPLICATIONS

Perhaps more than any of the other case studies, the Bosnian one offers empirical support both for those who are optimistic and those who are pessimistic about the prospects for win-win conflict resolution and reconciliation. In fact, what we will see here is that the same set of empirical factors can lead to either type of outcomes. The differences lie in the way that particular factor has 'played itself out' in various phases and aspects of the conflict.

1. *Developing and sustaining political will in the new international environment.* Bosnia offers us a classic example of why it is difficult to create and maintain the political will necessary for effective conflict resolution. For a variety of reasons, ranging from media coverage to domestic politics to the weakness of international institutions, politicians are slow to make a commitment to intervene in most cases even after the human catastrophe has begun to unfold. In Bosnia, the situation was complicated by the fact that the Cold War had barely come to an end, and political leaders around the world were struggling to find their bearings. Nearly a decade later, however, there is a growing realization that the international community will have to be involved in such circumstances, as we have seen most recently in Kosovo and East Timor. Nonetheless, as those two examples also indicate, that realization does not necessarily carry with it the commitment to find the political will to act before the conflict turns violent.

2. *Third parties.* It is hard to imagine how the combatants themselves could ever have stopped the fighting let alone reached an agreement like Dayton. However, the Bosnian case also shows us that not all third parties are effective. It may well be that a conflict that has the degree of violence and hatred we saw in the former Yugoslavia needs the kind of hard-nosed and coercive diplomacy of a Richard Holbrooke rather than the tact and patience of a George Mitchell or the earlier, failed mediation in Yugoslavia itself.

3. *Images of the enemy.* The hatred expressed in the statement in the box entitled 'Hatred and Victimization' (p. 169) may be unusual and extreme. Nonetheless, in most instances of intense conflict today, the stereotypes

psychologists have labeled the image of the enemy figure prominently. One of the missing elements in this case compared to the three earlier ones is a serious attempt to overcome them. The few that have been tried have had limited success, in part because they were poorly funded. The Neighborhood Facilitators Programme discussed earlier did not even last a year, because its funding was terminated. More important, Last makes the obvious point that overcoming the image of the enemy will take a long time, given both the history of tension among Serbs, Muslims, and Croats and the horrors of the most recent war (1999:3).

4. *Domestic politics and leadership.* That growing impatience with 'Dayton' is but one example of the role domestic politics has played, mostly in hindering the end of the fighting and the reconciliation since Dayton. The three Bosnian communities are still led by hard-line nationalist politicians. Despite the efforts of the High Representative and others, few moderate political groups and none that even raise the possibility of reconciliation have emerged (though the High Commissioner has been able to keep the ultranationalistic Nikola Poplasen from serving as president of the Republika Srpska). As we saw earlier, both the United States and the leading European powers failed to respond to the crisis effectively early on, and governments on both sides of the Atlantic are under considerable pressure to reduce their commitment to Bosnian reconstruction today.

5. *Patience and the long term.* The Bosnian case study most strongly reinforces a conclusion we have found in all four chapters in part 2 so far – the need for patience in building a long-term strategy in which significant progress toward reconciliation will only come slowly. The South African, Irish, and Israeli-Palestinian cases all involved protracted negotiations and transitions under what were less devastating conditions. Therefore, it only makes sense to assume that it will take at least as long to build a civil society or stable peace in Bosnia – if one can be built at all. However, even the supportive critics whose arguments have been raised in this chapter are already frustrated by the slow pace of change just a few short years after the fighting stopped.

6. *The changing role of force and the international community.* In one key respect, Bosnia is the most controversial case in this book, because it is the only one in which the international community used military force *as a conscious part* of the conflict resolution process. Most observers who come to international conflict resolution from a background in the peace movement have trouble with even the threat, let alone the use, of violence. Nonetheless, this case offers strong evidence for the proposition that force may sometimes be required to stop a conflict. It is a more open question whether the international community can then switch

gears and do an effective job of peacebuilding once it has done so.

Despite all its shortcomings, the international community is now willing to address conflict without waiting for the declaration of a cease-fire. There is no better example of that than the changing role of NATO (Yost, 1998). Whether we can realistically hope to move toward reconciliation after imposing our will on disputants as we have tried to do in Bosnia or Kosovo is an open question. However, there is no denying the changing role Western militaries are playing in places like Bosnia. As David Last (himself a Canadian officer and trainer of peacekeepers) points out (1999), IFOR and SFOR troops have been deeply involved with the efforts to rebuild Bosnian society both on their own and in conjunction with NGOs and official development agencies.

The American military now includes peacekeeping as part of the training of all senior officers. Canada and the various Scandinavian countries do the same for all officers.

In short, proponents of cooperative problem-solving would point to Dayton as a learning experience in which the international community in all its forms was developing its strategies and tactics as it was implementing them. Thus, it should hardly be surprising that they have so far been less than wholly successful from anyone's perspective. The challenge facing us is to draw the lessons that would allow us to hasten 'positive' developments on each of these six dimensions in future conflicts.

The pessimists could point to exactly the same examples and trends in urging caution. That is the case because they are undoubtedly correct that none of these obstacles is ever easy to overcome. And, if you subscribe to theories that stress either the aggressive side of human nature or the irreconcilable nature of ethnic divisions in the Balkans and elsewhere, we may never be able to make nonviolent conflict resolution the norm rather than the exception to the rule.

It remains to be seen how effective such innovations can be. Their track record in the former Yugoslavia is mixed at best. That, however, should hardly be surprising, given both the intensity of the conflict and the newness of these techniques, many of which were invented as they were implemented.

7. *Is peace more than the absence of war?* In conclusion, it is useful to return to the distinction made between conflict management and conflict resolution in chapters 5 and 4 respectively. Clearly, the Bosnian case at best offers an example of conflict management, with true resolution barely on anyone's political horizon.

As noted above, it may be that an end to the fighting and other conflict management goals are all we can hope for in the short term, given the history of the last decade, century, and millennium. Ironically, the absence of viable programs for reconciliation and the reconstruction of Bosnia's social and economic infrastructure also put the importance of 'true' conflict resolution in sharp relief.

Along those lines, consider what Baruch Spinoza wrote more than 300 years ago:

> Peace is not an absence of war, it is a virtue, a state of mind, a disposition for benevolence, confidence, justice.

Such sentiments have motivated citizens and scholars who are interested in peace and reconciliation ever since.

Realists and other, more pessimistic, observers doubt whether a disposition for benevolence, confidence, or justice is possible given everything from our human nature to the anarchic international political system. Indeed, they still equate peace with the absence of war, because it is the most they think we can accomplish.

This chapter alone cannot determine whether Spinoza's goals can ever be realized. It does, however, remind us that achieving 'merely' the absence of war can be a gargantuan task. And it leads this author, at least, to ask if we shouldn't lower our expectations and welcome the limited gains since 1995 – at least in the short run. In short, it would be wise for us all to ponder the following statement by Ivo Daalder and Michael Froman:

> So rather than insist that Dayton will have failed if Bosnia does not soon become a multiethnic democracy, it is better to accept reality and concentrate instead on safeguarding Dayton's biggest achievement ending the bloodiest war in Europe since World War II. (Daalder and Froman, 1999)

SELECT BIBLIOGRAPHY

Bunce, Valerie. 'Peaceful versus Violent State Dismemberment: A Comparison of the Soviet Union, Yugoslavia, and Czechoslovakia.' *Politics and Society* 27 (June 1999): 217–37.

Burg, Steven, and Paul Shoup. *The War in Bosnia-Herzegovina: Ethnic Conflict and International Intervention*. Armonk, NY: M. E. Sharpe, 1999.

Daalder, Ivo, and Michael B. G. Froman. 'Dayton's Incomplete Peace.' *Foreign Affairs* (November/December 1999). Accessed on 1 August 2000 from <http://proquest,umi.com>.

European Stability Institute. 'Reshaping International Priorities in Bosnia and Hercegovina.' Unpublished paper, 1999.

Fromkin, David. *Kosovo Crossing: American Ideals Meet Reality on the Balkan Battlefields*. New York: Free Press, 1999.

Holbrooke, Richard. *To End a War*. New York: Random House, 1998.

International Crisis Group. 'Is Dayton Failing: Four Years after the Peace Agreement.' Unpublished paper, 1999.

Judeh, Tim. *The Serbs*. New Haven: Yale University Press, 1997.

Last, David. 'Soldiers and Civilians in Peacebuilding: Reliable Partners?' Paper prepared for the 1999 Meeting of the International Studies Association, Washington, D.C.

Malcolm, Noel. *Bosnia: A Brief History*. New York: New York University Press, 1994.

Rieff, David. *Slaughterhouse: Bosnia and the Failure of the West*. New York: Vintage, 1995.

Rose, William. 'The Security Dilemma and Ethnic Conflict.' *Security Studies*, 9, no. 4 (October 2000): 1–55.

Sharp, Jane M. O. 'Dayton Report Card.' *International Security* 22 (Winter, 1997): 101–38.

United Nations. *The Blue Helmets*. New York: United Nations Press, 1996.

Woodward, Susan. *Balkan Tragedy: Chaos and Dissolution after the Cold War*. Washington D.C.: Brookings, 1995.

Yost, David. *NATO Transformed*. Washington, D.C.: United States Institute for Peace, 1998.

10

IRAQ

> If I make a peace proposal, then I'm the one who will have to make concessions. If the others propose one, then I can obtain concessions.
>
> –Saddam Hussein

In his remarkable speech to the United Nations General Assembly in December 1988, Soviet president Mikhail Gorbachev used the term 'new world order' to describe the international relations being born out of the ashes of the Cold War. Then, U.S. president-elect George Bush adopted the term to describe what he – and most of the rest of us – hoped would be a more peaceful world.

Yet, even before the Soviet Union disintegrated, the international community was plunged into a new and costly war following Iraq's August 1990 invasion of Kuwait, a war that led some pundits to call it a new world *dis*order instead. More than three-quarters of a million soldiers from thirty-five countries were deployed in Operation Desert Shield to the region while negotiations to convince Iraq to withdraw from Kuwait continued. In January 1991 negotiations broke down, and the war, dubbed Operation Desert Storm, began. Seven weeks of air strikes and a few days of surprisingly easy ground combat forced Saddam Hussein's troops out of Kuwait and dealt a terrible blow to Iraq's society and economy. Unlike what we saw in Bosnia and Kosovo, however, attention did not then shift to peacebuilding and other conflict resolution strategies.

Indeed, after the fighting stopped, the Gulf war allies and Iraq remain deeply at odds. Sanctions are still in effect. Skirmishes periodically break out between Iraqi and what remains of the UN-led forces of 1990–91.

The situation remains so bleak that some observers would argue that it does not make sense to include Iraq and the Gulf war in a book on conflict resolution. In fact, Iraq provides an excellent case for concluding part 2 of this book for three reasons.

First, it reminds us of just how hard and rare it is to achieve effective win-win conflict resolution. Second and ironically, by considering the causes of the continued conflict between Iraq and most of the rest of the world we will be able to see that forces that can achieve win–win conflict resolution yield positive-sum outcomes in sharper relief. Finally, the tragedy that has befallen Iraq both before and after the Gulf war should drive home yet again the normative conclusion that we need to find better ways of settling our disputes.

But at this point it is important to underscore that first and most important conclusion. This was clearly a case in which traditional approaches to conflict management and resolution failed, while the new ones first raised in chapter 4 never made it onto the political agenda.

There are many reasons why that has been the case. Responsibility for the failure is to be found on both sides of the conflict. One of the most important explanations for why the Iraqi case is different lies in the statement by Saddam Hussein that begins this chapter. He has certainly been reluctant to take the first steps toward reaching an agreement, because he is convinced that doing so would also require Iraq to make the first concessions, something he is unwilling to do. Although they would never speak so bluntly, the same case can largely be made for the leaders of what remains of the 1990–91 coalition. The Bush and Clinton administrations, in particular, were unwilling to make (m)any con-ciliatory gestures, because they were convinced that, given Iraqi behavior since 1990, they need not and should not have done so.

The point is not to cast blame on either or both sides. Rather, you should see that the stances both have taken have done little or nothing to bring an end to the conflict, especially in the years since the war itself.

THEORETICAL ISSUES

This chapter's theoretical focus is different from those of the previous four, because win-win conflict resolution and steps toward stable peace have never been options in Iraq's ongoing dispute with the international community. Here, though we will concentrate on many of the same explanatory themes that were raised in chapters 6 through 9, the challenge is to understand why a nonviolent solution to the crises involving Iraq has proved elusive both before and after the 1991 war itself. Thus, we will review:

- the way the end of the Cold War made new alliances and other geopolitical arrangements possible

- the weakness of international institutions and the international community in general, except under the most exceptional of circumstances
- the assertion made in earlier chapters that it is easy to at least chart out a hypothetical win-win outcome and that it is often a primary goal of foreign policymakers
- a certain conceptual looseness in the idea of a hurting stalemate that makes it a less useful analytical tool than it might have seemed in earlier chapters
- the way that misperceptions and other psychological factors as well as domestic politics can reinforce the kind of intransigence shown in the statement by Saddam Hussein that begins this chapter

---

A Common Problem

This chapter will be making a number of conclusions about what happened in Washington and Baghdad both before and after the Persian Gulf war. Those conclusions should really be read as assertions because of a problem all international relations scholars face, but that is particularly challenging here.

We do not have access to all the factual information we want or need.

As the description of the United States intelligence community later in the chapter attests, surprisingly little is actually known about Iraq. We do not have in-depth information about the working of the Baath Party's inner circle. Therefore, we are forced to rely on at best educated guesses about what motivates Saddam Hussein and other key Iraqi leaders (but see Post, 1992).

The United States, other Western governments, and the United Nations are much more open to journalists and scholars than is Iraq. However, even there, much information remains classified, and the political leaders involved have revealed primarily what they want the public or scholarly community to know and have withheld other material.

This is, in fact, a problem for all the case studies in this book, but it is particularly problematic here. What I have tried to do throughout is to rely on the most widely respected sources of information and draw on works that reflect the varied points of view on the conflicts.

IRAQ AND INTERNATIONAL RELATIONS BEFORE THE GULF WAR

Imperialism, Iraq, and the Rise of the Baath

As was the case with the other four case studies, the causes of the conflict with Iraq had their roots that stretch back hundreds of years and include both regional issues, the long-term impact of imperialism, and more (Marr, 1985, Denoeux, 2000).

The region now known as Iraq was almost certainly the birthplace of civilization. The first cities, systems of writing, and irrigation were developed over four thousand years ago in the fertile region between the Tigris and Euphrates rivers. The tower of Babel stood there. As recently as the thirteenth century, Baghdad was one of the world's leading intellectual centers, and the Muslim empire centered there dwarfed anything in Europe at the time.

Table 10.1   Iraq and the world before 1990

Date	Event
1919	Treaty of Versailles
1932	Iraq become legally independent
1958	Monarchy overthrown
1963	First Baath coup
1968	Baath comes to power for good
1979	Saddam Hussein takes control
1980–88	Iran–Iraq war

After that, the region, which has no natural defenses, was repeatedly invaded and overrun. In 1900 it was nothing more than a group of provinces of the crumbling Ottoman empire based in Turkey.

During World War I, the British offered a group of Arab leaders independence after the war if they helped defeat the Ottoman empire. The British reneged on their offer shortly after the war ended and carved up the Arab world from Egypt to Iraq with their allies, the French. The country they called Iraq was put together from eighteen provinces of the old Ottoman empire but did not include Kuwait, which many thought should have been part of it.

That decision created a country that is richly endowed with natural resources but also is plagued by ethnic and religious divisions. Over 15 percent of the world's proven oil reserves lie beneath Iraqi soil, enough to last at least 140 years at 1980s levels of production. Despite its location in one of the most arid parts of the world, the area between the Tigris and Euphrates rivers is fertile enough for Iraq to grow all the food it needs.

In short, Iraq was quite well off by regional standards before the invasion of Kuwait. Its cities were among the richest and most cosmopolitan in the Arab world. Literacy stood at 55 percent or more. Most people in the countryside as well as the cities enjoyed reasonable health care, had adequate housing, and could aspire to a middle-class standard of living. Iraq also offered more professional opportunities and personal freedoms to women than any of the other Arab states.

However, the British decision after World War I made Iraq all but ungovernable by anything but the most authoritarian regime, because it combined three groups whose histories were every bit as antagonistic as those we saw in the former Yugoslavia. About 95 percent of the population is Muslim. There is a small Christian minority – Tariq Aziz, who has held a number of key posts since 1990, for instance, is one. There was also a small Jewish population, but most Jews emigrated after the creation of Israel.

That apparent homogeneity, however, is misleading. Between 55 and 65 percent of the population are Shiites. They are part of a rather devout (and often militant) sect of Islam that is dominant in neighboring Iran. Virtually all the Shiites are ethnic Arabs. The rest of the population are Sunnis, who make up the overwhelming majority of the world's Muslim population. In Iraq, however, they are divided into two roughly equal – and antagonistic – communities. Independent Iraq has always been dominated by Sunni Arabs, including Saddam Hussein and most of his entourage. The rest of the Sunni are Kurds, who are part of a wholly different ethnic group. The world's nearly 30 million Kurds are spread across Iraq, Turkey, Syria, Iran, and Azerbaijan. The Kurds never accepted their incorporation in any of these states, and various (and often feuding) Kurdish groups have been fighting for their own country ever since 1919, when their hopes were thwarted by the Treaty of Versailles.

The British compounded the difficulties brought on by ethnic and religious differences by importing King Faisal I from what is now Saudi Arabia as Iraq's first head of state. Faisal and his successors were, at best, mediocre rulers who did little to forge a stable or legitimate regime after Iraq gained its nominal independence in 1932. The last king was overthrown in 1958, which began a series of coups and countercoups that left Iraq without an effective government for a decade.

By that time, the duplicitous role played by the British and foreign capitalists had reinforced three key Iraqi cultural values:

- a distrust of outsiders
- strong parochial loyalties to family, clan, and region
- acceptance of violence to settle political differences

In 1968 the Baath Party filled the power vacuum in Baghdad and has run the country with an iron fist ever since. The party was formed in the late 1940s as a pan-Arab and socialist party, whose primary goals was to unify the Arabs into a single state. The Baath came to power in Syria and Iraq, but its goal of Arab unity collapsed as those two states became rivals in the 1970s and then combatants in the Gulf war.

The Iraqi Baath Party has always been composed of a tiny elite, whose rule ranks among the most brutal of the twentieth century. Its regime was always repressive, but only after Saddam Hussein (1937–) took power in 1979 did it become all but totalitarian.

Iraq's Baath Party has become a tool of Saddam Hussein and his inner circle, which is composed mostly of his family and others from his hometown of Tikrit (Dawisha, 1999). The party controls everything, including the press, the schools, and all social organizations, including its Olympic committee and national soccer teams, which are run by Saddam's son, Uday. The regime is so powerful and repressive that one observer called it a 'republic of fear even before the invasion of Kuwait brought the country to the attention of the rest of the world' (al-Khalil, 1990). Four secret police bureaus monitor what Iraqi citizens do at home and abroad. Anyone who says anything against the regime risks arrest and execution. Tens of thousands of real and potential opponents have been arrested. Many have been tortured and/or summarily executed, including two of Saddam Hussein's sons-in-law. I could go on and present dozens of concrete examples, but the following story told by Elaine Sciolino of the *New York Times* is as good as any. She arrived at the airport in Iraq (named for Saddam Hussein, of course) and hailed a taxi to take her into town. Sciolino asked him what he thought of Saddam Hussein. The cabbie replied:

> 'This is car,' he says, patting his hand on the dashboard. 'But if Saddam says this is bicycle, it is bicycle.' He looks around anxiously and added: 'He could kill me for this.' (Denoeux, 2000:394)

The Iran–Iraq War

Academics and policy analysts understood that the Baath had already established an authoritarian regime in the 1970s. Few others cared, since the repression had yet to reach the proportions it would under Saddam Hussein. More important, Iraq was at most a minor irritant in global politics, even in the ticklish relations between Arabs and Israelis.

All that changed in 1979. As we have already seen, Saddam Hussein took control in Baghdad and ushered in what has now been twenty years of personalized and highly despotic rule. Meanwhile, fundamentalist Shiites led by the Ayatollah Ruhollah Khomeini (1902–89) overthrew the shah's corrupt dictatorship in neighboring Iran.

As the two most powerful countries in the region, Iran and Iraq had long been rivals for control of the Persian Gulf. Iran had also supported Kurdish rebels in northern Iraq. Now, the secular Baath worried that the religious fervor that had produced the Islamic revolution would spread to Iraq's Shiites. There was good reason for those fears, since Khomeini had lived in Iraq for years until he was thrown out by the Baath regime in 1978. Then, Egypt's involvement with the Camp David Accords cost Cairo its leadership role among militant foes of Israel, a role both Baghdad and Tehran coveted.

The new regime in Iran purged its army of officers who had been loyal to the shah. Iraq decided to take advantage of the decline in Iranian readiness and morale by invading on 22 September 1980. Contrary to Baghdad's expectations, the Iranian army held. The war would last eight years. During that time the front barely moved. However, hundreds of thousands of soldiers and civilians were killed on both sides. Iraq used chemical and biological weapons both on Iranian troops and on their own Kurdish citizens, the first time such arms had been used since World War I. Finally, the Iranian government was convinced that it could not win, and on 20 August 1988 agreed to a cease-fire that amounted, at most, to a marginal victory for Iraq.

For our purposes, Iraq's changing relations with the West during the 1980s are more important than the war itself. Policymakers in the West and the other Arab states had no illusions about Baghdad's intentions. The Baath was anti-Western, and Iraq had long had reasonably close ties to the Soviet Union.

The war against Iran, however, changed the geopolitical landscape. Iraq portrayed itself as defending the Arab world against the Persian and fundamentalist menace, gaining itself an estimated $40 billion in support from the wealthy Gulf oil states. Western governments seemed to adopt the Arab proverb 'my enemy's enemy is my friend.' Arms and development assistance poured into Iraq. For example, in 1987 no country received more agricultural aid from the United States. The West turned a blind eye to Iraq's use of chemical weapons on the Kurds and other human rights violations. When the war with Iran ended, the

Western consensus was that Iraq was run by a reasonably pragmatic leader who could and should be encouraged to further reform his regime.

THE GULF WAR

Whatever one thinks of the war and subsequent events, conventional wisdom in the West about the Iraqi regime certainly proved to be inaccurate.

Iraq emerged from the war with Iran deeply in debt, primarily to the other Gulf states it felt it helped defend by taking on Tehran. The most charitable explanation for Iraq's actions during the first eight months of 1990 is that it occupied Kuwait to solve those economic problems.

Moreover, we have to remember that Iraq was not a major focus of Western attention during 1989 and the first few months of 1990. Like almost everyone else in the world, policymakers on both sides of the Atlantic were preoccupied by the dizzying and confusing changes occurring behind the disappearing iron curtain. To the degree that they did worry about the Middle East, it was in trying to deal with the conflict between Israel and the Arabs as the Intifada gradually ground to an end.

In short, only low-level political appointees and career analysts in Western foreign ministries and intelligence agencies were paying much attention to Iraq. And, there was no consensus among them about either what Iraq was about to do or how the West should respond.

Some American analysts did point out that Iraq was a rogue state, whose unpredictable leadership could lead it to threaten the regional balance of power. However, given the other events sweeping the world, there was little enthusiasm for changing policy toward Baghdad in the Bush administration or in the governments of the major European powers. If anything, they encouraged expanded trade and other contacts with Iraq which, ironically, helped Baghdad rearm and speed up its programs to develop weapons of mass destruction. Even more important, in 1989 the U.S. intelligence community issued a national intelligence estimate that predicted Iraq would not pose a threat to any of its neighbors for a number of years. Indeed, in October 1989 the Bush administration adopted National Security Council Directive 26, which called for a policy of cooperation with Iraq on the assumption that it would be playing a more constructive role in global affairs (George, 1993:33–89).

As a result, Western governments were slow to respond when Baghdad began sending out ominous signals. On 24 February Saddam Hussein made a major speech in which he attributed hostile intentions to the United States for maintaining its fleet in the Persian Gulf.

Saddam Hussein

Toward the end of this chapter, we will see how demonization of Saddam Hussein and his regime contributed to what is now a decade-long dispute. Here, however, it is important also to see that the Iraqi regime has proved hard to deal with in part because Saddam Hussein *is* a brutal leader of what can only be considered a rogue regime.

Saddam Hussein was born in 1937 in a dirt-poor village a hundred miles from Baghdad. His father died before he was born, and he was abused by several of the relatives who helped raise him.

He moved to Baghdad at age eighteen and immediately got involved in revolutionary politics. Wounded in the Baath's first attempt to seize power in 1959, he then studied law in Cairo, the farthest he has ever been from Iraq for any extended period of time. He returned to Iraq, took part in the 1968 coup that brought the Baath to power to stay, became the second most influential person in the new regime, and rose to the top in 1979, when he forced Ahmad Hassan al-Bakr to resign.

Saddam Hussein has been a ruthless ruler who exerts all but total control over his entire country. Through a series of purges, he has turned the Baath regime into what is little more than a personal dictatorship. Thomas Friedman of the *New York Times* describes him as a thirteenth-century tyrant whose craving of weapons of mass destruction has turned him into the archetypical twenty-first-century threat.

Then, in June and July, Iraq demanded $30 billion from the Gulf states as payment for services rendered during the war. It also accused them and Kuwait, in particular, of exceeding agreed levels of oil production and driving prices (and hence Iraqi revenue) down. Finally, it raised the old, but not widely respected, claim that Kuwait legally should have been the nineteenth province of Iraq.

At the end of July, Iraqi troops massed near the Kuwaiti border. No one knew what their plans were. The U.S. intelligence community was split down the middle, about half the analysts thinking Iraq would invade, half claiming it would not. The uncertainties went both ways. The Iraqi regime went away from an (in)famous meeting with U.S. ambassador April Glaspie convinced that Washington would not stand in the way of an invasion.

There was uncertainty on the Iraqi side as well. Saddam Hussein and his immediate entourage seem to have assumed that the international community would not retaliate if he moved on Kuwait. What's more, the most recent evidence suggests that even people just outside the inner circle in Baghdad did not know what Saddam Hussein had planned. Tariq Aziz, for instance, apparently thought that Iraq would only seize part of the country to settle an old border dispute and tried to talk Saddam out of doing that (Cockburn and Cockburn, 1999:7–9).

In that atmosphere of uncertainty, Iraq's troops poured into its tiny neighbor on 2 August 1990. Within hours, it had taken over Kuwait City. The royal family fled along with many other prominent Kuwaitis.

By taking Kuwait, Iraq had also positioned itself to attack Saudi Arabia. Had it occupied that country as well, it would have controlled upward of a quarter of the world's proven oil reserves.

Table 10.2   Iraq and the world in the 1990s

Year	Events
1990	Invasion of Kuwait
	Operation Desert Storm created
	UN resolutions authorize sanctions, use of force
1991	Gulf war
	Uprisings by Kurds and Shiites
	UNSCOM created
1992	More violations of UN restrictions on Iraqi program developing weapons of mass destruction (WMD)
1993	Iraq formally accepts UN conditions on WMD
1994	Iraq moves troops close to Kuwait border
1995	Iraq acknowledges major WMD programs
	Saddam and Hussein Kamel and families defect and return. Saddam and Hussein Kamel executed
1996	Limited oil sales permitted for purchase of humanitarian aid
1997	Iraq tries to deny UNSCOM access to 'presidential' and other sites
1998	Iraq stops cooperating with UNSCOM
	UNSCOM leaves
	Latest round of air strikes begins and continues into 1999
1999	Iraq rejects plan for new UN inspection regime

At that point, the kind of conflict resolution techniques we have concentrated on throughout this book were not on anyone's agenda and for all intents and purposes have not been since then. Instead, the UN, the United States, and the rest of the allies engaged in a classic example of coercive diplomacy (Herrmann, 1994), combining negotiations with the threat of force in an attempt to stop Iraq from moving into Saudi Arabia and to compel it to pull out of Kuwait.

Within weeks, the UN Security Council passed a number of resolutions, the most important of which demanded that Iraq withdraw (Resolution 660), and imposed economic and other sanctions (661). Representatives of the UN and the world's powers met regularly with Iraqi officials. With the end of the Cold War, most of the world united against Iraq's invasion. The United States and the USSR did not completely agree on the tactics to use. Still, the two superpowers worked more closely together than they had at any point since World War II. Saudi Arabia, Syria, Egypt, and a number of smaller Arab states joined in condemning the Iraqi invasion and supporting the coalition's efforts to roll it back.

This point is worth underscoring. The end of the Cold War produced a sea change in international relations. The old bipolar division had disappeared, and the United States and United Nations could build a much broader coalition that was prepared to go much farther than at any point during the Cold War. Even though the allies were not able to prevent war, the six months between the invasion and the launch of Operation Desert Storm opened the door to a dramatic expansion of multilateral responses to aggression that undermined regional peace that has characterized international relations ever since.

Meanwhile, the United States took the lead in putting together Operation Desert Shield. The force, which would eventually top 800,000 soldiers, was designed to prevent Iraq from moving into Saudi Arabia and, it was hoped, eventually persuade it to withdraw from Kuwait.

In retrospect, some left-wing critics have taken the allies to task for their occasional rigidity and their frequent use of heated rhetoric laden with images of Saddam Hussein as an evil human being. Others suggest that U.S. president George Bush had all but given up hope on the diplomatic front as early as the first week of November. Conservatives, in contrast, argue that Bush was not tough enough in dealing with a leader who emerged from a culture in which toughness is respected and any sign of meeting one's adversaries half way is seen as a sign of weakness.

Most observers, however, are convinced that the most serious misperceptions and miscalculations occurred in Baghdad. It was at the height the crisis that Saddam Hussein uttered the words that begin this chapter in a meeting with a delegation from the PLO (Cockburn and Cockburn, 1999:8–9). They could have been used to describe the Iraqi leadership's attitude from 1990 onward. By all accounts, Saddam Hussein (though not necessarily his advisers) was convinced until the very last moment that the allies would not attack and, if they did, that his troops would prevail in what he called the 'mother of all battles.' He was also convinced that most of the Arab world would rise up with him to defeat what he saw as Western imperialism.

After nearly four months without a positive response from Baghdad, the Security Council voted on 29 November to authorize the use of force if Iraq did not withdraw by 15 January 1991. The United States and other coalition members engaged in nonstop diplomacy, trying to convince Saddam Hussein to withdraw and avoid war. Other states that were not affiliated with Operation Desert Shield tried to mediate, most notably the Soviet Union, which had had good relations with Iraq and had an able intermediary in future Russian prime minister Yevgeny Primakov.

The deadline came and went, and in the early morning of 17 January 1991 (Baghdad time), the allies started what turned out to be a thirty-nine-day air war. Unlike the case in Kosovo, the air campaign did not lead to an Iraqi surrender. Therefore, on 24 February the allies launched a ground attack. The Iraqi forces crumbled in the face of the superbly led and immensely better equipped coalition forces. Three days later, the Iraqis fled Kuwait, and President Bush announced a cease-fire. Bush has been severely criticized for not pushing on to Baghdad and removing Saddam Hussein and the Baath from power. To this day, Bush justifies himself by stating that the UN mandate only extended to liberating Kuwait. Many – though by no means all – observers are also convinced that such a campaign would have been far bloodier than Operation Desert Storm, in which fewer than 200 Americans were killed, most of them as a result of friendly fire.

AFTER THE GULF WAR

As we saw in the chapters on the former Yugoslavia and the Arabs and Israel, postconflict reconstruction and peacebuilding in general were on everyone's agenda by the time serious peace negotiations began. That was not true for Iraq.

The specifics of the allied policy toward Baghdad have changed on and off since 1991. However, there is not likely to be any thought of serious long-term conflict resolution as long as Saddam Hussein and his entourage are in power. If anything, the United States and its allies are (perhaps unintentionally) making that harder by continuing the UN-imposed sanctions that have contributed to the worsening of the average Iraqi's social and economic conditions without having a noticeable impact on the regime.

In short, there is no way that the conflict can be described as being on the road to resolution. Although there has not been fighting on the scale of the Gulf war itself, Iraq and the U.S.-led coalition have moved back and forth between an armed, tense standoff and periodic fighting since 1991.

In fact, conflict resolution arguably is not even a secondary goal of the leaders on either side. Thus, the United States and its allies have made

---

Useful Web Sites

The Middle East Network Information Center at the University of Texas provides a good comprehensive site for the entire region. <http://link.lanic.utexas.edu/menic>.

The *Middle East Report* is one of the best journals in the field. Its web site has its publications and more. <http://www.merip.org>.

The Iraq Action Coalition is one of the many groups trying to ease or end the sanctions against Iraq. <http://leb.net/fchp/irq.htm>.

The Iraq Foundation provides somewhat less one-sided views, but is squarely lined up against the regime in Baghdad. <http://www.iraqfoundation.org>.

The Iraqi government does not have much of a presence on the Internet. Its best site is run by its mission to the UN. <http://www.Iraqi-Mission.org>.

The Iraqi National Congress is the largest group operating in exile. <http://www.inc.org.uk>.

The U.S.-based Arms Control Association has some of the best statistics on the weapons programs and the attempts to limit them. <http://www.armscontrol.org/ASSORTED/iraqindx.html>.

The best online source on sanctions is by well-known peace studies professors Robert Cortright and George Lopez. <http://www.fourthfreedom.org/hottopic/sanctions-againstiraqfactsanalysis.html>.

The UNSCOM site is also a great source of material on the international community's response to Iraq as is the U.S. State Department's web site. <http://www.un.org/Depts/unscom> and <http://www.state.gov>.

the policy of dual containment of the feared expansionary ambitions of both Iran and Iraq a much higher priority (Fuller and Lesser, 1997). While we do not have access to the inner workings of the Iraqi elite, all the signs are that it is much more interested in holding on to power, maintaining its military strength, and continuing the development of its weapons systems than it is in reaching any sort of accommodation with the UN and the West.

The Immediate Aftermath

It is an open question whether war still fulfills the task assigned to it by Karl von Clausewitz – settling political disputes that could not be resolved otherwise. The Gulf war, at most, reached only one of the allies' goals, although it was clearly its most important. The allies were able to force Iraq out of Kuwait. However, they were not able to put an end to the tensions between Iraq and the international community; in many ways, the inconclusive end to the fighting left us with a more intractable situation.

Saddam Hussein and the Baath remained in power. President Bush and other Western leaders made ambiguous statements about the future of relations with Baghdad as long as he was still in control. The U.S. administration, in particular, issued statements that many Iraqi opposition figures felt urged them to take up arms to overthrow Saddam.

Within days of the cease-fire, Shiites in the south and Kurds in the north rose up against the government in Baghdad. The international community did little to help them overthrow the government. For logistical reasons, little could be done to help the Shiites, who were brutally repressed. The United States and its allies were able to assist the Kurds, who succeeded in setting up their own de facto state in northern Iraq, largely outside the control of the central government. No fly zones that Iraqi aircraft were not permitted to enter were created over the northern and southern parts of the country. But, as 1991 ended, Saddam Hussein was as securely in power as ever.

What we have been left with are four overlapping sources of continued tension rather than steps toward conflict resolution – many threats and several actual instances of fighting, years of inspections to uncover and eliminate Iraq's weapons of mass destruction and the technologies that could develop them, sanctions, and the not-so-subtle attempts to overthrow the regime in Baghdad.

Threats and Bombs

There have been a series of confrontations between the Western allies (see box) and Iraq since 1991, some of which have led to bombing campaigns. The most important of them include:

- January 1993. The United States fired forty cruise missiles at a factory suspected of being part of the nuclear weapons development program.
- June 1993. More cruise missiles were fired at Iraqi intelligence headquarters after reports that Baghdad had planned to assassinate former president Bush when he visited Kuwait.
- October 1994. The United States sent aircraft and over 50,000 soldiers to the region after Iraq massed its own troops near the Kuwaiti border.
- September 1996. The United States fired missiles at a variety of targets after Iraqi troops moved into Kurdish areas in the north.
- February 1998. UN secretary-general Kofi Annan defused a crisis over UNSCOM access to 'presidential sites' suspected of being used for weapons development.
- December 1998. About 450 cruise missiles and 650 bombing runs by conventional aircraft were launched following Iraq's decision to stop cooperating with UNSCOM once it became clear that it was closing in on Baghdad's biological weapons program.
- 1999. Repeated attacks by British and American planes were challenged by Iraqi fighters and radars.

Weapons Inspections

Many of those confrontations have revolved around the regime of weapons inspections. In spring 1991 the UN Security Council passed Resolution 687, which stated that economic sanctions would stay in place until Iraq complied with all UN demands. The most important of these was an end to its program to develop nuclear and other weapons of mass destruction (WMD). To that end, the UN created UNSCOM (United Nations Special Commission) to monitor Iraq compliance (or the lack thereof) with its demands. By the middle of 1991, it was clear that Iraq was not providing anything like a full disclosure of its inventory of weapons or its plans for developing new ones.

For the next seven years, Iraq played a political cat-and-mouse game with UNSCOM. It did whatever it could to deny the inspectors access to

---

The International Community

Operations Desert Shield and Desert Storm were remarkable coalitions that brought together an unprecedented number of countries, some of which would never have cooperated with each other during the Cold War. Although led (some would say dominated) by the United States, the coalition was also unprecedented in that it sought authority and legitimacy for its actions by getting the approval of the UN Security Council through 1990 and 1991.

The coalition is nowhere near as united following the dawn of the twenty-first century. The United States and Great Britain lead a dwindling number of countries that insist on full compliance by Iraq before sanctions can be lifted. The three other permanent members of the Security Council by no means countenance Iraqi actions, but they do think that enough progress has been made to ease or even end the sanctions.

Critics go so far as to suggest that the United States and Great Britain acted illegally in their 1999 and other recent bombing campaigns by not explicitly getting support for their actions from the Security Council.

Realistically speaking, British and American intransigence are such that it seems highly unlikely that sanctions will be fully lifted as long as Saddam Hussein and the Baath remain in power.

---

possible weapons sites as well as data on its progress. Over the years, UNSCOM was able to document that Baghdad had made more progress than had previously been suspected toward developing nuclear, chemical, and biological weapons as well as medium-range missiles. It provoked tremendous criticism from Iraq, including charges that it was little more than a cover for American officers such as former Marine captain Scott Ritter to spy for the United States. By the late 1990s, UNSCOM head, Richard Butler, had become a lightning rod for Iraqi criticism of the West in general and the United States in particular (even though Butler is an Australian). Throughout the period, the UNSCOM's actions and Iraq's reactions sparked numerous crises.

- 1991. Iraq made its first attempt to deny UNSCOM officials access to suspected weapons sites, refused to turn over documents about its nuclear weapons program, prevented the destruction of some dual-use technologies, and held UN officials for four days.

- 1992. Iraq continued to deny UNSCOM officials access to Department of Agriculture and other buildings suspected of being used for weapons research and development.
- 1994. Iraq threatened to stop cooperating with UNSCOM unless the embargo was lifted. The UN refused.
- 1995. The Iraqi government claimed it would refuse to give material on biological weapons unless the UN terminated its investigations into other weapons systems.
- 1997. Despite its differences over how to respond to Iraq, the Security Council unanimously passed resolution 1115, which ordered Baghdad to allow UNSCOM to complete its work as it saw fit.
- 1997–98. Iraq tried to block UNSCOM access to so-called 'presidential sites,' many of which were vast territories containing palaces and, it was alleged, weapons development facilities.
- 1998. Iraq again refused to cooperate with UNSCOM, and the UN removed it. Richard Butler resigned.
- 1999. The UN approved plans for a new inspection system. Iraq refused to cooperate.

Economic Sanctions

In fall 1990 the United Nations Security Council Resolution 687 imposed economic sanctions that prohibited just about all forms of foreign trade with Iraq. With the exception of the sale of some oil for the purchase of medicine and other humanitarian supplies (see below), the sanctions remained in place as of this writing.

The sanctions have also become the most controversial aspect of allied policies because of their impact on Iraq's society and economy. As David Cortright and George Lopez put it for an earlier period:

> For more than seven years, since August 1990, the people of Iraq have experienced almost complete economic isolation. The Gulf War with its intensive bombing campaign exacerbated the effects of sanctions and created what a March 1991 UN report described as 'near apocalyptic' conditions. (Cortright and Lopez, 1999)

Conditions have only worsened since 1991. Iraq has lost the equivalent of about $130 billion in oil sales. That money *could* have been used to purchase needed food, clothing, medicine, and other supplies and to fund the rebuilding of the country after the destruction of the two wars. The word 'could' was emphasized in the preceding sentence because Western supporters of sanctions are quick to point out that there is no reason to assume that the regime would have used the money for those purposes, given its track record both before and after 1991.

Directly and indirectly, the sanctions have taken a terrible toll. Study after study by the UN and other international institutions have confirmed Kofi Annan's conclusions in a report to the Security Council in late 1997:

> United Nations observers regularly report an exceptionally serious deterioration in the health infrastructure: a high infant mortality rate and high rates of morbidity and mortality in general, poor and inadequate storage conditions for supplies, an unreliable supply of electricity and back-up generators, faulty or non-functioning air conditioning, defective cold-storage, interrupted water supplies, broken/leaking sewage systems and non-functioning hospital waste disposal systems. (United Nations, 1997)

Estimates of the number of Iraqis who have died because of the public health and other consequences of the sanctions have topped 500,000, although those figures could well be wildly off the mark. Yet, even if they overestimate the fatalities by a factor of two, postwar deaths would still greatly outnumber the number of battlefield deaths.

It isn't just the number of deaths. A 1997 UNICEF study estimated that one-third of all Iraqi children under the age of five suffer from malnutrition. Clean drinking water is in short supply, as are almost all consumer goods. Hospitals lack basic medicine and other supplies. Inflation has destroyed the real value of most people's incomes. People in the former middle class have been reduced to selling books, televisions, and other consumer goods on the black market.

In 1996 the Security Council passed Resolution 986, which allows Iraq to sell $2 billion worth of oil every six months (that figure was raised somewhat in 1999) for the purchase of food and medical supplies. But even that money is deposited in UN accounts and is not controlled by the Iraqi government.

Critics have also pointed out that the sanctions have not had the desired impact on the regime (Byman, 2000). To be sure, it has grudgingly complied with most UNSCOM directives, which has dealt a crippling if not fatal blow to its weapons development programs. On balance, however, sanctions have not done much to compel Iraq to reach a final agreement with the international community.

In contrast, supporters of sanctions point out that the Iraqi government spends the money at its disposal for weapons and other programs instead of on the social and medical needs of its people. Thus, the regime has kept up the parts of its military permitted under UN rules. Black marketeers (most of whom are closely connected to the regime) are frighteningly wealthy. Members of the elite – including Saddam's two sons – live like kings, and the 'Iraqi people' built the ruler a sumptuous new palace in honor of his sixtieth birthday in 1997. Perhaps just as galling to many supporters of the regime are events like the 6 May 1999 opening of the new city of Saddamiat that has athletic stadiums, a theme park, and a 30-foot-tall bronze statue of Saddam Hussein.

Removing Saddam?

Finally, the United States and, to a lesser degree, its allies have unsuccessfully tried to remove Saddam Hussein from power. Because Iraq is so tightly controlled by the Baath, there is no 'inside the system' way of changing the leadership. In other words, the United States and its allies have 'had' to try to foment a coup.

It is against American and British law to assassinate the leader of another country, and there is no evidence that either government has tried to do so, though allied forces did target buildings Saddam Hussein was rumored to be in during the war. However, it is clear that either London or Washington would be delighted were Saddam Hussein to be killed as part of a coup.

To that end, the United States and Great Britain in particular have supported a number of Iraqi exile groups (no viable opposition exists or can exist inside the country). The largest of these is the Iraqi National Congress (di Giovanni, 2000). Like most such groups, it is made up of long-standing opponents of the Baath as well as more recent defectors. Intelligence agencies such as the CIA and MI6 have given these often-shady groups hundreds of millions of dollars, but they have never come close to toppling the regime. There have been some rumors of coup attempts. One group (apparently not supported by either the British or the Americans) nearly killed Saddam Hussein's son, Uday. The most spectacular defection from the regime came when Saddam's cousins and sons-in-law, the high-ranking Saddam and Hussein Kamel, fled to Jordan with their families. After their attempt to spark the opposition failed, they returned to Iraq, where both men were assassinated by the regime's troops.

Saddam Hussein's inner circle is smaller than it was in 1990. And, he undoubtedly has a weaker base of support than he did before the invasion of Kuwait. Nonetheless, it is hard to see how exile-based groups funded by the United States, Britain, or another Western power could topple the Baath. More important, there is no reason to believe that these groups would be noticeably more democratic or be better able to produce reconciliation with the West than the current regime in Baghdad has been.

THEORETICAL IMPLICATIONS

At this point, you might well be asking what this material has to do with conflict resolution. At first glance, the answer is remarkably little. No matter what your ideological perspectives on the continuing conflict with Iraq, you are unlikely to be able to discern any significant moves toward reconciliation or stable peace since the invasion of Kuwait.

If we dig a bit deeper, we can see that the failure to make progress toward working out those differences tells us at least as much about how conflict resolution does occur than the more successful examples covered in the preceding four chapters.

My goal here is not to argue whether or not Western or Iraq policy has been correct. In particular, I am not going to suggest that the West could have or should have tried to move toward reconciliation or stable peace at any point in the years after Saddam Hussein came to power.

Those are touchy and controversial issues, and taking a firm stand on them would make it harder for you to reach your own conclusions. Furthermore, in keeping with the purposes of this book and this series, it is more important to focus on the empirical conclusions about the conflict with Iraq and its theoretical implications, of which six stand out.

1. *Opportunities for cooperation in the changing international environment.* The Iraqi case does illustrate at least one of those opportunities for international cooperation, if not conflict resolution per se. The onset of the Gulf crisis marked the first time at least since the Korean War that the international community used an international organization to structure and justify the response to aggression. Indeed, before the Gulf crisis, it was impossible to talk about *the* international community, because the Cold War rivalry divided the major powers on almost every issue.

Operation Desert Shield and Desert Storm were led by the United States. However, the Bush administration went out of its way to see to it that these were international operations of unprecedented breadth and with unprecedented support from the United Nations. In fact, as we saw with the former Yugoslavia, it ushered in a period in which the major powers became more willing to intervene in the domestic affairs of rogue states. However, they only seem do so with at least the semblance of support from institutions that are beginning to take on some of the trappings of regional if not of global governance.

That pattern continued throughout the 1990s. All the major instances of intervention were carried out at least in the name of a regional organization or the United Nations. Critics are undoubtedly correct that this was often mostly a political fig leaf to give legitimacy to actions the United States planned to take anyway, as in the case of Kosovo. Nonetheless, even the limited shift toward the use of international organizations does seem to have set a precedent that can be expanded on in the future.

2. *The weakness of those international organizations.* We should not exaggerate the power exerted by the United Nations or the regional international organizations. After all, the international community's track record since the end of the Gulf war is largely one of failure to convince or compel Iraq to comply with UN resolutions. What's more, the UN in Iraq and NATO in Bosnia and Kosovo have been heavily dependent on a handful of powerful countries, especially the United States.

In other words, the international community can only exert the kind of influence it did in late 1990 and early 1991 under the most exceptional of circumstances. It requires political conditions that allow the formation of what amounts to a consensus among the major powers to act quickly and decisively to, for instance, raise, fund, deploy, and coordinate troops whether they are sent to keep, make, or impose peace. It is probably easier to do so today than it was in 1980 or 1970. However, for all the domestic and international reasons we have seen, that kind of political will is difficult indeed to muster and has been hard to sustain even with Iraq.

3. *The continued importance of traditional geopolitics.* The Iraqi case also reminds us that the changes that have swept the world since the mid-1980s have not eliminated traditional geopolitics. As a result, it shows us more clearly than any of the other cases how traditional theories and issues in international relations remain important and why it is difficult to achieve nonviolent solutions to conflicts that are primarily geopolitical in origin.

The crisis over Kuwait arose out of aggression of the most traditional variety. It wasn't just the invasion of Kuwait that bothered international policymakers, but it also was its broader implications for Saudi Arabia and the fragile balance of power in the Middle East as a whole.

The threat to regional security was complicated by two other issues. First, as many critics of the high-minded rhetoric coming from Washington, London, and other Western capitals pointed out, the conflict was as much about access to oil as national sovereignty or human rights. Second, political leaders in Washington and elsewhere after March 1991 were convinced that they had to take broader regional power dynamics into account. Thus, the Clinton administration felt the need to maintain a policy of 'dual containment' against Iran as well as Iraq, which left it reluctant to support Saddam Hussein's Shiite opponents lest they throw their own lot with the Iranians.

4. *Is there always a win-win solution?* In earlier chapters, I chose my words carefully in stating that it is almost always possible to chart out an intellectually plausible win-win solution to any international conflict. However, as this case makes clear, it is one thing to devise an intellectually plausible proposal. It is quite another to make it politically plausible.

In this case and perhaps others, such as the 1999 war over Kosovo, there has not been a realistic option for a nonviolent resolution of a conflict. Furthermore, policymakers often have to deal with rogue states whose leaders are not very open to the kind of discussion that can take parties toward a negotiated settlement. In such conflicts, when world leaders confront a sudden and, often, unpredicted crisis, they often have to act quickly, which makes it even harder to rely on preventive or coercive diplomacy, which typically take months if not years to have an impact.

This is not to suggest empirically or normatively that we should abandon attempts to seek win-win conflict resolution and stable peace or that we will not become more adept at doing so over the medium to long run. However, it does seem safe to conclude that whatever 'progress' the international community and individual states make, we are likely to face conflicts of this sort in which the use of force may be the only realistic path for one or more of the parties to take.

5. *Hurting stalemate?* The Iraqi case also shows us both the importance and some limitations of the concept of a hurting stalemate.

On the one hand, it is easy to argue that there has been little progress toward a definitive settlement because neither the Iraqis nor what is left of the Western alliance has concluded that it cannot win and that the costs of continuing the conflict have grown too great.

On the other hand, we can also see that there is a certain looseness to the concept that may make it a less useful analytical tool than it might have seemed in earlier chapters. In other words, it might seem, at first glance, that a hurting stalemate might be an objective state of affairs: the two sides get to a certain point at which victory is no longer an option and the costs are devastating. However, it should be clear from this chapter that it has a psychological or perceptual component as well. Thus, the hurting stalemate had not been reached when these lines were written, because leaders in Washington, London, Baghdad, and elsewhere were not yet convinced that it existed.

In short, a hurting stalemate actually can only lead to negotiations once the leaders involved decide that it exists. In this case, it has not come despite the deaths of hundreds of thousands of people. In Northern Ireland, it emerged after 'only' 3,000 people died during the course of the Troubles and was strongly reinforced by the 1998 bombing at Omagh that 'only' killed twenty-eight people.

This combination of objective and perceived conditions may be a more accurate way of rendering the idea of a hurting stalemate than the way it was used in earlier chapters and is usually presented in the literature. Conversely, it becomes a less useful concept for analytical or policy-making purposes, because it is much harder to predict or explain when leaders reach (or don't, as the case may be) the conclusion that it exists.

6. *Domestic politics and psychological dynamics.* Finally, this chapter provides us with the best insights into two ways that domestic political dynamics can render win-win conflict difficult, if not impossible.

First and most obvious is how images of the enemy and other stereotypes made both sides more intransigent and less constructive than they might otherwise have been. Leaders on both sides demonized each other. President Bush led other Western leaders in branding Saddam Hussein the 'second Hitler,' while Western rhetoric in general likened Iraqi policies to those of the Third Reich or the Soviet Union under Stalin. Iraqi attitudes toward the United States were no more conciliatory and got even more extreme afterward. For instance, the regime had a picture of President Bush inlaid into the entry to the hotel where Western journalists stayed in Baghdad, forcing them to step on it on their way in and out. Similarly, Saddam Hussein strode onto the balcony of one of his palaces and fired his pistol in the air in celebration the night Bush lost his bid for a second term in 1992.

This is not to say that there is no grain of truth in those stereotypes. The Iraqi regime is among the most ruthless and tyrannical in the world today – though it is a far cry from either Nazi Germany or the Soviet Union of the 1930s. As the psychologists who have done the most work on this subject point out, however, the most important factor is that such thinking in and of itself hinders any moves toward negotiation. People who invoke the image of the enemy tend to use rhetoric that sees their own side as 'in the right,' turns the other side into a caricature rather than a collection of real people and institutions, and places all the blame for the crisis on them. Under those circumstances, it is hardly surprising that such politicians (or average citizens) assume that the other side has to take the first step, because it is, after all, responsible for the conflict in the first place. Moreover, as the quote that begins this chapter implies, taking the first step toward peace can be viewed as a sign of weakness that one's 'evil' adversary will only take advantage of.

Second, we can see the importance of misperceptions and other difficulties in making effective judgments, which have played an important part in the mainstream literature on international relations since the 1960s. As we saw above, the United States and its allies lacked reliable intelligence information about the capabilities and intentions of the Iraqi government from the first days of the crisis in early 1990 until the end of the war. That led to an underestimate of Baghdad's expansionist intentions before August 1990 and an overestimate of its ability to resist the Western onslaught in 1991.

For its part, the Iraqi leadership also seems to have reached its share of mistaken conclusions about Western intentions. The (in)famous meeting between Saddam Hussein and Ambassador April Glaspie constituted one of many signals that Baghdad read incorrectly before it decided to invade Kuwait. Similarly, it appears that much of the leadership watched the Senate debate on authorizing the use of force on CNN and concluded that it was a sign of weakness and indicated that the United States would not have the courage to fight. Finally, since the end of the war, the Iraqi leadership has made numerous attempts to split and intimidate the 1990–91 coalition, which, so far at least, has had a minimal impact at least as far as the lifting of sanctions is concerned.

In short, the combination of stereotypical thinking and other biases plus frequent misperceptions combined to reinforce a predisposition against negotiation and win-win conflict resolution on both sides. While it is especially hard to extrapolate from this one, admittedly unusual example, there is enough supporting evidence in the international relations and psychological literatures to indicate that these kinds of dynamics are all too typically obstacles to the peaceful resolution of disputes.

SELECT BIBLIOGRAPHY

Batatu, Hanna. *The Old Social Classes and the Revolutionary Movement of Iraq: A Study of Iraq's Old Landed and Commercial Classes and of its Communists, Ba'athists, and Free Officers.* Princeton: Princeton University Press, 1978.

Bengio, Offra. *Saddam's Word: Political Discourse in Iraq.* New York: Oxford University Press, 1998.

Byman, Daniel. 'A Farewell to Arms Inspections.' *Foreign Affairs* 79 (January/February 2000): 110–32.

Cockburn, Andrew, and Patrick Cockburn. *Out of the Ashes: The Resurrection of Saddam Hussein.* New York: HarperCollins, 1999.

Cortright, David, and George Lopez. 'Sanctions against Iraq: Facts and Analysis.'
<http://www.fourthfreedom.org/hottopic/
sanctionsagainstiraqfactsanalysis.html>. Accessed 8 January 2000.

Dawisha, Adeed. 'Identity and Political Survival in Saddam's Iraq.' *Middle East Journal* 53 (autumn 1999): 553–67.

Denoeux, Guilain. 'Iraq.' In *Comparative Politics: Domestic Responses to Global Challenges*, edited by Charles Hauss, 393–432. Belmont, CA: Wadsworth, 2000.

Di Giovanni, Janine. 'The Enemy of Our Enemy.' *New York Times Magazine*, 20 February 2000, 46–49.

Fuller, Graham, and Ian Lesser. 'Persian Gulf Myths.' *Foreign Affairs* 76 (May–June 1997): 42–53.

George, Alexander. *Bridging the Gap*. Washington, D.C.: United States Institute for Peace, 1993.

Gordon, Michael, and Bernard Trainor. *The General's War*. Boston: Little, Brown, 1995.

Herrmann, Richard. 'Coercive Diplomacy and the Crisis over Kuwait, 1990–1991.' In *The Limits of Coercive Diplomacy*, edited by Alexander L. George and William E. Simons, 229–66. Boulder, CO: Westview Press, 1994.

Karsh, Efraim, and Inari Rautsi. *Saddam Hussein: A Political Biography*. New York: Free Press, 1991.

Al-Khalil Samir. *Republic of Fear: The Inside Story of Saddam's Iraq*. New York: Pantheon, 1990.

Marr, Phebe. *The Modern History of Iraq*. Boulder, CO: Westview, 1985.

United Nations. *Report of the Secretary General Pursuant to Paragraph Three of Resolution 1111 (1997)*. 28 November 1997.

11

CONCLUSION

We need to know the destination – if not in a precise way, at least in a generalized way. Before we actually translate something into reality, we must be able to dream about it. If we do a good job in identifying our destination, more innovations and changes will take place to help us reach it.

– Muhammad Yunus

As noted in chapter 1, this book and the series of which it is a part are based on the premise that a student of international relations can make tremendous progress in understanding general trends in the field by considering theories and case studies together. Now, having examined samples of both, we return to that premise both empirically and normatively.

The process of shuttling back and forth between theory and examples while writing this book worked for me. In particular, focusing on traditional theories and 'unsuccessful' cases like the dispute with Iraq led me, first, to challenge some of the conventional wisdom in the field and then to deepen my understanding about conflict resolution.

What follows, then, is my set of conclusions about what you have read so far. As you will see, they reflect the newness of the field and the uncertainties of our times. They also demonstrate equally vividly both the 'danger' and 'opportunity' sides of the global crisis we are in at the dawn of this new century and millennium. And, perhaps most important of all, they straddle the distinction between new and traditional theories raised in chapters 3 through 5 and suggest that we need to include them both in studying conflict resolution or any other international issue.

That is another way of saying that while these are my conclusions, they need not be yours. Indeed, people with whom I have worked on this and other projects over the years have reached markedly different conclusions based on the same evidence.

Put even more bluntly, my frequent use of terms like 'uncertainty' in the pages that follow suggests just how intellectually open the field is.

Table 11.1 Factors affecting conflict resolution

Factor	South Africa	Ireland	Israel/Palestine	Bosnia	Iraq
			A. International, New Theory		
Global system	End of Cold War and its impact on National Party and ANC leaders helps get them to rethink their position	Not very important, given Britain's role as one of the world's leading powers	Often an obstacle, but post-Cold War shifts also made progress possible	End of Cold War worsened conflict and slowed response by the international community	End of Cold War made coalition possible
Preventive diplomacy	—	—	—	Successful in Macedonia, not Bosnia	Failure
Track two	—	Minor and usually facilitated by outsiders	Critical especially for Oslo	Minimal	Virtually none
Third parties	—	Vital in building trust and brokering the 1998 and 1999 agreements	Hard to establish but vital for Oslo and negotiations afterward	Failure until Holbrooke mission	Virtually none

Peace imposition	—	—	Central	Not tried because regime remains in power
War crimes and restorative justice in general	Rejected	Many accusations but little activity in practice	Symbolically important but few arrests of key leaders	Not tried because regime remains in power
B. International, Traditional Theory				
Anarchy and sovereignty	—	Central, especially for Israel	Sovereignty eventually superseded	Violated by Iraq, superseded by allies
Humanitarian intervention	Marginal	Marginal	More important than negotiation until near the end	None until after the war
Coercive diplomacy	Marginal via sanctions	More a factor in Israel's conflict with Arab states	Important only near the end	Failed
Peace imposition	—	—	Central	Not tried because regime remains in power

Factor	South Africa	Northern Ireland	Israel and the Palestinians	Bosnia	Iraq
		C. Domestic, New Theory			
Media	Only outside SA	Probably marginal	Especially important in the U.S.	Limits of CNN effect	Central to lead-up to war, 'enemy' images. Not as important now
Reconciliation	Vital	On the agenda now, but little progress so far	Little conscious attempt to do so, but many projects at the grass roots	Very little	None
Stages	Remains to be seen	Few plans for next stage(s)	Conscious part of the process, especially at Oslo	Dayton does little beyond ending the fighting	None
Psychological dynamics	Key to reconciliation	Key obstacle to reaching an agreement	'Rejectionists' on both sides, but also efforts to bring the communities together	Critical – see the quote that begins chapter 9	Critical in the lead-up to the war

Developing win-win proposals	Important stage setter	Less important than the actual politics and negotiations	Less important than actual politics and negotiations	Largely ignored by leaders 'on the ground'	None (yet)
Asymmetry	More balance over time	More balance over time	Israeli domination remains an obstacle	Favored Serbs at first but balance shifts in 1994–95	Iraq is far weaker than West but can still resist imposition of many terms
Broader social and economic issues	Vital but unclear how much progress can/will be made	Indirect consequence, for example in increased foreign investment	Partially included in interim agreements	Massive destruction of social and economic infrastructure	Worsening conditions inside Iraq
Hurting stalemate	Vital	Vital, though it took years for all parties to see it	Central after the end of the Cold War and the Gulf war	Key goal of Holbrooke's policy to spark negotiation	None yet, despite the costs of the continued conflict, especially for Iraq
Leadership	Vital	With exception of John Hume and a few others, usually an obstacle	Vital	Vital and anything but constructive	More often than not, exacerbates the conflict

Factor	South Africa	Northern Ireland	Israel and the Palestinians	Bosnia	Iraq
Democratization	Vital	—	Important but uncertain in the PNA	Minimal progress	None
Domestic politics	Vital	1997 elections in Britain and Republic of Ireland	Vital, especially in shifts between Likud and Labor in Israel	Vital	Little difference between left and right in the West. Continuity in Iraq

TEN EMPIRICAL CONCLUSIONS ABOUT CONFLICT RESOLUTION

Table 11.1 summarizes what the five case study chapters showed us about the major theoretical issues raised in part 1. To make the table easier to follow, it is broken into four sections, covering domestic and international forces raised in the new and traditional theories respectively. The very uneven nature of the entries in the table's cells underscores the point made earlier that it is impossible to reach anything approaching definitive conclusions about international conflict resolution – at least at this point. Nonetheless, the following ten points do seem to emerge from the discussion in this book so far.

1. There Is No Blueprint for Conflict Resolution

Some of the more simplistic descriptions of win-win conflict resolution leave the impression that there is almost a cookie-cutter or step-by-step approach to conflict resolution. Everything we saw in the first ten chapters of this book demonstrates that such impressions are misleading at best.

The conclusions to follow do present some general principles that seem to affect the likelihood of win-win conflict resolution. However, they cannot be applied in anything like a routine manner for what should be an obvious reason. All conflicts are different, and those differences matter.

Consider, for example, the fact that the parties involved in the conflict in South Africa all but universally agreed that they had to share the same territory. That has not been true for most of the history of the Palestinian–Israeli conflict.

Along similar lines, we have also seen the importance of 'historical accidents,' which make any step-by-step approach all but impossible. Thus, in his memoir of the negotiations that culminated in the Dayton Agreement, Richard Holbrooke recalls that his team made a sudden, unplanned shift in their effort to forge an agreement between Greece and FYROM (former Yugoslavian Republic of Macedonia) in early September 1995. Had they not squeezed trips to Athens and Skopje into their itineraries, that critical agreement might never have been reached, because shortly thereafter Greek prime minister Papandreou became ill and retired, while Macedonian president Kiro Gligorov was incapacitated for months after an assassination attempt.

2. Nonviolent Conflict Resolution May Not Always Be Possible

In an earlier book, I agreed with colleagues who argue that nonviolent conflict resolution is always possible (Hauss, 1996). That may be true 'on paper.' However, each of the cases in part 2 suggests that being able to identify the outlines of such an agreement is one thing, but actually pulling it off is another.

Under the best of circumstances, turning the dreams into reality can take a depressingly long period of time. Under the worst of circumstances, a negotiated settlement is either virtually impossible or would be unacceptable if it were possible.

In chapter 10, we saw that the alliance might have eventually forced Iraq out of Kuwait by maintaining its sanctions after the January 1991 deadline. However, there is no guarantee that that would have happened; in fact, it is more likely that the U.S.-led coalition itself might have begun to splinter first.

More important, it is hard to see how the international community and Iraq could have come to a workable agreement at any point in the history of the conflict as long as the Baath regime remains in power in Baghdad. There is simply too much mistrust and hatred to imagine any U.S. administration, in particular, finding common ground with Saddam Hussein and his colleagues.

The same is probably true of the dispute between the U.S.-led alliance and the Serbian government over Kosovo. However, it is highly unlikely that any such agreement would have stopped Slobodan Milosevic's long-standing plan to ethnically cleanse Kosovo. As I tried to argue in chapter 9, it is entirely possible that the only way to start the region moving toward a more peaceful future was for the international community to intervene as it did in the air war and in the peacebuilding that followed. That process was just getting off the ground when these lines were written, and it is therefore far too early to tell if the ironical situation of using force to open the door to stable peace has any serious potential.

To see this point, consider Richard Holbrooke's description of the Bosnian Serb leadership:

> Headstrong, given to empty theatrical statements, but in the end, essentially bullies when their bluff was called. The Western mistake over the previous four years had been to treat the Serbs as rational people with whom one could argue, negotiate, compromise, and agree. In fact, they respected only force or an unambiguous and credible threat to use it. (Holbrooke, 1999:152)

Holbrooke may or may not have been right about the likes of Radovan

Karadzic and Ratko Mladic. What we can say with some certainty is that to the degree that one or more parties to a conflict hold values like those and act in the way he describes, win-win conflict resolution is all but impossible.

3. Reconciliation Is Critical

All analysts working on international conflict resolution stress agreements that end or ease the fighting that the parties to a conflict reach. However, as we look deeper into the full peace process, it becomes clear that formal agreements are never enough. To even come close to stable peace, reconciliation at the grassroots as well as the elite level has to occur.

That is not an altogether new point. It is central to the burgeoning literature on new forms of conflict resolution discussed in chapters 3 and 4. What does emerge from this study is the need to stress reconciliation more than most international relations specialists have.

What we have seen in the five cases is that efforts at reconciliation (in conflict resolution terms) or civil society building (in comparative politics terms) are just beginning to get the attention they deserve. But from both a normative and an empirical perspective, reconciliation needs to play a more important role in our thought and action regarding international conflict resolution.

Here, the work of David Bloomfield (1997) on Northern Ireland has far-reaching implications. He draws the distinction between the structural attempts to reach peace through formal, governmental agreements and cultural ones that stress changes in the values of all parties to the dispute. Focusing only on the former often leads to what Fen Osler Hampson (1996) calls 'orphaned agreements.' Under those circumstances, leaders reach an agreement as they did in Northern Ireland in 1998 and 1999. But, without social pressure to go further, they find it ever more difficult to find the additional common ground needed to push the peace process further. In perhaps the most tragic case of our time, you end up with situations like that in Cyprus, when a temporary agreement that divided the country into two antagonist and armed camps has continued for thirty-five years with no easing of tensions in sight.

4. Incremental Steps Can Be Enough ... For Now

This next point might seem to contradict the previous one at first glance.

Critics attack the Good Friday Agreement or the Oslo Accord as half measures that raised as many problems as they solved. That is not just true of international politics. To cite but one example, the limited gun control legislation passed in the United States since the mid-1990s is often scoffed at because it has so many loopholes and was never intended to get existing weapons off the street.

The case studies here suggest a somewhat different interpretation. To begin with, full-blown agreements to end the kinds of conflicts discussed in this book are virtually impossible to reach in a single negotiating cycle. There is simply too much tension, mistrust, and division for leaders to bridge all their differences.

That said, limited, incremental steps can mark major progress if two other things occur.

- They make the return to violence considerably less likely.
- They at least open the door to reconciliation, which, virtually by definition, takes a long time to engender.

Unfortunately, as the experience under the Binyamin Netanyahu government points out, the negotiations that lead to a first agreement provide no assurance that such subsequent steps will occur.

5. Leadership and Domestic Politics Matter

There is no mistaking Nelson Mandela for Saddam Hussein. The conciliatory attitude of the former and the hostile one of the latter go a long way toward explaining why the conflicts in South Africa and the Persian Gulf turned out so differently.

The role of individual leaders, however, is probably just a part of a much broader phenomenon that, as noted earlier, is usually minimized in international relations – domestic politics. When viewed through that lens, the emergence of a conciliator or an antagonist seem less like historical accidents. To be sure, the political viewpoints and personalities of the individuals considered in part 2 mattered and cannot always be explained in a satisfactory manner. However, domestic politics does make the emergence of certain types of leaders more or less likely in ways that echo the conclusion about incremental steps.

The type of political system a country has makes a tremendous difference. One version of the widely cited but controversial theory about the democratic peace holds that democracies tend not to go to war with each other because of the way politics is conducted inside them. Thus, emphasis is placed on compromise, coalition building, and other such values. In other words, it should come as little surprise that democracies tend to produce leaders who are most likely to be flexible and conciliatory. That is not an ironclad rule, since Mandela certainly did not come out of a democracy, and the Ulster Unionists have been in charge of their part of one of the world's oldest democracies.

Much the same holds for a country's culture. As Raymond Cohen (1997), in particular, has argued, some cultures do not lend themselves readily to the give and take of negotiation. As he has said at a recent conference, there are languages in which there is no term that is even roughly equivalent to reconciliation.

There is not a one-to-one link between democracy and the kind of culture that lends itself to this type of conflict resolution. To cite but the most important example here, there are scholars who argue that Mandela's willingness to reach out to the National Party leadership reflected both traditional African leadership patterns that stress respect for one's opponents and what he saw as the shared love of the country found among Blacks and Afrikaners alike.

In short, I am not arguing that the 'wrong' kind of culture or political system dooms a peace process. There are too many examples to the contrary. Rather, a democratic regime and a culture that stresses compromise or accepts diversity can help facilitate the end of fighting and the movement toward stable peace.

6. Third Parties Help, But Not All Third Parties Are Alike

Virtually everyone who writes about international conflict resolution stresses the vital role dispassionate third parties can play in brokering agreements. There are precious few examples like the South African one in which adversaries of long standing can hammer out their differences on their own.

The case studies, however, take the analysis of third parties further than one finds in the theoretical literature in two overlapping ways.

First, there are different types of third parties. George Mitchell is a classic example of a conciliator. As we saw in chapter 7, he based his entire political career on his ability to treat friend and foe alike with dignity and respect, skills he was able to use to build coalitions in the fractious United States Senate. Much the same is true of former U.S. president Jimmy Carter, whose successful conflict resolution interventions occurred in large part because he gained the personal and political respect of the parties.

Richard Holbrooke is very different. Even his supporters refer to him as a bulldozer. His critics use harsher terms like bully. Holbrooke would not have been an effective mediator for the Northern Ireland conflict. However, his pressurizing and, some would say, intimidating style was probably critical to the success of the Dayton Agreement after four years of tragic fighting.

Second, third parties need not always be neutral. Indeed, there are times when it is impossible or inappropriate for them to be. Many of Holbrooke's predecessors from the UN and European Union (EU) had tried to walk a fine line between the Serbs and their adversaries. That did not work in part because the Serbs were so much more powerful than the Croats and Bosnian Muslims and were intent on clinging to their plans for a Greater Serbia and in part because the Serbs were responsible for the lion's share of the atrocities committed as Yugoslavia fell apart.

Put simply, sometimes the international community has to intervene on one side or the other, as it has in both the former Yugoslavia and the Persian Gulf. Sometimes, a commitment to neutrality or the sovereignty of a state can paralyze the international community and keep it from getting involved, which was one of the main reasons there was no massive intervention to stop the killing in Rwanda even though virtually all observers agreed that such an intervention could have done so relatively quickly and easily.

7. Open or Secret?

These cases offer a mixed picture as far as one of the classic questions in the study of diplomacy is concerned. Should negotiations be held in secret or should they be open to public scrutiny?

Here, there is no question that the secrecy of the Norwegian channel was vital. Otherwise, it seems highly unlikely that the Palestinian and Israeli leaders who barely acknowledged each other's existence could get together, let alone make any progress. To be sure, some Jews and Palestinians had met informally before. But, the mere fact that it was illegal for Israelis to meet with members of the PLO until 1993 posed an all but insurmountable obstacle to any kind of public negotiation.

The same was true, to a lesser degree, in preparing the ground for formal negotiations in both South Africa and Northern Ireland. Thus, virtually no one in the African National Congress leadership – let alone the society in general – knew that Mandela had been meeting with top-level government officials in the late 1980s. Little news leaked out of meetings between Sinn Fein leaders and British civil servants until the last few days before the Downing Street Declaration was issued.

In short, secrecy is probably most useful in the early stages of negotiations. At that time, public awareness of even 'talks about talks' might scuttle the possibility of progress by strengthening opposition to them from hard-liners on one or both sides. Similarly, as the Dayton negotiations also showed, a news blackout can give highly antagonistic leaders more room for maneuver than they would otherwise have.

That said, the glare of the news camera or pressure from average citizens can also make an agreement more likely. In some cases, it is unavoidable, as in Northern Ireland, where leaks appear on an all-but-daily basis.

More often, however, openness can help when the visible intervention of national leaders or the public imposition of a firm deadline both builds up the pressure and also increases the possibility of reaching a deal. Both certainly occurred in the weeks before the Good Friday Agreement was reached. But, they did not help in the efforts of Blair, Ahern, and others to keep Northern Ireland's new institutions in place in early 2000.

8. The New World (Dis)order Matters

In the late 1980s, both Presidents Bush and Mikhail Gorbachev claimed that the end of the Cold War could usher in a new world order. With the Iraqi invasion of Kuwait and the other problems that have beset international relations since then, the pundits are more likely to talk about a new world *dis*order instead.

Whatever term you choose to describe the world we live in today, there is no question the changed international environment has made humanitarian intervention and new forms of conflict resolution more common than ever before. That does not mean that the international community always gets involved. It has largely stayed out of conflicts in which either solutions seemed unlikely or the interests (however defined) of the major powers were not involved. Intervention that has occurred has not always been particularly effective, something Americans saw most tragically in Somalia.

But the kind of approaches to international conflict discussed in this book are easier to employ for two main reasons.

First, there are no other overriding security issues that the states that can most readily intervene in conflict have to preoccupy themselves with. The Cold War is gone, and nothing of that nature has taken its place.

Thus, to cite but the most obvious example, NATO is now 'free' to take on the challenge of Bosnia or Kosovo, something that would not have been imaginable as recently as the late 1980s.

Second, the end of the Cold War division of most of the world between East and West no longer means that the United States and the Soviet Union routinely use their veto power in the Security Council to keep the UN from intervening in a crisis. And, perhaps most important of all, intervention does not carry with it the risk of escalation to a broader war that was often the case before the collapse of the Soviet Union.

9. The International Community

Conclusion 8 includes one of the greasiest terms used in this book – the 'international community.' It was rarely used before the 1990s, since the very idea of a world community made little sense during the Cold War years. Optimists think we have made major strides toward acting multilaterally. Indeed, virtually every instance of intervention if not every attempt at international conflict resolution was at least nominally organized through an international body. Critics point out that it is often little more than a code word or euphemism to describe the United States' self-assigned role as the world's policeman.

Wherever you come down on such issues, it is impossible to deny that international organizations are at least somewhat more important than they were before the end of the Cold War. The United Nations had a major spurt of peacekeeping and related activity in the mid-1990s. At that point, declining support from the United States, its related budgetary crisis, and difficulties on the ground cost the UN most of that momentum. In particular, the UN finds it all but impossible to mount the massive efforts that have been mounted in the former Yugoslavia.

In other words, whenever intervention is on the agenda, the world's leading powers have to be involved, because only they have the personnel and other resources to deploy tens of thousands of soldiers. That has shifted attention away from the UN to the EU and, especially NATO, which, coincidentally, was seeking a new role in the post-Cold War world. Attention has obviously been focused on NATO's role, given the two wars in the former Yugoslavia. But the EU has spearheaded economic reconstruction and the rebuilding of civil society in Bosnia and Kosovo. Since Oslo, it has also had a formal role in the Middle East peace process, focusing on issues involving refugees and water.

It's not just in Europe. The West African ECOWAS (Economic

Community of West African States) has sent peacekeepers to Liberia and Sierra Leone, and other regional efforts have been mounted to try to deal with the waves of fighting in the Democratic Republic of Congo (formerly Zaire).

To be sure, the United States has been the most powerful (and perhaps most arrogant) actor in most instances of intervention and conflict resolution. That should not, however, keep us from seeing that some important, albeit tentative steps have been taken toward giving international organizations limited power that transcends and sometimes limits the sovereignty of individual states.

10. The Uncertain Role of Force

The final conclusion is the most uncertain. More important, it is the most troubling for someone like this author who came to international conflict resolution with an ironclad commitment to nonviolence.

As noted earlier, it is hard to see how a nonviolent win-win outcome could have been produced in the Yugoslav and, to a lesser degree, Iraqi cases. Whether the blame lay primarily in Belgrade, Baghdad, or Washington really doesn't matter. The fact is that there were few plausible or practical strategies for avoiding violence in dealing with ethnic cleansing or the behavior of Iraq either before or after the Gulf war.

For a traditional international relations specialist or policymaker, that is to be expected. For ill or good, force is part and parcel of international life. For someone from my background, the use of force is troubling indeed, since the major work on such issues as reconciliation outside the academic community has always ruled out force of any kind, violent or otherwise.

Wherever you come down on the ethical aspects of the use of force, its use *as a part of the peacebuilding process* is so new that it is hard to assess. The United States' and NATO's attitudes toward their roles in Bosnia and Kosovo were unprecedented. They reluctantly used air power to stop what they took to be an even more egregious use of force by the Serbs. There is nothing new to that, of course. What is new is making the use of force part of a longer-term strategy of conflict resolution, reconciliation, and the building of stable peace.

The first signs from Kosovo and Bosnia are not encouraging. As we saw in chapter 9, little progress has been made in rebuilding Bosnia. And, in what might be as powerful a metaphor for these difficulties, on the day I started writing this book, the bombing campaign began in Kosovo. On the day I finished the final draft of this book, KFOR (the NATO Kosovo Force) peacekeepers were stoned by furious Serbs in Mitrovica.

THE ROLE OF DREAMS AND PASSION

I began this book with a statement by Philip Gourevitch about the passions the study of conflict and its resolution provokes. I wish to end it by returning to passion and the normative issues that eddy around it.

As everything in this chapter so far has suggested, writing this book has left me less optimistic about the short-term possibilities for nonviolent international conflict resolution. However, it did nothing to reduce my commitment to it as a practical long-term goal.

It is hard to find a scholar from any intellectual school of thought who doesn't consider the carnage described in this book unacceptable. It does not require being a visionary to be convinced that we have to find a better way of settling our disputes. That said, it would be easy to read the more pessimistic cases in part 2 as reinforcing the realists' argument that the goal of making nonviolent conflict resolution the norm is a utopian fantasy.

The more successful cases in part 2 also point us toward a way of meshing what do seem to be somewhat idealistic goals with the harsh realities of international life. To see that, consider the words of Muhammad Yunus that begin this chapter.

Yunus does not work on international conflict resolution. Instead, he is the founder of the Grameen Bank, which is widely (but not universally) thought to hold an important key to development not just in the third world but poorer sectors of the industrialized democracies as well. It is a point one also finds among the more visionary writers in the corporate world.

As Yunus suggests, it is easy to focus on – and sometimes be depressed by – the specifics of daily political life. However, real progress – especially progress toward something new – requires a combination of what he calls dreaming about one's goal and of empirical analysis.

It is the goal that grabs our attention and then provides us with the motivation to continue even when the 'real world' is providing us with at best a mixed message about ever reaching it. That's the normative side. The goal also offers us a benchmark against which to measure that progress and learn how to do things better the next time. That's the empirical side

That point about the interplay of passion and the often harsh realities of day-to-day politics was driven home to me by the last paragraph of

George Mitchell's (1999) book on the peace process in Northern Ireland. The book hit me hard. I had long been a fan of Mitchell's. I lived in Maine during his years in the Senate and had even had a bit role in one of his campaign ads. Then I lived in the United Kingdom for the first three years of Mitchell's involvement in the peace talks. During that time, a conflict I had paid little attention to became a part of my daily life as well as his. I had been at the site of two of the IRA's bombings just a day or two before the blasts went off. I twice had to leave shopping malls because of bomb threats.

Thus, I was delighted by the way he had helped turn dreams into tangible progress in Northern Ireland and dashed out to buy his book the day it was published. Even so, I was not prepared for its last lines.

Mitchell became a father at one of the low points in the talks. In the book, he frequently muses about the world he was leaving Andrew and the sixty-one children born on the same day in Northern Ireland. He ends his book with his dream:

> [t]o return to Northern Ireland in a few years with my young son, Andrew. We will roam the countryside, taking in the sights and smells and sounds of one of the most beautiful landscapes on earth. Then, on a rainy afternoon (there are many in Northern Ireland) we will drive to Stormont and sit quietly in the visitors gallery of the Northern Ireland Assembly. There we will watch and listen as the members of the Assembly debate the ordinary issues of life in a peaceful democratic society: education, health care, agriculture, tourism, fisheries, trade. There will be no talk of war, for the war will have been long over. There will be no talk of peace, for peace will by then be taken for granted. On that day, the day on which peace is taken for granted in Northern Ireland, I will be fulfilled. (Mitchell, 1999:188)

SELECT BIBLIOGRAPHY

Bloomfield, David. *Peacemaking Strategies in Northern Ireland*. Basingstoke: Macmillan, 1997.

Cohen, Raymond. *Negotiating across Cultures: International Communication in an Interdependent World*. Rev. ed. Washington, D.C.: United States Institute for Peace, 1997.

Hampson, Fen Osler. *Nurturing Peace: Why Peace Settlements Succeed or Fail*. Washington, D.C.: United States Institute for Peace, 1996.

Hauss, Charles. *Beyond Confrontation: Transforming the New World Order*. Westport, CT: Praeger, 1996.

Holbrooke, Richard. *To End a War*. New York: Random House, 1998.

Mitchell, George. *Making Peace*. New York: Knopf, 1999.

SELECT BIBLIOGRAPHY

This is not intended to be a comprehensive bibliography. Given the booming interest in conflict resolution, doing so would produce a document as long as this book as a whole. Therefore, this bibliography only includes the works cited in the text that, on balance, include all the major works in the field plus others that are less well known, but that I found useful in writing this book. It is also organized by topic, with theoretical and general works first and those on the case studies at the end.

GENERAL

Albin, Cecilia. 'The Global Security Challenge to Negotiation: Toward a New Agenda.' *American Behavioral Scientist* 38 (1995): 921–49.

Anderson, Mary B. 'Humanitarian NGOs in Conflict Intervention.' In *Managing Global Chaos: Sources of and Responses to International Conflict*, edited by Chester Crocker, Fen Osler Hampson, and Pamela Aall, 343–54. Washington, D.C.: United States Institute for Peace, 1996.

Anderson, Mary B., and Peter J. Woodrow. *Rising from the Ashes: Developmental Strategies at Times of Disaster*. Boulder, CO: Westview, 1989.

Avruch, Kevin. *Culture and Conflict Resolution*. Washington, D.C.: United States Institute for Peace, 1998.

Ball, Nicole. 'The Challenge of Rebuilding War-Torn Societies.' In *Managing Global Chaos: Sources of and Responses to International Conflict*, edited by Chester Crocker, Fen Osler Hampson, and Pamela Aall, 601–22. Washington, D.C.: United States Institute for Peace, 1996.

Boulding, Kenneth. *Stable Peace*. Austin, Tex.: University of Texas Press, 1978.

———. 'Moving from Unstable to Stable Peace.' In *Breakthrough: Emerging New Thinking: Soviet and American Scholars Issue a Challenge to Build a World beyond War*, edited by Martin Hellman and Anatoly Gromyko, 157–67. New York: Walker, 1988.

Boutros-Ghali, Boutros. *An Agenda for Peace*. New York: United Nations, 1992.

Burton, John, ed. *Conflict: Human Needs Theory*. London: Macmillan, 1990.

Buzan, Barry. *People, States, and Fear: An Agenda for International Security Studies in the Post-Cold War Era*. London: Harvester Wheatsheaf, 1991.

Caplan, Pat, ed. *Understanding Disputes: The Politics of Argument*, Oxford, U.K.: Berg Publishers, 1995.

Capra, Frijtof. *The Turning Point: Science, Society, and the Rising Culture*. New York: Simon and Schuster, 1982.

Carnegie Commission for the Prevention of Deadly Conflict. *Preventing Deadly Conflict*. New York: Carnegie Commission, 1997. Also available at <http:www.ccpdc.org>.

Cohen, Raymond. *Negotiating across Cultures: International Communication in an Interdependent World*. Rev. ed. Washington, D.C.: United States Institute for Peace, 1997.

Coles, Robert. *The Call of Service: A Witness to Idealism*. Boston: Houghton-Mifflin, 1993.

Cortright, David, ed. *The Price of Peace: Incentives and International Conflict Prevention*. Lanham, Md.: Rowman and Littlefield, 1997.

Crocker, Chester, Fen Osler Hampson, and Pamela Aall. *Managing Global Chaos: Sources of and Responses to International Conflict*. Washington, D.C.: United States Institute for Peace, 1996.

Donohue, William A., with Robert Kolt. *Managing Interpersonal Conflict*. Newbury Park, Calif.: Sage, 1992.

Eiliasson, Jan. 'Humanitarian Action and Peacekeeping.' In *Peacemaking and Peacekeeping for the New Century*, edited by Olara A. Otunnu and Michael W. Doyle, 203–14. Lanham, Md.: Rowman and Littlefield, 1998.

Evans, Gareth. 'Preventive Diplomacy and Conflict Resolution.' In *Peacemaking and Peacekeeping for the New Century*, edited by Olara A. Otunnu and Michael W. Doyle, 61–88. Lanham, Md.: Rowman and Littlefield, 1998.

Feil, Scott R. *Preventing Genocide: How the Early Use of Force Might Have Succeeded in Rwanda*. New York: Carnegie Council for the Prevention of Deadly Conflict, 1998.

Fisher, Roger. *International Conflict for Beginners*. New York: Harper Colophon, 1969.

Fisher, Roger, and William Ury. *Getting to Yes*. New York: Penguin, 1981.

Frank, Jerome, and Andrei Melville. 'The Image of the Enemy and the

Process of Change.' In *Breakthrough: Emerging New Thinking: Soviet and Western Scholars Issue a Challenge to Build a World beyond War*, edited by Martin Hellman and Anatoly Gromyko, 199–208. New York: Walker, 1988.

Friedman, Thomas L. *The Lexus and the Olive Tree: Understanding Globalization*. New York: Farrar, Straus and Giroux, 1999.

George, Alexander L., David K. Hall, and William E. Simons. *The Limits of Coercive Diplomacy*. Boston: Little-Brown, 1971.

George, Alexander L., and William E. Simons, ed. *The Limits of Coercive Diplomacy*. Boulder, CO: Westview, 1994.

Gleick, James. *Chaos: Making a New Science*. New York: Viking, 1987.

Gourevitch, Philip. *We Wish to Inform You That Tomorrow We Will Be Killed With Our Families*. New York: Farrar-Strauss-Giroux, 1998.

Gowing, Nik. *Media Coverage: Help or Hindrance in Conflict Prevention*. New York: Carnegie Commission on Preventing Deadly Violence, 1997.

Haass, Richard. *Conflict Unending*. New Haven: Yale University Press, 1990.

Hampson, Fen Osler. *Nurturing Peace: Why Peace Settlements Succeed or Fail*. Washington, D.C.: United States Institute for Peace, 1996.

Hauss, Charles. *Beyond Confrontation: Toward a New World Order?* Westport, Conn.: Praeger, 1996.

————. *New London Day*. 16 May 1999. Accessible at <http://classweb.gmu.edu/classweb/chauss/index.htm>.

————. *International Relations: Confrontation, Cooperation, Continuity, and Change*. Belmont, CA: Wadsworth, forthcoming.

Hellman, Martin and Anatoly, Gromyko, eds. *Breakthrough: Emerging New Thinking: Soviet and Western Scholars Issue a Challenge to Build a World beyond War*. New York: Walker, 1988.

Holbrooke, Richard. *To End a War*. New York: Random House, 1998.

Horsman, Matthew, and Andrew Marshall. *Beyond the Nation State*. London: HarperCollins, 1995.

Janis, Irving. *Groupthink*. Boston: Houghton-Mifflin, 1983.

Jervis, Robert. 'Hypotheses on Misperception.' *World Politics* 20 (April 1968): 454–79.

————. *System Effects: Complexity in Social and Political Life*. Princeton, N.J.: Princeton University Press, 1997.

Johnson, David W., Roger T. Johnson, Bruce Dudley, and Douglas Magnuson. 'Training Elementary School Students to Manage Conflict.' *Journal of Social Psychology* 135 (February 1997): 673–86.

Joulwan, George A., and Christopher C. Shoemaker. *Civilian-Military Cooperation in the Prevention of Deadly Conflict: Implementing Agreements in Bosnia and Beyond*. New York: Carnegie Commission on the

Prevention of Deadly Conflict, 1998.

Kaplan, Robert D. 'The Coming Anarchy.' *Atlantic* 273 (February, 1994), 44–76.

——. *The Ends of the Earth: A Journey at the Dawn of the 21st Century.* New York: Random House, 1996.

Keen, Sam. *Faces of the Enemy: Reflections on the Hostile Imagination.* New York: Harper and Row, 1986.

Kelman, Herbert C. 'The Interactive Problem-Solving Approach.' In *Managing Global Chaos: Sources of and Responses to International Conflict,* edited by Chester Crocker, Fen Osler Hampson, and Pamela Aall, 501–19. Washington, D.C.: United States Institute for Peace, 1996.

Kittani, Ismat. 'Preventive Dipolmacy and Peacemaking: The UN Experience.' In *Peacemaking and Peacekeeping for the New Century,* edited by Olara A. Otunnu and Michael W. Doyle, 89–110. Lanham, Md.: Rowman and Littlefield, 1998.

Kriesberg, Lewis. 'The Development of the Conflict Resolution Field.' In *Peacemaking in International Conflict: Methods and Techniques,* edited by I. William Zartman and J. Lewis Rasmussen, 51–80. Washington, D.C.: United States Institute for Peace, 1997.

Kuhn, Thomas. *The Structure of Scientific Revolutions.* Chicago: University of Chicago Press, 1969.

Last, David. 'Soldiers and Civilians in Peacebuilding: Reliable Partners?' Paper prepared for the 1999 Meeting of the International Studies Association. Washington, D.C.

Lederach, John Paul. *Building Peace: Sustainable Reconciliation in Divided Societies.* Washington, D.C.: United States Institute for Peace, 1997.

Lipschutz, Ronnie D., and Susanne Jonas, eds. 'Beyond the Neoliberal Peace: From Conflict Resolution to Social Reconciliation.' *Social Justice,* special issue. 25, no. 4 (1998).

Lund, Michael S. *Preventing Violent Conflict: A Strategy for Preventive Diplomacy.* Washington, D.C.: United States Institute for Peace, 1996.

Mearsheimer, John. 'Back to the Future: Instability in Europe after the Cold War.' *International Security* 15 (1990a): 5–56.

——. 'Why We Will Soon Miss the Cold War.' *Atlantic Monthly* 266 (1990b): 35–50.

Miall, Hugh, Oliver Ramsbotham, and Tom Woodhouse. *Contemporary Conflict Resolution.* Oxford: Polity, 1999.

Minow, Martha. *Between Vengeance and Forgiveness: Facing History after Genocide and Mass Violence.* Boston: Beacon Press, 1998.

Muravchik, Joshua. 'Promoting Peace through Democracy.' In *Managing Global Chaos: Sources of and Responses to International Conflict,* edited by Chester Crocker, Fen Osler Hampson, and Pamela Aall, 573–86.

Washington, D.C.: United States Institute for Peace, 1996.

Natsios, Andrew S. 'An NGO Perspective.' In *Peacemaking in International Conflict: Methods and Techniques*, edited by I. William Zartman and J. Lewis Rasmussen, 337–64. Washington, D.C.: United States Institute for Peace, 1997.

Nye, Joseph. *Understanding International Conflict: An Introduction to Theory and History*. Upper Saddle River, N.J.: Prentice Hall, 1998.

Ogata, Sadako. 'Humanitarian Responses to International Emergencies.' In *Peacemaking and Peacekeeping for the New Century*, edited by Olara A. Otunnu and Michael W. Doyle, 215–31. Lanham, MD: Rowman and Littlefield, 1998.

Otunnu, Olara A., and Michael W. Doyle, eds. *Peacemaking and Peacekeeping for the New Century*. Lanham, MD: Rowman and Littlefield, 1998.

Pruitt, Dean G., and Peter J. Carnevale. *Negotiation in Social Coflict*. Pacific Grove, CA: Brooks/Cole, 1993.

Ramonet, Ignacio. 'Nouvel ordre global.' ('New World Order') *Le Monde Diplomatique*, June, 1999. <*http://www.monde-diplomatique.fr/1999/06.RAMONET*>. Accessed 19 June 1999.

Rose, William. 'The Security Dilemma and Ethnic Conflict.' *Security Studies* 9, no. 4 (Autumn 2000): 1–55.

Rosenau, James. *Turbulence in World Politics: A Theory of Change and Continuity*. Princeton, N.J.: Princeton University Press, 1990.

Rosenau, James, and Mary Durfee. *Thinking Theory Thoroughly*. Boulder, CO: Westview, 2000.

Russett, Bruce. *Grasping the Democratic Peace: Principles for a Post-Cold War World*. Princeton: Princeton University Press, 1993.

Senge, Peter. *The Fifth Discipline: The Art and Practice of the Learning Organization*. New York: Doubleday Currency, 1990.

Sharp, Jane M. O. 'Dayton Report Card.' *International Security* 22 (Winter 1997): 101–38.

Singer, Max, and Aaron Wildavsky. *The Real World Order*. 2d ed. Chatham, N.J.: Chatham House, 1996.

Snow, Donald M. *Uncivil Wars: International Security and the New Internal Conflicts*. Boulder, CO: Lynne Reiner, 1996.

Stremlau, John, and Francisco R. Sagasti. *Preventing Deadly Conflict: Does the World Bank Have a Role?* New York: Carnegie Commission on Preventing Deadly Conflict, 1998.

Strobel, Warren P. *Late-breaking Foreign Policy: The News Media's Influence on Peace Operations*. Washington, D.C.: United States Institute for Peace, 1997.

Susskind, Lawrence, and Sarah McKearnan. 'Enlightened Conflict

Resolution.' *Technology Review* 98 (1995): 70–74.

United Nations. *The Blue Helmets: A Review of United Nations Peace-Keeping*. 3d ed. New York: United Nations 1996.

Waldrop, M. Mitchell. *Complexity: The Emerging Science at the Edge of Order and Chaos*. New York: Simon and Schuster, 1992.

Wallensteen, Peter, and Margareta Sollenberg. 'After the Cold War: Emerging Patterns of Armed Conflict.' *Journal of Peace Research* 23 (1995): 345–60.

Weart, Spencer R. *Never at War: Why Democracies Will Not Fight One Another*. New Haven: Yale University Press, 1998.

Weiss, Thomas. *Military-Civilian Interactions: Intervening in Humanitarian Crises*. Lanham, MD: Rowman and Littlefield, 1999.

Weiss, Thomas, and Cindy Collins. *Humanitarian Challenges and Intervention: World Politics and the Dilemmas of Help*. Boulder, CO: Westview, 1996.

White, Ralph. *Fearful Warrior: A Psychological Profile of U.S.-Soviet Relations*. New York: Free Press, 1984.

Wilson, James Q. *The Moral Sense*. New York: Free Press, 1993.

Yankelovich, Daniel. *The Magic of Dialogue: Transforming Conflict into Cooperation*. New York: Simon and Schuster, 1999.

Zartman, I. William. *Ripe for Resolution*. 2d ed. New York: Oxford University Press, 1989.

Zartman, I. William, and J. Lewis Rasmussen, eds. *Peacemaking in International Conflict: Methods and Techniques*. Washington, D.C.: United States Institute for Peace, 1997.

SOUTH AFRICA

Bornstein, David. *The Price of a Dream: The Story of the Grameen Bank*. Chicago: University of Chicago Press, 1997.

Crawford Neta, and Audie Klotz, eds. *How Sanctions Work: Lessons from South Africa*. London: St. Martin's, 1999.

Goodman, David. *Fault Lines: Journeys into the New South Africa*. Berkeley, CA: University of California Press, 1999.

Klotz, Audie. *Norms in International Relations: The Struggle against Apartheid*. Ithaca, N.Y.: Cornell University Press, 1995.

Mandela, Nelson. *Long Walk to Freedom*. Boston: Little-Brown, 1994.

Meredith, Martin. *Nelson Mandela: A Biography*. London: Hamish Hamilton, 1997.

Sparks, Allister. *The Mind of South Africa*. New York: Ballantine, 1990.

————. *Tomorrow Is Another Country: The Inside Story of South Africa's*

Negotiated Revolution. London: Arrow Books, 1997.

Thompson, Leonard. *A History of South Africa*. Rev. ed. New Haven, CT: Yale University Press, 1995.

Waldmeier, Patti. *Anatomy of a Miracle*. New York: Penguin, 1997.

Yunus, Muhammad. *Banker to the Poor: Micro-Lending and the Battle against World Poverty*. New York: Public Affairs Press, 1999.

NORTHERN IRELAND

Bloomfield, David. *Peacemaking Strategies in Northern Ireland*. Basingstoke: Macmillan, 1997.

————. *Political Dialogue in Northern Ireland*. Basingstoke: Macmillan, 1998.

Coogan, Tim Pat. *The Troubles: Ireland's Ordeal 1966–1996 and the Search for Peace*. Boulder, CO: Roberts Rinehart, 1996.

Hoge, Warren. 'Roadblock to a Peace Pact: Irish Mostly Say "No." ' *New York Times*, Washington Edition, 3 July 1999a, 7.

————. 'Pledges by Ulster Rivals Break the Deadlock at Talks.' *New York Times*, Washington Edition, 17 November 1999b, A3.

Holland, Jack. *Hope against History: The Course of Conflict in Northern Ireland*. New York: Henry Holt, 1999.

Lloyd, John. 'Ireland's Uncertain Peace.' *Foreign Affairs* (September–October 1998) 109–23.

————. 'The Troubles That Won't Go Away.' *New York Times Magazine*, 12 December 1999, 89–93.

McKittrick, David. *The Nervous Peace*. London: Blackstaff, 1996.

Mitchell, George. *Making Peace*. New York: Knopf, 1999.

O'Toole, Fintan. 'The Ulster Conundrum: The Words Used to Broker Peace Have Become Stumbling Blocks.' *Washington Post*, 11 July 1999, B4.

Stevenson, Jonathan. 'Peace in Northern Ireland: Why Now?' *Foreign Policy* (Fall): 41–54.

Toolis, Kevin. *Rebel Hearts: Journeys within the IRA's Soul*. New York: St. Martin's, 1995.

IRAQ AND THE GULF WAR

Al-Khalil, Samir. *Republic of Fear: The Inside Story of Saddam's Iraq*. New York: Pantheon, 1990.

Batatu, Hanna. *The Old Social Classes and the Revolutionary Movement of*

Iraq: A Study of Iraq's Old Landed and Commercial Classes and of Its Communists, Ba'athists, and Free Officers. Princeton, N.J.: Princeton University Press, 1978.

Bengio, Offra. *Saddam's Word: Political Discourse in Iraq*. New York: Oxford University Press, 1998.

Cockburn, Andrew, and Patrick Cockburn. *Out of the Ashes: The Resurrection of Saddam Hussein*. New York: HarperCollins, 1999.

Gordon, Michael, and Bernard Trainor. *The General's War*. Boston: Little, Brown, 1995.

Herrmann, Richard. 'Coercive Diplomacy and the Crisis over Kuwait, 1990–1991.' In *The Limits of Coercive Diplomacy*, edited by Alexander L. George and William E. Simons, 229–66. Boulder, CO: Westview Press, 1994.

Karsh, Efraim, and Inari Rautsi. *Saddam Hussein: A Political Biography*. New York: Free Press, 1991.

BOSNIA

Bunce, Valerie. 'Peaceful versus Violent State Dismemberment: A Comparison of the Soviet Union, Yugoslavia, and Czechoslovakia.' *Politics and Society* 27 (June 1999): 217–37.

Burg, Steven, and Paul Shoup. *The War in Bosnia-Herzegovina: Ethnic Conflict and International Intervention*. Armonk, N.Y.: M. E. Sharpe, 1999.

Daalder, Ivo, and Michael B. G. Froman. 'Dayton's Incomplete Peace.' *Foreign Affairs* (November/December 1999). Accessed from <http://proquest,umi.com> on 1 August 2000.

European Stability Institute. 'Reshaping International Priorities in Bosnia and Hercegovina.' Unpublished paper, 1999.

Fromkin, David. *Kosovo Crossing: American Ideals Meet Reality on the Balkan Battlefields*. New York: Free Press, 1999.

Holbrooke, Richard. *To End a War*. New York: Random House, 1998.

International Crisis Group. 'Is Dayton Failing? Four Years after the Peace Agreement.' Unpublished paper, 1999.

Judeh, Tim. *The Serbs*. New Haven: Yale University Press, 1997.

Last, David. 'Soldiers and Civilians in Peacebuilding: Reliable Partners?' Paper prepared for the 1999 Meeting of the International Studies Association, Washington, D.C.

Malcolm, Noel. *Bosnia: A Brief History*. New York: New York University Press, 1994.

Rieff, David. *Slaughterhouse: Bosnia and the Failure of the West*. New York:

Vintage, 1995.

Sharp, Jane M. O. 'Dayton Report Card.' *International Security* 22 (Winter 1997): 101–38.

United Nations. *The Blue Helmets*. New York: United Nations Press, 1996.

Woodward, Susan. *Balkan Tragedy: Chaos and Dissolution after the Cold War*. Washington, D.C.: Brookings, 1995.

ISRAEL AND THE PALESTINIANS

Ciment, James. *Palestine/Israel: The Long Conflict*. New York: Facts on File, 1997.

Gerner, Deborah. *One Land, Two Peoples*. Boulder, CO: Westview, 1994.

Rabinovich, Itamar. *Waging Peace: Israel and the Arabs at the End of the Century*. New York: Farrar, Straus and Giroux, 1999.

INDEX